CENTRAL AFRICA: CRISES, REFORM AND RECONSTRUCTION

Edited by

E.S. D Fomin & John W. Forje

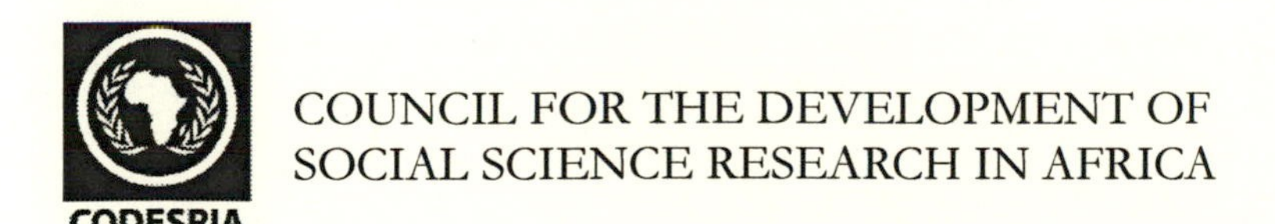

COUNCIL FOR THE DEVELOPMENT OF
SOCIAL SCIENCE RESEARCH IN AFRICA

Avenue Cheikh Anta Diop Angle Canal IV, BP 3304, Dakar, 18524 Senegal.
http:\\www.codesria.org

ISBN: 2-86978-151-2

Typeset by Djibril Fall

Cover designed by Ibrahima Fofana

Printed by Lightning Source

CODESRIA would like to express its gratitude to African Governments, the Swedish Development Co-operation Agency (SIDA/SAREC), the International Development Research Centre (IDRC), OXFAM GB/I, the Mac Arthur Foundation, the Carnegie Corporation, the Norwegian Ministry of Foreign Affairs, the Danish Agency for International Development (DANIDA), the French Ministry of Cooperation, the Ford Foundation, the United Nations Development Programme (UNDP), the Rockefeller Foundation, the Prince Claus Fund and the Government of Senegal for support of its research, publication and training activities.

Contents

Section II

The Weird Wind of Democratisation and Governance

About the contributors

Valentine Ameli is Senior Lecturer in the Department of Public Law and Political Science, Dschang University, Cameroon. She is also a visiting lecturer, Law Department, University of Buea in Cameroon.

Margaret Ayike is a lecturer at the International Relations Institute of Cameroon (IRIC) in Yaounde, Cameroon.

Susanna Yene Awasom lectures at CEFAM, Buea/Cameroon. She studied Law and Economics at the University of Yaounde where she obtained an LLB She obtained her Maîtrise in Public Law and a Postgraduate Diploma in Managerial Economics (Diplôme des Techniques en Quantitatives de Gestion) from the University of Yaounde and Douala respectively.

Oladiran Bello is currently a PhD candidate at Cambridge University, UK. His research and consulting interests are resource-control politics and economic agendas in African conflicts, and the roles of corporate actors and states' elites in resource wars in the Great Lakes region. Bello's doctoral research analyses the roles of mineral-prospecting networks and corporations in peace building in the DR Congo.

Victor Cheo is a lecturer in the Department of Journalism and Mass Communication, University of Buea, Cameroon. He studied in University of Yaounde 1, Cameroon and University of Ibadan, Nigeria. He has contributed book chapters and articles in scholarly journals. His current research interest is environmental communication.

E.S.D. Fomin has a Doctorate in History from the University of Yaounde. He is the author of four books, has published several scientific articles, and participated in many seminars, conferences, and symposia.

John W. Forje is currently Archie Mafeje Fellow at the African Institute of South Africa, Pretoria. He was educated at the Universities of Lund (Sweden), Hull and Salford (UK), receiving his Fil Kand, M.Soc.Sc: MA and PhD in Political Science and Science and Technology Policy. He is a Lecturer in the Department of Political Science, University of Yaounde II-Soa; and a Visiting Lecturer, University of Buea, Cameroon. He is author of a number of books and articles.

Ntangsi Max Memfih is a Senior Lecturer and Coordinator of the Short courses programme in the Faculty of Social and Management Sciences of the University of Buea. He is an economist with more than seven scientific publications to his credit. He is a bona fide member of CODESRIA and many other scientific organizations.

George Ndoh Mbanga is a Senior Lecturer in Economics in the University of Yaounde II, Cameroon.

Henry Muluh is a lecturer of broadcasting in the department of Journalism and mass Communication at the University of Buea, Cameroon. He studied at the University of Kent and City University of London in the United kingdom. His research interests are in the evolution of the modern mass media and media production. He has published journal articles and book chapters.

Arsene Honore Gideon Nkama holds a doctoral degree in economics and an Assistant Professor in Yaounde II University. He was a Ph.D. Fellow at the United Nations University Institute of Advanced Studies (UNU/IAS), Tokyo, Japan in 2000 where he contributed to UNU/IAS Working Paper Series. He has published papers and contributed to reports on Cameroon some main ones which include Cameroon's Poverty Reduction Strategy Paper, Cameroon Development Policy Review.

Walter Gam Nkwi is a Lecturer in the Department of History, Faculty of Arts, University of Buea in Cameroon where he graduated with an MA in history with a minor in archaeology. He is currently working on his PhD, and his research interests are in socio-cultural and economic history.

Ian Taylor holds an MPhil from the University of Hong Kong and a DPhil from the University of Stellenbosch in South Africa. He is currently a Lecturer in Africa Politics at the School of International Relations, University of St. Andrews, United Kingdom. Prior to joining the School he was a Senior Lecturer in the Department of Political and Administrative Studies, University of Botswana. His research interests are in International Political Economy, with a specific regional focus on Africa. He is also interested in regional security as well as critical theories relating generally to both multilateralism and regionalisation. He has just finished writing a book on the New Partnership for Africa's Development (NEPAD).

Emmanuel Yenshu Vubo is a Senior Lecturer in Sociology and Head of Department of Sociology and Anthropology at the University of Buea. He obtained a doctorate in Sociology from the University of Yaoundé in 1991. He has published several scholarly journal articles and contributed to book chapters in the domain of sociology and social anthropology. He is currently working on civil society in both traditional and contemporary contexts and the role it can play in the search of development alternatives.

Vukenkeng Andrew Wujung obtained the Licence and the Maîtrise-ès-Sciences Economiques from the University of Yaoundé and is currently completing a Ph.D. thesis in Economics at the University of Yaoundé II. He is currently a tutor of economics and trainer of modern pedagogy in the Arts with the Presbyterian Secondary School, Batibo. His other research interests are in environmental protection.

Introduction

E.S.D. Fomin & John W. Forje

Central Africa is a geographical nomenclature as it is used here in the designation of the area covered by the CODESRIA anniversary conference held in Douala, Cameroon from 4–5 October 2003. The sub-region has never been a single political entity. The area was never governed by one supreme ruler. Neither the great Bakongo kings of Pre-European Congo region nor the French colonial Equatorial African Empire embraced the totality of the region as represented in the area covered by the conference. The area covered is massive in landmass with over fifteen independent states albeit sparsely populated. It extends from Burundi and Rwanda along its eastern limit to Cameroon in the west and from Angola in the south, to the Republic of Chad to the north.

The sub-region shares quite a lot in common geographically as well as in the development issues (Crises, Reform, and Reconstruction) that constitute the theme of this Conference. It is largely covered by a dense equatorial rain forest, one of the largest and varied in biodiversity, remaining rain forests in the world today. This forest jungle seems to have inhibited the frequent creation of large scale states in this region in the past as compared to the Sudan region of Africa. The area is drained almost entirely by the great Congo River and its tributaries. They and other rivers that drain directly into the Atlantic Ocean such as the Sananga, Wouri and the Mungo provide over sixteen thousand kilometres of navigable waters (Murray 1866:47). Water transport was therefore the most reliable means of communication and transportation in the sub-region in the past and it is still important especially in the Democratic Republic of Congo. It was the main means through which trade was conducted between the hinterlands of this region and its Atlantic coast at the Gulf of Guinea. The African traders, the European explorers, the slavers, and the European colonial agents used these rivers as the key means of transportation in the early commercial transactions involving ivory, slaves and forest produce from this region. River transportation was indeed a great uniting factor in the dense and difficult jungle of this central African sub-region.

The transport and communication problems of Central Africa are only some of the difficulties that the geography of this area has imposed on its history of development. The western and eastern portions of the region are mountainous thus compounding the problem of road and railway construction and they have remained undeveloped in most parts of this region. The torrential rainfall, high humidity and insects carrying diseases are also some of the natural factors that have beset the development of this region. Yet the geography of Central Africa is more a blessing than a curse. In addition to the wonderful timber resource and other forest riches, the hydroelectricity potentials of the many huge rivers are enormous.

The subsoil of the region was once and still to some extent abounds with many highly valued minerals and large quantities of crude oil reserves. After many years of colonialist and neocolonialist exploitation of these riches, little or nothing is there in terms of development, to attest to the tremendous wealth that foreign imperialists and their African collaborators have looted from the whole sub-region since the fifteenth century when this area came under the infamous trans-Atlantic slave trade. Here begins the saga of the numerous development problems of the region which is better told in its history than its geography.

Historically the Central African sub-region has many common experiences. It is peopled largely by Bantu speakers who spread into the region supposedly from the area around the present day Cameroon–Nigerian southern borders in the first millennium BC (Shillington 1989: 138). The Bantu met in this region the pygmies who are one of the oldest autochthonous peoples of Africa. Unlike the Bantu who spread across to East and South Africa, the pygmies have remained attached to the heartland of the Central African forest. They are among the purest races of the world today. Not much is known about their civilization other than that they are very good dancers and experts in the medicinal plants of the huge Central African rain forest.

The Bantu appeared to have evolved a high civilization before the advent of the trans-Atlantic slave trade that ravaged the area and prepared it for yet an unprecedented pillage by European colonizers. This civilization was characterized among other aspects by State building, agriculture and iron workings. But this did not last long. The trans-Atlantic slave trade and its ramifications ruined it. At the height of the trade in this area, that is from 1790–1799, Central Africa exported some 340,110 slaves being the highest region then along the Atlantic coast of Africa. In fact from 1660–1870 the region lost over 3,821,769 persons to the Atlantic slave trade, according to conservative estimates, constituting 40.3 percent of the slaves exported from the Atlantic coast of Africa during the period (Eltis 1989:17). Colonization is one of the major ramifications of the slave business in

Central Africa as well as the other parts of Africa. As a matter of fact, it was more about the control of the river Congo and its fabulously rich hinterlands that the European Powers held the Berlin Conference of 1884-1885 to regulate the use of this great water way and the acquisition of colonial territories in other parts of Africa.

And as the outcome of this scramble for Africa by European imperialists, Central Africa suffered the colonial yoke of almost all European imperialist states. Thus Germany colonized Cameroon; Belgium grabbed Congo Leopoldville and Rwanda – Burundi; France amassed Congo Brazzaville, Central African Republic, Gabon and Chad; Portugal occupied Angola, Sao Tome and Principe while Spain took Equatorial Guinea. Even the British who were initially absent here came in later to exercise colonial influence over the British Cameroons when Germany was defeated and ousted from Cameroon in the First World War. Central Africa appeared therefore to have had the lion's share of different European colonial influences. Some papers of this conference have linked the terrible persistent crises and underdevelopment in this rich sub-region to the legacy of colonialism and its ramifications.

The role of the difficult physical environment, the multiplicities of conflicting ethnic entities, the bad colonial legacies and the purposeless African political elite are all to blame for the development woes of Central Africa. The theme of this conference, "Crises, Reform and Reconstruction" greatly inspired scholars who took part in it to study and discuss in an eclectic manner the development problems of this sub-region. Reading through the papers presented in English which are contained in this publication we find it necessary to subdivide them, for better appreciation, into two sections according to the closeness of the issues they treat thus:

- Nation building and regional integration: Problems and prospects
- The weird wind of democratization and governance

In this introduction we have hinted just on the main arguments and conclusions of each section to enable readers better appreciate Central Africa from the perspective of this conference.

Nation Building and Regional Integration: Problems and Prospects

The papers in this section focus on different problems and prospects of nation building and regional integration in Central Africa. It is important to note that the problems of nation building in this sub-region are inherent in the way all the states here were created. The nation states in the sub-region are all patchworks of ethnic entities put together haphazardly by European colonialists. Some of them, like Cameroon, have over two hundred and above of these ethnic groups. However, the very small states like Equatorial Guinea, Congo Republic, the Republics of Rwanda and Burundi are fairly homogenous in ethnic composition yet ethnic related conflicts are also a big hindrance to nation building among them as it is in the large states with many traditionally organized societies. And since nation building is all about melting ethnic differences to create a national culture, it is bound to be difficult in this region where ethnic groups are plentiful.

The papers in this section that treat crises which emanate from ethnicity, identity and citizenship see crises arising from these issues as disturbing new developments in the body politic of most states in Central Africa. All colonialists who exploited this region used favoured ethnic groups in the indirect rule, which they practiced in some parts of their colonies. But ethnic conflicts became a major disturbing phenomenon in the politics of this region only after 1990. From then the sub-region and other parts of Africa were caught up in the wind of change that started in eastern Europe. In almost all countries in the sub-region there were ethnic related conflicts that went a long way to complicate the frequent political upheavals of the period.

The haphazard manner in which the colonialists lumped together these ethnic entities to create the present nation states in the sub-region and the way they and their African collaborators treated the non-collaborators are at the origin of the ethnic antagonism that has beset the building of strong states and modern politics in Central Africa. As one reads through the other papers of this section it is discovered that the perpetration of this ethnic phenomenon in the politics and governance of this region is to blame squarely on the Central African political elite that is purposeless, greedy, tribalistic and more often than not these elites are neocolonialist agents with little or no concern for the welfare of the people they govern.

The discourse on nation building as seen in this section of this publication is centred more, understandably, on problems than solutions. In the first place no colonial power in the area succeeded in creating a viable nation state before terminating its colonial rule. After independence, many states were engulfed in interminable internal ethnic related conflicts that made nonsense of the so-called nationhood. Secondly, neocolonialism seems to thrive well in weak states with chaotic economies and administration, which has been the case in states in Central Africa. From these persistent internal conflicts, the prospects of building viable nations in the sub-region in the short run are slim.

The political ramifications of ethnic conflicts seem to have affected all states in the sub-region but not in the same proportion. Ethnic conflicts for example appear to have had greater negative influence on the politics of the Great Lakes countries (Rwanda and Burundi); the Democratic Republic of Congo and the Republic of Cameroon than in the rest of other states. Bangarwanda who are Congolese of Rwandese origin are ethnically discriminated against in citizenship matters in the Democratic Republic of Congo. This denial of citizenship to groups on the basis of ethnic origin, their length of stay in the country notwithstanding, is responsible for the Banyamulenge problem in DR Congo. In this Great Lakes area peoples of neighbouring states often promote these conflicts. They exploit the maltreatment of persons of their ethnic origin in a neighbouring state to intervene in the body politic of that state as in the case of DR Congo and her neighbours.

The situation in the Republic of Cameroon is slightly different. In the first place no one ethnic group in Cameroon is so overwhelming in size and influence to dictate the pace of development singlehandedly. Secondly, the ethnicity, identity and citizenship problems of Cameroon are not complicated by individuals from neighbouring states. In his paper Vubo Emmanuel Yenshu shows how the regime in Cameroon had to recourse to *de facto* alliances to win ethnic support. Such alliances are built throughout the country by the appointment of elites from ethnic groups to top government positions. This might explain why Cameroon governments since the 1990s are unusually very large. Most governments have had on the average over forty ministers, taking both senior and junior ones together. This is because every ethnic entity wants to be represented in government as a sign of recognition and appreciation for voting for the regime in power.

The problem is also seen in the multiparty aspect of the political life of Cameroon. In fact the greatest problem of plural party endeavour in this country is plurality itself. Cameroon counts over 180 political parties most of them drawing support only from the ethnic groups of the founders. Very few of them enjoy support across ethnic boundaries. The party in power uses only patronages and sinecures to buy support from other groups. Ethnic identities have sometimes been revised to accommodate more persons. The Sawa identity of the Douala people in Cameroon had never considered the Bakweri component of the South West Province seriously until when the present prime minister, Mr. Peter Mafany Musonge of Bakweri origin was appointed prime minister of Cameroon in 1996.

The political repercussions of the resurgence of ethnicity in the political life of this sub region have also been marked on Rwanda and Burundi. The genocide in Rwanda in 1993, which is the outcome of an ethnic conflict that pitted the Hutu against the Tutsi, is the most glaring and unfortunate example of the ramifications of ethnic antagonism in the body politic of this region. The phenomenon is not quite serious in the other smaller countries in the region and this might explain why no papers specifically addressed it in the context of such countries at this conference. But ethnicity and citizenship crises which are traceable to the concept of autochthones as opposed to *allogenes* are quite rife in the politics of many African countries today. Ethnic related conflicts have therefore affected negatively aspects of national development in Central Africa. The so-called national governments that rule these patchworks of ethnic entities pursue policies that antagonize rather than unite their peoples. In fact identity and citizenship crises which are rife in most countries of the sub-region are a byproduct of this sad lack of purposeful national governments. Even military governments that have ruled in almost all states in the region have often also resorted to the perpetration of ethnic adhesion while singing the meaningless song of national unity without real nations.

The efforts mobilised in creating regional blocs in Central Africa as a way of fostering regional integration and development has a checkered history as some papers in this section clearly demonstrate. Attempts to create regional economic blocs here were started in 1958 when the former French colonial administrative union, called French Equatorial Africa, that grouped all French colonies of Chad, Congo, Gabon and Central Africa Republic was dismantled. It was replaced in 1959 by *Union Douanière Equatoriale* (UDE). Many of its members had obtained autonomy from France. The UDE became UDEAC in 1964 when the Federal Republic of Cameroon, the former British and French UN administered territories that united in 1961, joined the union. Arsene Honore Gideon Nkama shows in his paper that UDEAC suffered severe vicissitudes and became a white elephant and gave way to CEMAC which took on Equatorial Guinea as a new member. He is quite optimist in his conclusion that with careful planning and greater political association among member states of CEMAC, the community could become a viable economic bloc.

There is no doubt that Central Africa has the potential of becoming a great economic entity, given even what is left now of the tremendous resources it once had but that is not quite foreseeable from the rest of the papers in this section. The other papers show many internal and external inhibiting factors to the recovery of what is left of the resources of the region for public interest. Some of the key factors discussed include: the burden of foreign debt and the problem of economic integration.

The general worry about the future of the much talked about economic integration of Central Africa is that the political situation in the region is not conducive to economic growth even within member countries of the region. Economic integration has to proceed not precede political stability in this sub-region which is notorious for political chaos. If one were to borrow experience from elsewhere one would discover that the prerequisite for membership of the European union is the practice of democracy and good governance. Few if any ruler of the states in the sub-region is democratically elected. As a result instability is rampant and the economies of most countries here are in shambles. Indeed, the region has some of the poorest and heavily indebted countries in the world.

As a matter of fact, nation building and regional integration in Central Africa are two development processes that must be pursued vigorously but the latter following the former. In other words the tremendous wealth of Central Africa shall never benefit its peoples unless the nation states in the sub-region become veritable nations. The integration of their economies and to an extent their political life must come as a way of working together to maximize the economic and social benefits of co-operation among member nations. It is in this way that these states can cope with other problems that engender crises and underdevelopment in the region.

Central Africa is the only one of the three major petroleum producing regions of Africa (North, West and Central) that has nothing to show in terms of development to justify its oil wealth which has been exploited since the 1970s. Although the oil output from Central Africa is smaller in comparison with that from each of the other two regions, oil producing states here are more in number than in the other regions. In fact while Nigeria is the only petroleum producer in West Africa and Algeria and Libya in North Africa, the Central African producers include Angola, Cameroon, Congo Republic and Gabon. Equatorial Guinea and Chad just joined this club recently. The production from these countries put together is substantial.

Central Africa is second again only to South Africa in the continent in the production of highly valued non-petroleum minerals. Diamond, gold and uranium are among the minerals found in the sub region. The Democratic Republic of Congo leads the region in the non-petroleum minerals whose reserves are much and varied. Like Angola, DR Congo, the greatest producers of these minerals in the sub-region, has little or nothing to show for the wealth that these minerals have generated for nearly half a century. As a matter of fact, the mineral wealth of these states has brought them conflicts and destruction rather than peace and development. But the saga of the rich mineral wealth of this region does not tell it all.

The Congo rain forest was once one of the greatest single concentrations of tropical rain forest in the world. And the region has produced and is still producing the greatest quantity of tropical timber in the world again without much to show in development generated from it. On the contrary, timber companies, which are largely foreign, destroy with impunity the flora and fauna, the environment and the transport infrastructures in the region. It is only in recent years in many of the timber producing states in this region that timber companies have been compelled to pay royalties to affected rural communities for development. Countries of this sub-region with rich tropical rain forests include Cameroon, Central African Republic, Congo Republic, DR Congo and Angola. Unfortunately most of them are among countries that are listed as the poorest in the world.

The mineral wealth of DR Congo was at the origin of its plunder by the colonialists and is still largely responsible for the activities of the neocolonialist aggressors in that country. The exploitation of the petroleum riches of Central Africa is more recent than that of diamond and other minerals. Those of Equatorial Guinea and Chad are most recent and known to be quite substantial (Zafar and Kubota 2003). But the two countries like the others in the sub-region are not ruled by democratically elected governments. Though this sub-region has lost a lot in the past in oil revenue to foreign exploiters as well as to unscrupulous nationals, oil revenue remains a big fraction of the revenues of most CEMAC countries. Some papers in this section are devoted to the measures that could be taken to redress the misuse of the rich mineral and petroleum wealth of this region by greedy and senseless ruling elites and their collaborators. Some of them see in the fiscal policies of the states concerned, budgetary measures, structural adjustments and the management of foreign debt as the best away of addressing this problem. In fact the degree of the economic misery in this sub-region is attested by the fact that many states here are the poor and heavily indebted.

In the structural adjustment conditionality of the International Monetary Fund (IMF) to which most countries here have gone cap in hand since the 1980s, the reform of the fiscal policy, the budgeting of state revenues, liberalization of the economy and the fight against corruption in government and corporate bodies are paramount. But the weaknesses are so deep rooted that few countries have met the conditionality satisfactorily. The IMF loans have failed to restore the economies in the region to health. The reasons for this are obvious. First most of these states hardly meet the IMF conditionality before getting the loans. Secondly the IMF has not succeeded in ensuring that corrupt regimes do not use the monies given them for selfish purposes.

'If you think structural adjustment is going to turn Zaire around, you are a bit naïve. An economic program does and cannot change a social malaise.' Zaire was one of the first Central African states to do structural adjustment business with the IMF but Mobutu was unable to sustain it. He accused IMF of re-colonization and dropped the measures in 1988 (Harden 1990:56). The social malaise that has inhibited reforms in fiscal policies, budget management and the liberalization of the economies of the states in this region is corruption whose corollaries are nepotism, tribalism and clientelism in government business. The measures put in place by some of the states to fight corruption and its attendant evils cannot achieve much since the wide spread corruption emanates largely from high government officers some of whom are the untouchables in the positions they occupy in their countries. This malaise must be fought from top to bottom not the reverse as it is practiced in these states.

Tackling this problem at the level of CEMAC is not easy as the practice is competition not cooperation as it should be. Business at the level of individual states as well as in CEMAC is often stifled by a fiscal policy which is bedevilled by corruption and incompetence, consequently inimical to a dynamic economy. Generally there is this growing poverty in the region as the years go by. It is no exaggeration that most countries in the region are poorer now in their per capita incomes and social and economic livelihood than they were in the first ten years of independence. The reason for this sad situation must be sought in the very bad regimes that have presided over this wealth and the destinies of these states since the 1980s. These dictators in all the cases were caught up unprepared in a wind of change which they have spent these resources resisting.

Andrew W. Vukenkeng and Walters Nkwi in their papers have departed from the general trend, in the other papers of this section, of perceiving the problems of nation building in Central Africa from the political and economic perspectives. Vukenkeng stresses in his paper the urgent need to promote environmental education among the youths in Cameroon secondary schools as a way of building a strong and healthy nation. He commends the effort being made in this direction by the Presbyterian Church in Cameroon. A good perception of other dimensions of nation building in Central Africa whose rich environment is under going rapid destruction but his scope is rather too narrow. Nkwi, also using a lone example in his paper shows how cult art could be a factor of unity among peoples, indeed, a type of resilience in nation building. Using the Afo-a-kom of the Kom people of the Western Grassfield of Cameroon he shows how the theft, brief sojourn at the United States of America and the return to Kom of this religious art object awakened great national sensitivity that could be harnessed for meaningful nation building endeavour.

The Weird Wind of Democratization and Governance

Before the 1990s all the countries in Central Africa were ruled by either the military or single party civilian dictatorial regimes, some of them dating back as far as the mid 1960s. Joseph Desiré Mobutu seized power as a military dictator in Congo Kinshasa (DR Congo) in 1965 while Amadou Ahidjo tricked all the active political parties in Cameroon into one party (Cameroon National Union, CNU) under him in 1966. The trend went on fast and the region was soon under unprecedented military and party dictatorships.

In Central African Republic (CAR), Bukasa, (a military dictator) even went further and crowned himself emperor. It would be recalled that CAR. was and it is still perhaps the poorest country in the sub-region. In Chad, CAR and Congo Republic the frequent change of military governments through coups d'états made the bad situation even worse. In Cameroon and the DR Congo where dictators ruled for many years people were cowed to submission and there was apparent peace but little development and progress. In Angola the civil war whose parties were backed by the West and East, supporting the rebels and government respectively, the military remained in control for many years before the advent of this weird wind of democratization.

It was in this messy military and civilian absolutism that this wind from eastern Europe caught up with the states of Central Africa. Many if not all the dictators considered the reforms involved in this revolution (multiparty democracy, good governance, transparency and the conduct of free and fair elections) as foreign and inapplicable to their states and as a result resisted the changes. Some have continued to do so while others albeit timidly have tried some of the changes.

The response of these dictators to the changes and the effects that it has had on the region are some of the issues discussed in the chapters of this section.

A number of the papers have shown how the resistance mounted by these dictators unleashed waves of violent pressure in most countries of the sub-region. This violent pressure took the form of civil disobedience and ghost town measures in many areas. Civil disobedience involved non-payment of taxes and bills to utility corporations like those concerned with the distribution of water and electricity which were state owned in most countries in the region at the time. The ghost town activities included the non opening of business premises in the urban cities. The enforcement of these measures often led to violence and the destruction of property. Governments were in serious financial stress and could hardly pay civil servants. Under this pressure, Gabon, Congo Brazzaville, Chad, Congo Kinshasa, Central African Republic, succumbed and organized national conferences as a starting point to the multiparty democratization and liberalization that the masses wanted. The Cameroon government of president Paul Biya rejected the idea of the national conference but finally gave in to a less exacting tripartite conference in 1991.

These conferences appeared to have achieved little or nothing in terms of advancing democratization and liberalization in any of these countries. Nonetheless, progressive forces were unleashed all over the region often with terrible consequences. The genocide in Rwanda, the civil war in Burundi, in Congo Republic and DR Congo were all in a way manifestations of this wind of change which found vent in ethnic hatred. Even the foreign military adventures which brought DR Congo to the brink of partition are all byproducts of these internal political upheavals which left most states badly shattered. In his paper Ian Taylor sees some of the ramifications of this phenomenon in the chaotic political economy of DR Congo, which external adventurous fortune seekers have exploited to foment conflicts and violence in the sub-region. In Cameroon the disturbances reached its apogee in the presidential elections of 1992, when the leading opposition candidate, John Fru Ndi was purportedly robbed of victory by the incumbent old guard president Paul Biya through underhand methods. The situation in Cameroon today like the one in other countries of the sub-region is that of an impasse to borrow the apt words of Valentine Ameli Tabi, the author of the paper 'Cameroon: Tribulations of a Democratic Transition'. Since 1992, elections have been regularly conducted in Cameroon but the complaint against those elections is that they lack transparency, fairness and freeness. For many of these countries, election is the luxury they cannot afford now. In Chad, CAR, Congo Republic, DR Congo and even Gabon to an extent, elections are out of the question for now.

One of the ramifications of the chaotic democratic situation in Central Africa is the reckless abuse of human rights by governments as well the radical elements of the opposition forces. In chapter eleven, Margaret Ayike has shown how the rights of children in this region are flagrantly abused. The loss of jobs by parents as result of political victimization, the ruinous cuts in salaries by governments unable to pay civil servants as well as the loss of property through arson associated with violent demonstrations affect many parents and consequently the children. Many in the sub-region can not go to school because their parents can not afford the expenses.

The rights of children have also been directly abused in these agitations for democratization and good governance. Many politicians are known to have pushed children to the forefront of their demonstrations and accompanied confrontations with conservative government forces to the extent that many children in the sub-region are incapacitated for life. The future appears to hold very little for them. The situation is an anxious one because the misery and hardship that the process has occasioned have produced posts seekers not statesmen that these politicians ought to be. However, human rights abuse which appears to be endemic in the sub-region is not just the byproduct of democratization but more that of bad governance which is a long standing phenomenon in Central Africa.

The vicissitudes of the civil society is also seen by Susanna Awasom as a fundamental setback in this struggle to build a democratic culture in the sub-region. Central Africa must reform politically to reap the fruits of sub-regional and continental cooperation. CEMAC, COPAX, NEPAD and even the AU will not take this sub-region out of economic woes unless the states therein are politically strong and stable. The political leaders of this region should learn to derive their power from the masses through the ballot box in elections which are free and fair. It is also hoped that these sub-regional and continental organizations would put the pressure necessary on dictators who still rule in many of the states of the region to submit to meaningful democratic practice. It is high time that other African states should take interest in the reconstruction of this very rich but poorly governed sub-region of the continent. In fact the various types of conflicts that have bedevilled this sub-region have largely exploited this chaotic political situation and bad governance.

Analysing the causes and nature of political crises in Central Africa, E.S.D. Fomin shows in chapter nine how the exclusion policy based on ethnic or cultural antagonism is often at the root of political tension in the sub-region. This policy involves keeping other elites out of governance on ethnic and intra-ethnic prejudices. The governance of states in the sub-region has since the colonial era promoted ethnic, clannish, and regional exclusion to the detriment of healthy democratic practice. Political conflicts which have brought Burundi, Rwanda and many states in the sub-region to the brink of destruction are rooted in this policy. The politics of exclusion has bred some of the most catastrophic conflicts in the region in terms of human casualties. The Rwandese conflict of 1993 claimed close to one million lives being the worst in recent history of the sub-region.

Burundi, DR Congo, Congo Republic and Chad have lost many human lives and valuable property in exclusion provoked political conflicts.

The focus of some papers in this section is on peace building as a way of ending conflicts and promoting reconstruction in this conflict torn region. John W Forje sees the solution to the endemic political conflicts and bad governance in Africa in general and Central Africa in particular in the rethinking of the political will and empowerment of the masses. The masses who are the worst victims of conflicts in the region should be empowered through political education and poverty alleviation measures. The main cause of the lack interest in politics among the masses in Africa is poverty. In states where elections are organized the politicians, often those of the party in power get their votes usually by purchase or intimidation of the electorate. The dictators that preside over the destinies of most states in this sub-region might eventually be ousted only by mass uprisings as it happened in recent years in Eastern Europe. This might sound as if we are advocating violence as a solution to the political intransigence that breed conflicts in most parts of Africa. Mass uprising, emanating from political awareness, as a means of doing away with political dictators is perhaps the lesser of the two evils.

The rhetoric about union governments as a way of circumventing exclusion in the governance of many states in this sub-region has not yielded much fruit. In the Great Lakes area, the belated role of the international community to end conflicts in that region by creating power sharing governments on ethnic basis has brought only precarious peace. In fact, despite the earnest effort of great world leaders including the venerable Nelson Mandela, peace is yet to return to these Great Lakes states. In DR Congo many attempts to organize a union government have ended in naught and military dictatorship has continued to reign. In Cameroon, the government in power has circumvented the call for a union government by absorbing hand picked political parties into what is usually called in that country as presidential majority. Unfortunately union governments have come to mean that the party that takes the others into its government will continue to remain in power while varying its allies as it is the situation in Cameroon and Gabon.

There is a school of thought that sees a lasting solution to these vexing politically motivated conflicts in the creation of a new political structure for the sub-region. The new structure most advocated is federalism which is bastardised in many states of the region now as decentralisation. Of course a decentralised government is, strictly speaking, a unitary government (Awa 1976:2) The ethnic, cultural and physical composition of most states in the region coupled with the many ills of over centralisation, which has bedevilled government business in the countries of the sub-region since independence, require that any meaningful attempt at reconstruction must adopt a federal set-up. The decentralisation into federated or regional unites is a way forward which is also prescribed by international donors but the old guards are toying with it. Where decentralised units are created like in Cameroon and Gabon but with very little power devolved to them from the centre, the evils of over centralisation (corruption, favouritism, nepotism and the lack of development) will persist. The regimes in power here resist federalism because it is the antithesis of dictatorial power with its attendant evils of anti-democracy and bad governance. These evils are indeed incarnated in over centralisation which is fashionable all over the sub-region.

It is our hope that this CODESRIA initiative of bringing scholars regularly together to dialogue on the development problems of Africa will yield fruit. Africanist scholars shall through this eclectic intercourse get to understand better the development problems of the continent which affect them as individuals and challenge them as scholars who are the top cream of their societies. As

> men of high intellectual enterprise, (we) must contribute
> to the common culture, where we talk to each other,
> not just about the facts of nature …
> but about the nature of the human predicament,
> about the nature of man, about law,
> about the good and the bad,
> about morality, about virtue, about politics
> in the Aristotelian sense
> (Robert Oppendeheime in Bernard Fonlon, 1969:81).

Many African intellectuals have not sufficiently preoccupied themselves with the deteriorating political and economic developments in the continent. The dictators that rule most states in this continent have impoverished, emasculated and rendered intellectuals impotent to the extent that many of them do not raise their voices against the corruption, nepotism, favouritism, and bad governance that characterised all the states of the sub-region. In fact some of them have joined these dictators for various pecuniary and other reasons. They shamelessly lick their boots and dance to their tunes for political positions which put them fittingly in this clique that exploits their country and renders the masses miserable. In all states in the sub-region, highly qualified men and women have been appointed to cabinet positions in government. Such appointments are often based on ethnic considerations and party loyalties and many who take them usually dance to the tune of these dictators. Thus these so-called intellectuals are often strong defenders of these dictatorial regimes.

They put their scholarly know-how to the justification of the wrongdoings of such regimes. The CODESRIA initiative might help to enable scholars appreciate and get concerned with the development predicament of Africa which emanates from bad politics and governance. Their lack of concern or passive involvement in the struggle has been perhaps the absence of deserving academic fora like the

CODESRIA 30th Anniversary Conferences. The papers of the Central African conference, some of which form the subject matter of this publication, are interesting and constitute a wonderful starting point of involving scholars in the development endeavour of this continent. We find in the exercise a wonderful way of empowering scholars who should be the avant-gardes of the fight against ills that have continued to undermine development in Africa.

Section I

Nation Building and Regional Integration: Problems and Prospects

1

Regional Economic Blocs in Central Africa: What Went Right and What Went Wrong?

Arsene Honore Gideon Nkama

Introduction

Regional economic integration stands for special economic agreements between countries in a specified geographical area or between two or more geographical areas. These agreements lead to a differential treatment in trade and even in investment policies for member countries in comparison with non-member countries. The potential impacts of such an economic grouping can be static on the one hand and dynamic on the other. The static impact refers to changes occurring in the equilibrium market price and quantity before and after the creation of the economic grouping. This can lead to trade creation or trade diversion. For a given product, trade creation appears when high cost production is substituted by low cost production because of regional integration, while economic diversion occurs when low cost production is substituted by high cost production. Trade creation is a positive impact of regional integration in contrast to trade diversion. Among the dynamic impacts of economic integration, one can have an increased competition and then better performance of producers, increased investment, economies of scale, political and economic commitment, and socio-political stability.

Conscious of the benefits of regional integration, Central African countries adopted some measures in the earlier independence period, others during the 1970–1980s. They constituted a strategy of development in which regional integration played an important role. In the Central African sub-region, the pursuit of economic integration still faces a lot of challenges. The sub-region lags behind many other African sub-regions in term of economic integration. This paper is concerned with the achievements and challenges of Central African economic blocs in view of the increasing sub-regional benefits in the global economy. The paper is organised as follows. Section one presents the development of regional economic blocs in Central Africa. Section two is an analysis of tools of regional integration in each regional economic bloc while section three deals with the sub-region intra-trade. In section four, the last section, I discuss some policy recommendations.

The Development of Regional Economic Blocs in Central Africa

Central African States are grouped into four sub-regional economic blocs: (i) the Economic Community of Central African States (ECCAS); (ii) the Economic and Monetary Community of Central Africa (CEMAC); (iii) the Economic Community of Great Lakes Countries (CEPGL); and (iv) the Lake Chad Basin Commission (LCBC). These regional groupings have sometimes the same objectives and many of them overlap. In this section, I present each bloc starting with the CEMAC, the eldest, as its development can help us understand the development, achievements and failures of the others.

The Development of CEMAC

The Equatorial Customs Union: 1959–1961

Before independence, Chad, Congo, Gabon and Oubangui-Chari (former name of Central African Republic) formed French Equatorial Africa (FEA). France administered FEA as a single territory. Brazzaville was the capital. Following reforms adopted under the 'Loi-Cadre' in 1956, there had been a slight movement towards political decentralisation in favour of FEA. In 1958 most of the FEA member countries became autonomous. But countries needed to maintain their economic and political links not only with the metropolis, but also with other FEA member countries. For Oubangui-Chari and Chad, it was necessary to have access to the sea through Gabon. In addition to this, the two countries were poor and less industrialised. They needed to secure their financial sources as their main revenue came from other member countries, notably Gabon (CEA 1981:10-11). Congo was the most industrialised country. Because of weak domestic demand the country needed to preserve its FEA market for its manufactured products. Gabon, which had been the main supplier of funds in the federation budget, was hostile to the federation. Finally, supported by France, the four member countries of FEA signed on January 17, 1959 a convention creating the Union Douaniere Equatoriale- UDE (Equatorial Customs Union). The convention entered into force on June 23, 1959.

The UDE-Cameroon 1961–1964

Cameroon formed a German protectorate after 1884. In 1918 following the German defeat in World War I, Cameroon was divided into British Cameroon and

French Cameroon. French Cameroon became autonomous in 1957. This was a consequence of the French 'Loi-Cadre' of 1956. Gabon had important commercial links with Cameroon while Congo feared the entry of Cameroon to UDE, basing its arguments on the fact that Cameroon's products would be very competitive relative to those from Congo, leading to a decline in the country's market share. Taking into account the fact that Cameroon was a member of CFA zone and then member of the regional central bank – BEAC – France encouraged Cameroon's entry to UDE. A convention regulating Cameroon-UDE partnership was signed in 1961. UDE became UDE-Cameroon. UDE-Cameroon was a partial free zone between two equal parties: UDE on the one hand and Cameroon on the other.

The UDEAC 1964–1996

The treaty establishing the Central African Customs and Economics Union (UDEAC) was signed on December 1, 1964 between Cameroon and the member countries of the Equatorial Customs Union. The treaty entered into force on January 1, 1966. The five UDEAC founding members were Cameroon, Central African Republic (CAR), Chad, Congo and Gabon.

The main UDEAC objectives were to establish gradually a common market in Central Africa area; to eliminate obstacles for intra-regional trade in order to benefit from domestic markets' extension; and to reinforce unity among member countries. UDEAC institutions are: the Council of head of State (the supreme organ), the Management Committee composed of two ministers from each member country, and the General Secretariat, the executive organ based in Bangui, capital of Central African Republic.

UDEAC faced a deep crisis two years later. CAR withdrew in 1968 and rejoined UDEAC the same year. Chad withdrew in 1968 and re-entered in 1985, while Equatorial Guinea was admitted into the Union.

The CEMAC 1996

The treaty creating the Communauté Economique et Monetaire d'Afrique Centrale (CEMAC) was signed in 1996 (treaty and additive conventions) and entered into force on January 1, 1998. It was a case of UDEAC being relabelled CEMAC. Actually CEMAC is a single market of about 30 million people over a territory of approximately 3.02 million square kilometres. The territory, population and Gross Domestic Product of CEMAC are unequally shared among member countries. CEMAC is largely dominated by Cameroon that accounts for about 45 percent of its total GDP, followed by Gabon (about 25 percent of CEMAC GDP). Chad, Congo, Central African Republic and Equatorial Guinea each represent less than ten percent of the Community's GDP.

Other Sub-regional Economic Blocs in Central Africa Area

The ECCAS

The Economic Community of Central African States (ECCAS) was established in 1983 and includes all CEMAC member countries. Other ECCAS member countries are Burundi, Democratic Republic of Congo, Rwanda and Sao Tome and Principe. Angola maintained observer status until 1998 when it formally joined the community. ECCAS is the largest regional group in central Africa, but displays disparities in economic and trade indicators amongst member states.

ECCAS aimed to promote regional economic co-operation and establish a Central African Common Market. The treaty establishing ECCAS emphasised that the Community would promote and strengthen harmonious co-operation and self-sustained development in the fields of industry, transport and communications, energy, agriculture, natural resources, trade, customs, monetary and financial matters, human resources, tourism, education and training as well as the movement of persons.

The LCBC

Cameroon, Chad, Niger and Nigeria set up the Lake Chad Basin Commission (LCBC) in 1964. The group was enlarged with the entry of Central African Republic in 1994 and could enlarge further with Sudan's intention to become a member. The main objectives of the commission are: monitoring the region's water resources; promoting the conservation and optimal utilisation of these resources; and ensuring their use in support of irrigated agriculture, fisheries, livestock, reforestation and different other development activities in the region. During the last three decades, the water resources of Lake Chad and its main tributaries – the Logone and Chari rivers – have been seriously reduced as a result of combined rainfall deficit and increased utilisation of water by an increasing local population. According to UNDP the water of the lake has dropped to its lowest level in 3,500 years, and its surface area has been reduced to less than one-tenth of its former size. An important summit of heads of states was held in N'Djamena in August 2000 in order to concert action to protect the disappearing lake.

The CEPGL

Burundi, Democratic Republic of Congo and Rwanda, three ECCAS member countries, form the Economic Community of the Great Lakes Countries – Communauté Economique des Pays des Grands Lacs – CEPGL. The CEPGL was created in 1976 to promote regional economic co-operation and integration among its member countries. This regional grouping faces the same problems as other groupings of Central African States. The CEPGL has to solve the social instability as well as the civil war problem before any development programme can be feasible. The creation of each economics bloc leads to the adoption of tools of integration. A critical analysis of these tools is presented below.

Tools of Regional Integration in Central Africa

The tools of regional integration in Central Africa differ from one bloc to another. In the CEMAC these tools changed radically during the customs duty reform of 1994. In ECCAS, CEPGL and LCBC, these tools at times are announced but are not implemented.

In the CEMAC

Any analysis of tools of regional integration in the CEMAC should distinguish at least two main periods: the pre-reform period (before January 1994), and the post-reform period (after January 1994).

Before the 1994 Customs Duty Reform

The original treaty of Brazzaville envisaged a customs and even a monetary union. Member countries envisaged the removal of trade and non-trade barriers among themselves and the adoption of common barriers for goods imported from non-members. But the treaty was revised in 1974, leading to the facto abolition of common external tariffs.

The tools of regional integration in CEMAC can be found in Part II of the treaty establishing UDEAC. Article 28 of the Treaty stipulated that the Customs Union between the UDEAC member States would comprise a common external tariff (hereafter CET) in their relations with third countries; the free movement, exempt from all import duties and taxes, of unprocessed products originating in the member countries; a special preferential regime – the Single Tax (ST) regime – applicable to imports of industrial products originating in the Union, and a search for ways of gradually eliminating restrictive trade practices among member countries.

The CET

The Common External Tariff comprised the customs duty ('droit de douane'), the entry duty ('droit d'entrée') and the import turnover tax ('taxe sur le chiffre d'affaires a l'importation'). CET was imposed on c.i.f. prices of imported goods. The rates of customs duties varied widely from one good to another. The rates were also country-specific. While looking at the 1988 edition of UDEAC external tariffs, one realises that these taxes varied from 0 to 30 percent and from zero to 120 percent for customs duty and entry duty respectively. The import turnover tax was fixed at 10 percent of c.i.f. price plus the customs duty and the entry duty without any discrimination.

The Complementary Tax

The complementary tax (CT) on imports differed from one state to another. This tax existed in addition to the common external tariff. The CT was the main source of protection against other member countries because its rates were fixed independently. The utilisation of the complementary tax (which varied from 0 to 150 percent – see 1988 edition of UDEAC tariffs) as revenue and protection tool underlines the fact that UDEAC did not have a true common external tariff. In Table 1, one can observe the impact of the complementary tax in creating tax differentials among member countries in UDEAC. In this way the policy of harmonising import taxes had been a failure in UDEAC.

The Single Tax

UDEAC companies that exported to other member countries were given single tax status. That means companies could import input materials free of tax. On intra-regional sales, they were to pay the single tax on their ex-factory sales. The Management Committee individually determined the rates of the single tax. The tax was said to be single because the taxation of final products was substituted for all other local taxes. The rates of the single tax were generally lower than the customs duty, which otherwise would had been applied to manufactured goods traded among these countries. The principle of variable single tax rates was admitted during a six-year transitional period during which the differences were to be gradually reduced following annual revisions. The variable principle was adopted in order to serve distributive ends because relatively less industrialised countries – Chad and CAR notably – argued that uniform rates of taxation would advantage the more relatively industrialised countries - Cameroon and Congo – (Mytelka 1975:141). Unfortunately, the tax, which was to be harmonised progressively and achieve uniformity by 1972, was subject to substantial variations. Studying the bargaining behaviour of UDEAC decision makers as reflected in the pattern of single tax rates, Mytelka (1975) found that variations in single tax rates were a positive function of the demand for compensation within UDEAC and a negative function of responsiveness with which these demands were met. The more industrialised a country, the higher the rates of taxation on that country's products in sales in other UDEAC member countries (correlation = +.82). The higher the level of industrialisation, the lower the rate of taxation on other UDEAC products sold domestically (correlation = -.93).

During the 1980s, even if some rates were uniform (soap products for example) the situation can be illustrated by rates applicable to paints. Cameroon's paints were taxed 11 percent in Cameroon, lower than all other UDEAC member countries' paints sold in Cameroon. CAR taxed its product at 12 percent. This rate was lower than rates applied to Cameroon, Congo and Chad's products. Gabon taxed its products at 12 percent, lower than all other UDEAC products,

Table 1: Import tariff levels in UDEAC in 1988 – selected products

	UDEAC Common external tariff	Common external tax + Complementary tax					
		Cameroon	CAR	Chad	Congo	E. Guinea	Gabon
Plastic products	60.5	65.5	70.5	60.5	75.5	60.5	65.5
Aluminium sheets	38.5	48.5	48.5	38.5	43.5	38.5	43.5
Cigarettes	66.0	216.0	91.0	66.0	116.0	66.0	96.0
Paints	66.0	76.0	76.0	66.0	76.0	66.0	71.0
Beer	132.0	222.0	216.0	132.0	192.0	132.0	212.0
Chocolate	60.5	70.5	70.5	60.5	70.5	60.5	60.5
Vegetable oils	49.5	49.5	64.5	49.5	54.5	49.5	49.5
Textiles	55.0	65.0	70.0	55.0	70.0	55.0	60.0
Cosmetics	132.0	152.0	152.0	132.0	147.0	132.0	147.0
Sugar	99.0	119.0	99.0	99.0	124.0	99.0	104.0
Soap	49.5	59.5	59.5	49.5	54.5	49.5	54.5

Source: computed using the 1988 edition of the UDEAC tariffs.

except CAR's products. This situation can be viewed as protection against other member countries' products. The rate of Gabon's products in CAR is 12 percent being viewed as responsiveness to Gabon rates applied to CAR products. In Gabon, Cameroon's products are taxed 16 percent in response to the 16 percent of the main Gabonese manufacturer's products in Cameroon, even though two other Gabonese producers benefit from lower taxation. This behaviour of responsiveness or reciprocity even reprisal can be well observed between Cameroon and Congo the two relatively industrialised countries. CEP, a Cameroonian paints producer was taxed 18 percent in Congo while Savconco, a Congolese paint producer, was also taxed 18 percent in Cameroon. CAR products are favoured in other UDEAC countries. Paints from the Gabonese main producer are taxed 84 percent in Chad. That can be explained as a result of revenue needs in this country.

To sum up, a couple of explanations can be given for the variation and the non-uniformity of the single tax in UDEAC. First from the side of imports, the more a country imported from other member countries, the more this country tended to apply high rates in order to increase tax revenues or to protect its industry. In contrast, the lower the level of imports, the lower the rates of single tax for other partners' products in order to show its conformity with the sub-regional spirit of integration. Second, as regards exports, the more a country exported to its partners, the more likely this country was to be in favour of low single tax rates to stimulate its sales in UDEAC. The less a country exported in UDEAC the more likely it was importing more from its partners and if so, the higher the rates applied to its partners' products in order to compensate itself (tax revenue purposes).

The single tax failed in two main ways. First it reduced intra-regional trade to products under this regime. Second, taxes that were supposed to be uniform by 1972 were subject to important variations due to national egoism. The intra-union trade of manufactured goods was restricted to those produced by firms under the Single Tax regime. In fact, UDEAC did not achieve a common external tariffs and fiscal policy harmonisation. It did not reflect a real customs union as goods and services could not move freely. On the contrary, each UDEAC member country used tariffs to protect itself against its neighbours. For these reasons and several others, the World Bank proposed reforms for UDEAC tariffs in order to improve and simplify their structure, and to improve the revenue generating capacity and competitiveness of domestic manufacturing activity. The new reform that was adopted in 1994 led to the single tax abolition and its replacement by the Generalised Preferential Tax (GPT).

Table 2: Matrix of single tax rates of paints (product no. in tariffs: 32.09.21)

Producers	Rates as of the following dates	Country of sale				
		Cameroon	CAR	Congo	Gabon	Chad
CEP (Cameroon)	18/ 6/71	11	18	18	16	
CENTRACOL (RCA)	18/ 6/71	12	12	12	12	
CHIMIE (Gabon)	28/ 7/77	12	12	12	12	
SAV (Congo)	12/ 7/84	18	18	12	14	
ABA (Gabon)	26/ 7/85	16	12	18	12	84
IPEINT (Chad)	15/12/86	18	18	18	18	18
GPL (Gabon)	16/12/87	12	12	12	12	12

Sources: Different decisions of Management Committee in different years.

After the New Customs Duty Reform

In recognition of the limits of the former UDEAC tariffs, the World Bank and UDEAC Secretariat agreed in 1988 to undertake customs duty reform in the sub-region (MINFI 1995). The main recommendations of the reform were presented in the World Bank report No 9747-AFR of 30 June 1992. The act of reform was published in June 1993 and entered in force on 1 January 1994. The simplification of tariff structure, the abolition of the complementary tax, and the replacement of the single tax by the generalised preferential tax were the main results of the regional tax reform.

The New Common External Tariff

The new common external tariff of CEMAC comprises two taxes: a customs duty (CD) and a temporary surcharge tax (TT).

The CD is a function of the product category. Four imports categories are distinguished. The set custom duties are 5 percent for category 1; 10 percent for category 2; 20 percent for category 3 and 30 percent for category 4. Category one regroups essential goods (medicines, books); Category two regroups raw materials and capital goods. Products appearing in Category three are intermediary goods. General consumption goods are represented in Category four.

The objective of a temporary surtax was to protect each member country's industry against dumping. Producers applied for the temporary surtax before being protected by this tax. But not every good could benefit from the tax as a list of products that were eligible to the tax was presented in an annex of the reform act. A product elected to the temporary surtax regime was to be protected for not more than two years and could not benefit from the tax again. This tax was eliminated in June 2000.

The Generalised Preferential Tax

The generalised preferential tax (GPT) is applied to products manufactured in CEMAC and sold in another member country. The GPT is the main foundation of industrial co-operation in CEMAC intra-regional trade. GPT rates were gradually reduced to zero in 1998 and were already zero on local textile products at its adoption. This tax represented 20 percent of the CET from January 1994 to December 1995. During this period, a non-CEMAC product of category 4 for example sold in CEMAC was taxed at 30 percent (CET). An equivalent CEMAC product sold in another CEMAC member country was taxed 6 percent (20 percent of 30 as GPT). The GPT rate was 10 percent of CET from January 1996 to December 1997. The GPT rate has been zero since 1998, meaning that there is a duty-free regime for CEMAC products sold in CEMAC. This tax was applied on the sales of all products satisfying the rule of origin that is, being recognised as a CEMAC product.

Tools of Regional Integration in other Regional Economic Blocs

For the ECCAS, in the trade domain, each ECCAS member country was supposed to refrain from the introduction of any new customs duty and from increasing customs duties applied vis-à-vis another member as a first step. As a second step, member countries were supposed to progressively reduce and eliminate customs duties between themselves and establish an external common customs tariff. The aims regarding intra-trade are to see a situation of duty-free goods for intra-community trade, the absence of local tax differentiation between domestic products and community products, and the elimination of non-tariff restrictions and prohibitions in intra-community trade. As pointed out by Mshomba (2000: 191), Cameroon alone contributed over 80 percent of the region's exports during the 1994-1996 period. But the country only imported about 4.5 percent of other countries' exports in the region. ECCAS has yet to move towards a free trade area. Social instability in the sub-region as well as lack of political commitment has contributed to the stagnation of regional integration among ECCAS member countries.

The following constitute some other important points of principle (if not altogether practice) regarding economic integration in ECCAS: freedom of movement, residence and right of establishment; cooperation in the monetary, financial and payment fields; cooperation in agriculture and food; cooperation in industry; cooperation in infrastructures and equipment, transport and communication as well as in science and technology, energy and natural resources, human resources and social affairs.

In CEPGL tools of regional integration are not very different from those seen in the CEMAC, while in the LCBC these tools are concentrated on the salvation of Lake Chad as the lake contributes not only to living standards in the region, but also plays a major environmental role.

The literature divides economic integration into progressive stages: the preferential trading arrangement, the free trade area, the customs union, the common market, and the economic union. The preferential trading arrangement refers to the reduction of tariff and non-tariff barriers among member countries. The free trade area consists of the elimination of trade barriers among member countries, while the customs union is a free trade area augmented by adopting a common external tariffs applicable to non-member countries. The common market is a customs union plus free movement of factors of production. The economic union refers to a common market ameliorated by harmonising economic policies. Complete economic integration can be observed if the economic union unifies its economic and sectoral policies.

A question that may come to mind is to discover in which stage each Central African economic bloc finds itself. Without being very critical, I think Table 3 can give a tentative answer to this question.

Table 3: Central Africa en route to Regional Integration – The current status

	Preferential Trading Arrangements	Free Trade Area	Customs Union	Common Market	Economic Union
CEMAC	YES (1961)	YES (1998)	YES (1998)	NO	NO
ECCAS	YES	NO	NO	NO	NO
LCBC	NO	NO	NO	NO	NO
CEPGL	YES	NO	NO	NO	NO

Because of the lack of political commitment in the implementation of the tools of regional integration in Central Africa, many sub-regional economic blocs still have to move towards a free trade area. This situation explains why intra-regional trade remains underdeveloped compared to other sub-regional groupings.

Intra-regional Trade in Central Africa

An analysis of Central African intra-trade should keep an eye on what happens in other economic groups in developing countries. To do so, I selected at least one economic group from each developing area. The Association of South East Asian Nations (ASEAN) established in 1967 represents Asia. For Latin America I selected the Latin America Economic Integration Association (LAIA) which was created in 1960. Caribbean islands are represented by the Caribbean Community (CARICOM) established in 1973 and based on the Caribbean Free Trade Association founded in 1968. The three regions were chosen in order to obtain further details regarding intra-regional trade in developing countries. But the must obvious comparison for this analysis is between CEMAC and ECCAS on one hand, and other Sub-Saharan African economic groupings on the other. These groups include, for eastern and southern Africa, the Common Market for Eastern and Southern Africa (COMESA 1981) and the Southern Development Community (SADC 1992). The Economic Community of Western African States (ECOWAS 1975) and the West African Economic and Monetary Union (UEMOA 1974) represent the West African area.

Table 4: Intra-trade of group as percentage of total exports to each group

	1970	1975	1980	1985	1990	1995	2000	1990–2000
CARICOM	4.2	4.8	5.3	6.3	8.1	12.1	14.6	12.00
LAIA	9.9	14.2	13.9	9.2	11.6	17.3	12.9	14.97
CEPGL	0.4	0.3	0.1	0.8	0.5	0.5	0.8	0.60
COMESA	7.4	5.6	5.7	4.4	6.3	6.0	4.8	5.61
ECCAS	9.8	2.3	1.4	1.7	1.4	1.5	0.9	1.30
ECOWAS	2.9	3.9	9.6	5.1	8.0	9.0	9.6	9.41
SADC	4.2	1.0	0.4	1.4	3.1	10.6	11.9	8.80
CEMAC	4.9	2.7	1.6	1.9	2.3	2.1	1.2	1.75
UEMOA	6.1	12.6	9.9	8.7	12.1	10.3	13.0	11.19
ASEAN	22.4	16.7	17.4	18.6	19.0	24.6	23.0	22.15

Source: UNCTAD (2002)

Data assembled by UNCTAD show that intra-regional trade is well developed among Asian countries. For this group, a ten-year average of intra-trade as percentage of total exports of the group varied from 17 percent to 22 percent during 1970–2000 period. Apart from the decade 1980–1990 where ASEAN intra-trade represented about 18 percent, this percentage is always greater than 20 percent, reaching a peak of 24.6 percent in 1995. In Latin America, intra-trade generally represents more than 10 percent of total exports for LAIA during the period considered. By contrast, Sub-Saharan African intra-trade is very weak. This weakness varies from one group to another. But an observation of general trends shows that UEMOA has the advantage. During the 1970s, intra-trade of UEMOA created just few years before represented approximately 9 percent of the region total exports. This rate is gradually increasing year by year and represents an average of 11.2 percent during the 1990–2000 period. In contrast, CEMAC whose rate was 4.9 in the 1970s dropped sharply and never reached this level again. The sub-region recorded a 1.7 average during the 1990–2000 period. Intra-trade in CEPGL has yet to reach 1 percent. ECCAS is not doing any better than CEMAC. Its rate that was about 10 percent in 1970 has declined sharply. It actually represents about 1 percent according to recorded data for the year 2000. The average for 1990–2000 is 1.3 percent. Regional integration in Central Africa, thus, faces several obstacles, among which are a lack of political commitment, weak complementary economies and social instability.

Concluding Remarks: Towards a New Vision of Economic Integration in Central Africa

If it is evident that from unity comes strength, it is also very clear that from strengthened unity comes development. So the quality of the 'unity' formed is a very important element for its future. Central African States already form a unity in the ECCAS. But this unity still needs to be strengthened for the development of the sub-region. For this reason, a new vision of integration is necessary. This vision should shift from the traditional trade policies characterised by import-substituting development with high external trade barriers for non-member states, to a model that takes into account political, social as well as economic effects of integration. Such a shift would help in better assessing the opportunities for deeper integration, and thereafter, rapid economic development for member countries. That means simple trade liberalisation is no longer the only important step for regional integration, but that trade liberalisation should be accompanied by the deeper harmonisation of domestic policies. In this way, apart from convergence criteria (like those of CEMAC), the Central African sub-region should clearly define a regional development plan centred on a joint infrastructure policy. This infrastructure policy would be the foundation of a deeper and generalised trade liberalisation policy in agricultural trade, in intermediary products, in final products, as well as in investment in equipment and human capital. A deeper liberalisation of agricultural trade would ensure the achievement of food security in the sub-region and would supply raw materials to local industry. Liberalisation of intermediary products would accelerate industrial development and so increase the sub-region's competitiveness as it would lead to cost reduction. Further real liberalisation of final products would reduce the sub-regional dependency on manufactured goods and increase the intra-regional trade with all its advantages. Free movement of human and non-human capital would increase investment as well as productivity and, with increasing intra-trade, that would lead at a higher level to productivity growth decline in the unemployment rate, and overall economic development.

References

Bela, L., 1995, *Régime de la Taxe Unique et la Coopération Economique au sein de l'Union Douanière et Economique de l'Afrique Centrale (UDEAC)*, RPI, CODESRIA.

Bela, L., 1996, *Efficacité Comparée en 1991 des Firmes Camerounaises et Centrafricaines Agréées au Régime de la Taxe unique*, RPI, CODESRIA.

CEA - Commission Economique des Nations Unies pour l'Afrique, 1981, Mission d'Evaluation de l'UDEAC, Rapport, Libreville.

CEMAC, 1998, The 1998 edition of the CEMAC tariffs.

Kitchen, R. and Sarley, D., 1992, 'Industrial Efficiency and Policy Reform: The Central African Customs and Economic Union (UDEAC)', *Industry and Development*, January 57-80.

Maxwel, S., 1989, *Etude Provisoire sur la Réforme Tarifaire et Autres Incitations Industrielles de l'UDEAC*, Yaoundé, June.

Ministère de la Coopération, 1962, *Etudes de l'Economie Camerounaise en 1957*, Paris.

Ministère de la Coopération, 1962, *République du Congo: Comptes Economiques année 1958*, Paris.

Ministère de la Coopération, 1963, *RCA Comptes Economiques année 1961*, Paris.

Ministère de la Coopération, 1965, Ré*publique du Tchad: Comptes Economiques 1961 –1963*, Paris.

MINEFI, 1995, *Revue des Douanes Camerounaises Premier Trimestre 1995.*

Mshomba, R. E., 2000, *Africa in the Global Economy*, Boulder: Rienner.

Mytelka, L. K., 1975, 'Fiscal Politics and Regional Redistribution', *Journal of Conflict Resolution*, Vol. 19, No. 1, March.

UDEAC, 1988, The 1988 edition of the UDEAC tariffs, UDEAC.

UDEAC, 1995, *Annuaire du commerce inter-Etats – année 1993*, UDEAC.

United Nations, 2002, *Handbook of International Trade and Development Statistics.*

World Bank, 1992, Regional Cooperation for Adjustment: A Program of Trade and Indirect Tax Policy Reform for Member Countries of UDEAC.

2

The Paucity and Irregularity of Anglophone Newspapers in Cameroon

Victor Cheo and Henry Muluh

Introduction

Cameroon's mass media are a reflection of the country's colonial and traditional heritage; a heritage in which the media always served as channels for the dissemination of information supporting various causes, on behalf of various sources of power– traditional rulers, colonial administrators, the government or political parties (Muluh & Ndoh 2001).

However, the media's orientation changed with the advent of democratisation and the passing of Laws on Freedom of Association and of the Press in 1990. Since information is knowledge and power, there is need for Anglophone and Francophone newspapers to provide information to the over fifteen million Cameroonians, on issues of varied interest ranging over socio-political, economic and cultural issues. Twelve years after the passing of the 1990 laws, the press in Cameroon in general and the Anglophone private press in particular, has taken on the colouration of an organ that suffers from high professional inadequacies, make-believe journalism and has actually become moribund. But Cameroonian society, involved and interested more than ever before in the socio-economic and political climate, characteristic of the state of politics today, still continues to depend on the papers.

There are fewer Anglophone newspapers compared to Francophone newspapers. *The Post* and *The Herald* are the only two regularly published Anglophone papers. These two papers which purport to be national in outlook, are effectively present in only five out of the ten provinces of the Republic of Cameroon —South West, North West, Littoral, Centre and West provinces. The English-speaking community in the other five provinces (East, South, North, Far North and Adamawa) have little or no access to these newspapers. Worse still, when some of them eventually obtain these papers either through friends or relatives, the information therein is stale or outdated. And while some who manage to lay their hands on the papers complain about the stale nature of the news, there are others who are glad even for these old copies. Hence they depend on the Cameroon Radio-Television (CRTV) network programme *Luncheon Date* for information about their immediate surroundings and other parts of Cameroon. Of course radio has its own disadvantages. First of all the reports are usually brief and lacking in circumstantial details. Secondly, as a result of the transient nature of radio, once you miss *Luncheon Date* there is nothing to fall back on.

Another very acute problem confronting the Anglophone community in Cameroon is the fact that their choice of newspapers is limited to two: *The Post* and *The Herald*, the only regularly published Anglophone newspapers. It can hardly be both because Cameroonians besides not having the financial wherewithal generally do not have a reading culture. Even the state-owned bilingual daily, *Cameroon Tribune*, that is presumably distributed to at least all major towns and cities cannot address this problem because it usually has less than ten percent of its stories in English. Thus stories in English from any part of Cameroon are fortunate if they feature in the news.

While some Cameroonians have attributed the problem regarding the paucity and irregularity of the Anglophone press to non-viability, others contend that the problems are more complex. One issue is the vibrancy of the press. Anglophone newspapers in particular and Cameroonian newspapers in general need to be vibrant before being competitive. For example there is virtually no competition between Anglophone and Francophone newspapers to the extent that Anglophones who are bilingual will readily go for Francophone newspapers.

What then are the reasons for this paucity and irregularity? The following hypotheses may help explain the possible reasons.

- Anglophone newspapers are not aggressive enough in their newsgathering exercise and consequently cannot stand the heat of competition from other private newspapers, especially the Francophone press.
- Publishers of Anglophone newspapers do not have financial backing sufficient to manage and sustain their publications.
- Anglophone newspapers lack professional writers who can write interesting and objective news stories or reports in order to attract readership and advertisements.
- The Anglophone press is highly partisan, articulating only Anglophone socio-political problems.
- Anglophone newspapers by virtue of the fact that they are serving a minority are unable to attract the amount of advertising necessary for newspaper viability.

Methodology

Two methods were used for this study, both qualitative and quantitative. There was first of all sampling of opinion from lecturers of mass communication, advertisers and vendors who gave an appraisal of Anglophone newspapers in Cameroon. Secondly, some newspaper publishers and/or senior reporters were also asked to suggest possible reasons as to what hampers the smooth functioning of their papers. Finally two newspapers, one in English and the other in French were content analysed to critically examine some differences relating to the number of adverts, types of adverts, the news hole, professionalism and writing skills.

Brief Historical Background

Following the outbreak of World War One Germany's hold on Cameroon came to a radical end with her defeat by a joint British and French expeditionary force (Ngoh 1990). In March 1916, and acting on instructions from Paris and London, the French general Aymerich and British general Dobell provisionally divided the country into two 'zones of influence' which were to be administered by the French and British for the duration of the War (Ngoh 1990). After the War, Cameroon became a mandate of the League of Nations, formed in 1919. The League in turn transferred the mandate to France and Britain, which administered a divided Cameroon until 1960/61 (Eyongetah et al. 1974:78). For four decades each part was governed by a different colonial power whose policies reflected its own historical development and experience. The history of the two divided parts of Cameroon became part and parcel of the history of French Equatorial Africa and British Nigeria (Eyongetah et al. 1974:81). One result was the development of bilingualism as Cameroonians had to speak either English or French or both.

The Declining Fortunes of the Anglophone Press

Unlike in the predominantly French-speaking Cameroon, no newspapers existed in the English-speaking part of Cameroon before 1940. The only exceptions were some monthly magazines circulated among teachers, one of which was *The Cameroon Chronicle* (it later on changed its title to *The West Cameroon Teachers Journal*), which was published by the Basel mission in Victoria (Limbe). Pre-independent Nigerian newspapers (*The Daily Times*, *The West African Pilot, The Cameroon Voice, Eastern Outlook*) were the first to be circulated in the British-ruled English-speaking part of Cameroon, today referred to as the North West and South West provinces. The first English-language newspaper to be founded in Cameroon was *Kamerun Times* on 9 December 1960. The creation of the Cameroon Printing and Publishing Company (CPPC) by Mr and Mrs Nchami and Chief Victor Mukete lead to the eventual launching of this newspaper, which fervently sang the reunification creed. At times it sounded as if it were the propaganda organ of Dr John Ngu Foncha's Kamerun National Democratic Party (KNDP), since it was founded at the time that Anglophone Cameroon was faced with the choice by plebiscite of becoming independent as part of Nigeria, or through reunification with Francophone Cameroon. The KNDP was in support of reunification. Another paper expressing the contrary views, *Cameroons Champion*, soon hit the kiosks weeks after the publication of *Kamerun Times*. Its first editor was Wem Mwambo and the publisher was the late Motomby Woleta who was the then Secretary General of Dr. E. M. L. Endeley's Cameroon People's National Congress (CPNC) party. The paper's column, 'Spitfire' was dedicated entirely to the cause of maintaining Southern Cameroons within the Federation of Nigeria. By that time, some 71 news organs, predominantly the news bulletins of political movements, were already being published in the French-speaking part of the country. Significantly, between 1960 and 1966 when the first Cameroonian Press Law (Law No. 66/LF/18 of 21 December 1966) was passed, twenty-six Anglophone newspapers (see Appendix) were published, partly as a result of the fact that they were still governed by the very liberal Nigerian Press Ordinance.

The first Cameroonian Press Law arose as a result of a major political event on 1 September 1966: The merging of all political parties to form the Cameroon National Union (CNU). The Ahidjo government in its attempt to wipe out political opposition, needed to control public opinion (Eyinga 1986). This was made possible through a draconian law, the 1966 Press Law, which installed a firm system of censorship of the press. Newspapers had to be deposited at the Ministry of Territorial Administration or at the Divisional Officers office prior to publication. This pre-publication censorship lasted up and until 1990 when the Law on Freedom of Association and of the Press was passed. The 1966 Press Law also imposed harsh imprisonment terms for various offences.

The Law affected the Anglophone Press adversely. It led to the demise of many Anglophone newspapers; to the banning of some papers; it resulted in the arrest and detention of some Anglophone journalists like Patrick Obenson and Charlie Ndi Chia. Some Anglophone journalists became frustrated and either quit the profession (Bonnu Innocent) or left the country to work or study abroad.

Attempts by Anglophone journalists through the West Cameroon Association of Journalists, founded in 1969 with Jerome Gwellem as President, to oppose the severe restrictions, and to unite Anglophone journalists and mobilise them against oppressive measures, failed. Some newspapers continued to appear but stopped publication soon after their launch. Between 1966 and 1981 when an amendment to the 1966 Press Law was signed (Law No. 81/244 of 22 June 1981), only two Anglophone newspapers (*Cameroon Times* and *Cameroon Outlook*) managed to survive. Thirty or so papers appeared and disappeared, all of which supported the regime, in most cases for lack of other viable options. Most were heavy on sports and avoided politics (Gallagher 1991). The 1981 Law made life even more difficult for the Anglophone Press. All existing or would-be newspapers had to be registered under tough new conditions. The procedure for approving newspapers for publication became more complicated as proprietors had to provide a large deposit of 500.000 FCFA; and two ministries were involved in the censorship of newspapers. The Ministry of Information and Culture registered and controlled the newspapers while the Ministry of Territorial Administration checked the contents of each edition of a newspaper before publication. Only four Anglophone newspapers (*Cameroon Post, Cameroon Times, Cameroon Outlook* and *The Day Dawn*) were registered after the 1981 law.

The period between 1981 and 1990 (the law of liberalisation) was a very difficult one for the Anglophone press. In addition to the new conditions for registering newspapers, the government treated all newspapers with suspicion, and kept insisting on the need to maintain law and order. Secondly, the government was neither prepared to give information nor tell the truth to newspapers, which thus ended up publishing stories based on rumours. For example, three events made government-press relations reach an all-time low in 1984. These were the bloody 6 April foiled plot to overthrow the government which led to the death of over one thousand Cameroonians; the 16 August gas explosion at Lake Njindom in the West province in which thirty-seven people died; and the 30 August Douala Airport fire disaster that claimed the lives of three persons and destroyed a Boeing 737. These incidents left Cameroon awash with rumours ranging from questions over casualty figures to the actual or imagined causes of these tragedies. Instead the Head of State on 20 September 1984, in an address to the nation warned: 'Do not systematically take what you are told for gospel truth. You must think, analyse, listen to the radio or read the papers... The truth comes from above and falsehood from below' (President Biya's Address to the Nation, 20 September 1984).

This increased government suspicion of private newspapers and led to confrontation between the government and the press. A number of newspapers and journalists were penalised. In 1984, the distribution of *Cameroon Times* was stopped and its editor Ndi Chia and publisher Jerome Gwellem were arrested and detained for writing an article that criticised some of the vices of society. The boss of the Ministry of Information and Culture organised a seminar for private journalists on 18 October 1984 but did not invite the Anglophone press. During the Yondo Black trial in April 1990 (accused of illegally trying to form a new party) journalists were expelled from the court. In May 1990 Paddy Mbawa (*Cameroon Post*) and Jerome Gwellem were detained for being in possession of a press release from the new political party, the Social Democratic Front (SDF) launched on 26 May 1990). This of course adversely affected especially Anglophone newspapers, which were heavily censored.

With the winds of change sweeping from the East, Cameroonians demanded the institution of a democratically elected system of government. Of course the newspapers played a major role in this popular demand leading to the passing of the Law on Freedom of Association and of Mass Communication (Law No.90/

052 of 19 December 1990). Freedom of the Press did not imply that journalists could cover and publish any story. According to Gallagher (1991) 'a new law concerning social communication... was both good and bad news for the press. While reaffirming that the liberty of communication is a central pillar of democracy, the Assembly added 'this liberty of expression, more than any other, can be a great danger for democracy if it is exercised without limits' (Gallagher 1991). Under the new law authorisation was no longer required before publication of a newspaper. A simple notification to the proper authorities was sufficient. The law also opened up access to more sources of state information, previously tightly guarded. The same system of total or partial censorship (post-publication censorship) was maintained till 1996 (Law No. 96/04 of 4 January 1996), but limited to any material judged dangerous to public order or morality as interpreted by the authorities of the Ministry of Territorial Administration (MINAT). MINAT used public security as a rationale for continuous censorship. A good number of stories were blotted out in 1991 editions of *Cameroon Post* and the English edition of *Le Messager*. The *Herald* newspaper had 16 of its stories censored within a period of one year, from February 1995 to February 1996. This was the period just before the 21 January 1996 multiparty elections, and most of the stories were very critical of the government. Yet there was provision in the new law for newspapers to challenge censorship decisions. (A decision by the censor can be appealed to a judge who has one month to make a decision).

Empirical Analysis

Advertising and circulation are the main sources of revenue for newspapers. While advertising acts like a drug to the newspapers, circulation serves as a live-wire. Hodgson (1993:144) states that advertising is the main source of newspaper revenue though varying in percentage from paper to paper.

Our findings reveal that out of the 25 issues each of *Le Messager* and *The Herald*, published for two months – June and July 2001 – *Le Messager* had 303 adverts while *The Herald* had 109. Though the adverts in both newspapers are classified *Le Messager* is more organised in the way it places its classified adverts. *Le Messager* allocates a full page devoted to classified adverts, while *The Herald* has very sketchy classified adverts scattered all over its pages. It was also realised that *Le Messager* enjoyed more full-page advertisements than *The Herald*. The one full page advert recurring in *The Herald* is the Paris Mutuelle Urbaine Camerounaise (PMUC) advert, while *Le Messager* receives full page adverts from several big companies like CANAL+, MTN, MOBILIS, BICEC, SONEL, Western Union, TOTAL et ELF, KADJI BEER, Aeroport du Cameroun, SCM, CAMI-Toyota, TEXACO, SONARA, ECOBANK and Cameroon AIRLINES. Most if not all of these companies are in Douala. There is therefore the likelihood that most advertisers would prefer to advertise in media which are nearer their business, thus giving preference to proximity.

The findings further reveal that the adverts in *The Herald* vary from full page to 1/25 page including unclassified adverts and legal notices. Those of *Le Messager* vary from full page to 1/6 page. Even the advert rates differ in both newspapers. It is important to note that these rates are not standardised. They are very flexible. The circulation of a newspaper is the number of copies it sells each day or week per issue. As far as revenue collection is concerned, circulation has a causal relationship or is inextricably linked to advertising. This is because a higher circulation rate results in greater solicitation for adverts. However, before newspapers are circulated, they must be printed and the number of copies printed is a function of the circulation figures. We also observed that *The Herald's* present print run varies between 2,000 and 5,000 depending on the state of affairs. On the other hand, *Le Messager* prints at least 10,000 copies of every issue while *The Post* prints at least 3,000 copies and as much as 5,000 copies.

Some journalists advanced the following reasons as to why Anglophone papers are irregular. According to Asong Ndifor of *The Herald*, Anglophone papers hardly survive because of lack of market research, few professional writers and limited finance. Moreover, conflicts in the newsroom cause people to break away and create their own papers with similar editorial policy and style (*Cameroon Post* and *The Post* or *The Heron* by Christopher Azieh formerly of *The Herald*).

Charlie Ndi Chia, editor-in-chief of *The Post*, contends that Anglophone newspapers lack the enabling environment to survive. There are no industries to support newspapers and no political patronage for Anglophone newspapers. He supports this point by alluding to one Beti newspaper *Le Patriote* that is very viable because it is funded by the Betis who presently are the ruling elite. They can use their position to divert advertising to their papers. He adds that most of these big industries are owned or controlled by the Bamilekes and the Betis, and for this reason they place their advertising in a Bamileke or Beti paper. For example, the Bamilekes have over a 40 percent share of Les Brasseries and UCB.

Chia further says most of the government ministries are headed by Francophones. Anglophones who hold posts of responsibility in the government are quite few. Any paid government advert will normally go to a Francophone newspaper. Besides the aims of advertisers are to target the largest audience. Advertisers will prefer to advertise in Francophone newspapers which have a much larger potential audience (Francophones make up four-fifths of the population).

With regard to how aggressive Anglophone newspapers are, Ndi Chia says *The Post* is very aggressive. Its journalists undertake objective reporting and carry out a lot of investigations before writing a news story – unlike the Francophone newspapers that have documents leaked to them by Francophone government officials. Asong Ndifor of *The Herald* says 'aggressiveness' is a function of what each newspaper institution defines as news. To *The Herald*, 'news is something somewhere, somebody wants to hide'. News to *Cameroon Tribune* concerns what happens in government circles.

No doubt Ndi Chia of *The Post* argues that Francophone newspapers are more sensational than Anglophone newspapers, which are writing for a marginalised and oppressed audience. One of its main objectives is therefore to correct the injustice done to Cameroonians. On the other hand Gallagher (1991) suggests that the difference between the two 'is partly a product of the colonial tradition of the newspaper as propaganda tool, but also derives from the more opinion-oriented tradition of French journalism... Papers based in the Anglophone area frequently contain more factual reporting, but most papers make little attempt to hide their ideological orientation, even in 'news' articles' (Gallagher 1991).

The obvious conclusion is that Anglophone newspapers have financial constraints since they find it difficult to obtain advertising. Even the few advertisements that come in are not priced at the same rate as in Francophone newspapers. This is probably due to the limited audience for English-language papers, which means circulation is comparatively lower than for the Francophone press. Dissatisfaction then creeps in as staffers are poorly paid and this leads to demoralisation amongst the workers.

An Appraisal of the Anglophone Newspaper

Out of the ten university lecturers whose opinions were sampled as to their choice of newspaper – Anglophone or Francophone – a majority prefer reading Anglophone newspapers, firstly because they are in English and secondly because they treat pertinent issues related to Anglophones. They also prefer these newspapers because they are more critical in the way they interpret, analyse and evaluate issues. The few who prefer Francophone newspapers do so because they have more access to information concerning the government, are more investigative, and less sensational. This is true also for our own findings. Most Anglophone newspapers look at issues very narrowly. Furthermore, payola has a major negative impact on the content of the newspapers. Facts end up being distorted, leading to disinformation.

According to a couple of vendors sampled, they sell more copies of *The Post* newspaper than *The Herald* probably because *The Post* is regarded as an opposition newspaper while *The Herald* is not. To the vendors, *Le Messager* is the most solicited newspaper.

Some Conclusions

Historically, the Anglophone newspaper has been irregular as a result of the press laws, which for close to a quarter of a century since independence were draconian, making life very difficult for an infant press which was modelled on an Anglo-Saxon tradition of unrestricted freedom of expression.

The main problem facing the Anglophone newspaper is that of inadequate finance. Newspapers in Cameroon generally do not benefit from regular advertising. Consequently advertisements, which are a principal source of revenue, fluctuate. Moreover, advertisements in Anglophone newspapers are mostly local retail advertisements or adverts which look more like announcements. These adverts do not meet the criteria as exhibited on the advertisement rates of these newspapers. Consequently, the rates are subject to negotiation. This militates against a healthy revenue from advertising. According to Zebaze Paul of the National Printing and Publishing Corporation (SOPECAM – the publisher of *Cameroon Tribune*), despite government subvention *Cameroon Tribune* cannot survive without advertising.

The location of Anglophone newspapers is a point of concern. Most of the newspapers are located where business is less keen. There are no industries to support the newspapers and canvassing for adverts in distant places becomes a major problem as the newspapers lack transportation and telephone facilities. In addition the absence of good communication infrastructure like a road network makes it difficult to cover stories and distribute newspapers to all parts of the country. Circulation too has its own problems. Payments by vendors are irregular and inconsistent as they often allow clients to read newspapers on the stands.

Conflicts of interest and lack of understanding amongst the Anglophone journalists often result in quarrels, which usually end up in separation. Staffers abandon a newspaper to form their own newspapers with similar styles and editorial policies.

The practice of advocacy and partisanship also has a negative impact on the Anglophone newspaper. The newspapers tend to concentrate on the coverage of events in line with their ideologies, paying particular attention to some topics at the expense of others. Anglophone newspapers try to articulate the socio-political aspirations of Anglophones who make up only one-fifth of the total population of Cameroon. Besides, newspapers in Cameroon tend to cover stories within their area of jurisdiction and in addition newspaper attention to local civic affairs, environmental and developmental issues has been downplayed and preference given to other issues, especially politics (Abungwo 2001). Furthermore, newspapers tend not to cover the entire country objectively. This implies the Anglophone newspapers target a very limited audience. The circulation of the newspapers is bound to be very low and of course not encouraging to the advertiser, the main source of income for newspapers. This leads to a paucity and irregularity of Anglophone newspapers, which find it difficult to survive.

Bibliography

Abungwo, O., 2001, 'The Scope of Coverage of National Newspapers', unpublished B.Sc. Dissertation, University of Buea.

Eyinga, A., 1986, *Introduction à la Politique Camerounaise*, Paris: L'Harmattan.

Eyongetah, T. and Brain, R., 1974, *A History of the Cameroon*, Yaoundé: Longman.

Gallagher, D., 1991, 'Public and Private Press in Cameroon. Changing Roles in the New Pluralism', http://www.lightingfield.com/cameroon/contents.html

Hodgson, F., 1993, *Modern Newspaper Practice. A Primer on the Press*, Oxford: Butterworth.

Ngoh, V., 1990, *Cameroon: 1884-1985. One Hundred Years of History*, Yaoundé: CEPER.

Nyamnjoh, F., 1996, *Mass Media and Democratisation in Cameroon*, Friedrich Ebert Stiftung Foundation.

SOPECAM, 1991, *Cameroon: Rights and Freedoms. Collection of Recent Texts.*

Takougang, J. & Krieger, M., 1998, *African State and Society in the 1990s: Cameroon's Political Crossroads*, Westview.

Tudesq, A., 1995, *Feuilles d'Afrique: Etude de la Presse de L'Afrique Subsaharienne*, Talence, MSHA.

Appendix I

Anglophone Newspapers published between 1960 and 1966:

Black Express
Buea Tribune
Cameroon Contact Magazine
Cameroon Daily Express
Cameroon Mirror
Cameroon Monitor
Cameroon Observer
Cameroon Pilot
Cameroon Spokesman
Cameroon Star
Cameroon Workman
Cameroon World Journal
Cameroons Champion
Cameroons Economic Rehabilitation
Kamerun Times (Changed to *Cameroon Times* after independence)
Cameroon Statesman
Daily Life
Iroko
Pioneer Magazine
Sports Cameroon
Sunday Times
The Citizen
The Hero
The Spark
Victoria Evening Star
Western Mail

3

The Management of Ethnic Diversity in Cameroon: The Case of the Coastal Areas

Emmanuel Yenshu Vubo

Introduction

The crisis of co-existence between erstwhile autonomous ethnic entities within the nation-state structure as it exists in contemporary Africa is an acute problem. This can be attested to by the multiplicity of ethnic conflicts (both armed and unarmed), the crisis of the tribalistic orientation of the state, and tensions between communities either as historic entities or as aggregates brought together by the nation-state structure or its derivative in the form of urbanisation, bureaucratic organisation, industrialisation, plantation economy etc. These processes have been generated with unequal speed within the territorial confines of the state. This crisis only goes to compound other social crises orchestrated by modern capitalist development such as unemployment, crime, lack of democratic representation, uncontrolled urban growth, juvenile delinquency, alienation of local peoples, and the commoditisation of tribal land. Our aim in this work is to revisit the question of conviviality within the coastal region of Cameroon and examine the strategies employed by the current regime in coping with the crisis posed by the coexistence of peoples of different ethnies within this area. We are working from the hypotheses that:

i) Far from being the product of political manipulation, the predicament of local peoples is real;
ii) Local peoples' interpretation of the crisis in terms of the presence of 'strangers' or non-natives is simply a social category of analysis and explanatory model in the absence of viable civic education and strategies towards citizenship;

iii) The regime's attitude to this situation has bordered on feeding on social cleavages and disorder and exploiting the plight of local peoples, while posing as the protector of and guarantor of the rights of minorities that it only vaguely defines;
iv) The crisis deepens in the absence of viable strategies to tackle essential problems that generate it.

The 1996 Elections and the 'Spectre of Democracy'[1]

A brief chronology of some events on the Sawa Movement will help situate us on the question in focus. On the 10 February 1996 three thousand indigenous inhabitants of Douala City[2] (Duala, Bassa and Bakoko), who are collectively known as Sawa, marched in protest against the election of non-natives as mayors in 'their city'. According to the organisers of the march they were dissatisfied with the fact that out of five councils in which the opposition Social Democratic Front (SDF) party won the municipal elections of January 21, 1996, only one of the mayors was an indigene. The Sawa interpreted this as proof of Bamileke hegemonic intentions, the Bamileke constituting the bulk of the SDF party and a demographic majority in Douala city. The protesters carried placards which read: 'Démocratie oui, Hégémonie non'. (Democracy yes, Hegemony no); 'Pas de démocratie sans protection des minorités et des autochtones' (No to democracy without the protection of Indigenous Peoples); 'La majorité ethnique n'est pas l'expression de la démocratie mais de l'expansionnisme' (Ethnic majority is not an expression of democracy but that of expansionism).

In an address to the protesters, the chief organiser of the march, Chief Ekwalla Essaka Deido, who is one of the heads of the traditional corporate groups of the Duala, declared that every Cameroonian who wanted to become mayor had to go back and stand for elections in his native council. In an interview with the state-run daily newspaper, *Cameroon Tribune*, he claimed that the Sawa had the exclusive right to become mayors in their native land and went ahead to argue that although non-natives had bought and occupied land from natives, the former could not claim such land as their homeland. Other prominent Duala natives questioned the possibility of non-natives (in this case Bamileke) becoming mayors in Douala when even in Bamileke land natives of one town (e.g. Dschang) could not become mayors in other towns (e.g. Bafoussam). They also questioned the Land Law of 1971 for making it possible for people to occupy land in an 'anarchical' manner.

Sawa chiefs later petitioned the Head of State on the issue, complaining about certain ethnic groups that were bent on flouting the principle of peaceful coexistence between Cameroonians, thus constituting a threat to national unity. They claimed that they had been taken for granted and their hospitality misconstrued by ethnic groups with hegemonic intentions. Native Douala city inhabitants were mobilised through indigenous associations such as the Kod'a Mboa Sawa (the Sawa Household) and protest marches that the radical press interpreted as manipulations by government. The governor of the South West Province was reported to have explained the poor performance of the ruling CPDM party in his province by the presence of settlers, i.e., immigrants, (*The Herald*, 19–21 February 1996).

Later on, the elected Mayor of the Douala III Council, Mr. Souob Lazare, a Bamileke, was expelled from the SDF party for failing to comply with the party's directives to appease the natives by placing a native as mayor of that council. In view of these incidents the SDF decided to make sure that other councils during these elections amply represented native interests.

In the same month, Presidential Decree No. 96/031 appointed indigenes as government delegates (with supervisory and over-riding powers over elected municipal councils) in metropolitan areas where the SDF won elections in towns considered Sawa (Douala, Limbe, Kumba). It was an occasion for the Sawa to meet and 'congratulate the head of state' for heeding their call to put a check to the hegemony of non-natives in 'their cities'. This was interpreted by the radical press – controlled for the most part by Bamileke businessmen – as a travesty of democracy since people who did not win the elections were imposed on the council structures. Indeed the opposition SDF has continued to treat these appointments, a prerogative of government, as an attempt to subvert the principles of democracy where the fortunes of the party in power are waning, especially as the appointees were all militants of the ruling CPDM party which had lost elections in those areas. In fact some of the appointees had run for the elections to the councils and failed.

On the 6 July 1996, a banker of Bamileke origins and deputy co-ordinator of the Social Democratic Front in the Littoral province was dismissed from the party for anti-party activities. Poo'lah, a youth cultural organisation for the mobilisation of the Bamileke ('Organisation culturelle de la jeunesse pour la conscience Bamileke'), blamed the provincial co-ordinator of that party, a man of Sawa origins, of being the brain behind his sacking. It went ahead to interpret this act as falling within the framework of a plan hatched by Sawa chiefs and elite to dispossess the Bamileke of their 'vital space' ('espaces vitaux'). It also reminded the mayor of the dominantly Bamileke nature of the party and thus of the fact that he owed his position to the latter's votes, eventually calling on the party's authorities to stop the anti-Bamileke plot.

On 10 July 1996, fifteen Sawa Chiefs led by the most senior of them, Prince René Bell, were reported to have gone round the prestigious quarter of Bonapriso, a predominantly native Duala residential area, inspecting houses belonging to non-natives. They were said to have entered the homes of the latter ordering them to quit or renegotiate the value of the land on which they had built. Again, Poo'lah considered this act as provocative and indicated its readiness to react.

On 8 March 1997 chiefs from the South West and Littoral provinces (Sawa), met in Kumba. During this meeting, the Prime Minister - of Bakweri origins - declared that the incumbent President of the Republic as well as the ruling CPDM party stood for the protection of minority rights and the preservation of the rights of indigenous peoples. He therefore called on them to vote for him in the next elections if they wanted their rights as indigenous minorities to be protected.

This has brought into focus the question of the role of indigenous groups in cosmopolitan areas in the conduct of affairs in what they consider their homeland. This is principally an issue of the relation of a people to the land and a history. An ethnocentric press, developed with the indigene/non-native question in focus, aids groups that raise such issues. On the one hand is the Sawa press (*Elimbi*, *Muendi*, *Fako International* or *Mendi me Fako*) and on the other Bamileke run press (*Ouest Echo*, *Nde Echo*), which transpose the debate from the streets and neighbourhoods to the public place. The Sawa press accused the newspapers predominantly controlled by the Bamileke of intellectual terrorism, characteristic of Bamileke hegemony (*Elimbi*, No. 26, June 1997) while the former read either governmental manipulations, political blackmail or a crisis of identity in political terms to the extent that *Elimbi*'s columnist, Eyoum, felt that this would henceforth constitute the crux of the political debate (*Elimbi* No. 41, 26 June 1997). In several parts of Cameroon, especially in the South West Province, people are considered indigenes (sons of the soil), 'settlers', immigrants, non-natives or *come-no-go* – a Pidgin English expression for permanent immigrants. The governor of the latter province is reported to have requested that residence permits be issued to immigrants from other areas before they could vote during the legislative elections of 17 May 1997. Many non-natives feel they have been disenfranchised by this move that they hold was intended to favour the party in power.

What provoked this debate and public restiveness was a constitutional provision, which empowers the state 'to ensure the protection of minorities and... preserve the rights of indigenous populations' (Law of 18 January 1996 to revise the constitution of 1972). The constitution goes further to require that chairmen of the Regional Councils must be indigenes (Article 57(3)). The regional structures themselves were introduced as part of solutions to the problem of local peoples in lieu of a popular request for federalist structures that would have made for local autonomy and initiative. Even then these measures have not become reality due to the reluctance of the incumbent regime, which is very protective of centralist structures and fearful of strong regionalist feelings that it views as tantamount to secession. Other provisions of the constitution require that parties running for pluralistic elections within the list system take into consideration the sociological composition of the area when compiling lists in order to ensure that certain peoples are not under-represented at the level of decentralised organs of the state (Municipal Councils, Regional Councils). One reading is that these provisions are meant to protect people who have come to constitute ethnic minorities in heterogeneous areas, but this would equally raise the critical question of who is a minority and who can be classified as indigenous peoples eligible for having their rights protected.

After the first term of office, the Social Democratic Front and other opposition political party saw a steep decline in the vote in these areas following the twin legislative and local elections of 23 June 2002, a fact that could be attributed to large-scale disenfranchisement of potential non-native electors. The dream of the protesters and those arguing in favour of indigenous people's rights became reality as the majority of the councils in the coastal area were composed essentially of natives, as were the parliamentarians elected during the twin elections of 23 June 2003. The disenfranchisement of non-natives, which had secured this victory for the local elites, equally served the party in power, the Cameroon Peoples' Democratic Movement, as the natives had come to identify themselves in the majority with it.

In an earlier examination of the same question I had posited that this situation was the result of the ambivalence with which local peoples experience a modernisation of their living space either as people who have lost total control of their own destiny or as people who find benefits in this modernisation (Yenshu 1998: 34–36). My argument was that the predicament of the coastal peoples was largely the result of modern peripheral capitalism operating to dislocate local peoples, thus situating the roots of the problem in the local history of modernisation. What we are interested in here is not the problem of causes or origins but the way the modern state structure has handled this question. This is tantamount to posing the question of how successive elites have handled the question of plurality and how a citizenry was being constructed out of the motley of social groups that suddenly constituted Cameroon, without making of it a nation (Levine 1964). Levine (1964), in characteristic western conceptions of plurality within the Third World context, argued that, although nationalism had support in Cameroon, the greatest obstacles to its being translated into a factor of integration was the country's diversity, which expressed itself in a variety of particularisms. He went further to argue that such particularisms tended to drown the concept of national unity when translated into political demands, as these raised a Babel of conflicting voices. Our own reading of the situation is different (probably due to the fact one is writing almost four decades away): the argument is that the failure of the national unity project (see Amin 1998:48-72) is the result of the inefficacy of policies promoted by successive political regimes. Ambiguous in nature, they professed a vague formula of national unity which fluctuated between tough administrative coercion inherited from the colonial regimes and romantic fraternalism. It is in this scheme of things that we are going to analyse the management of ethnic diversity as a solution to the predicament of the dislocated coastal peoples. We will trace this predicament from colonial times until the present moment and show how the insensitivity and near callousness of the colonial regimes and the successor state as a style of management of diversity has been a total failure.

Capitalist Modernity and its Crisis in a Context of Ethnic Diversity: The Case of the Coastal Region of Cameroon

The problems posed by the protesters have their roots in the development of the coastal region of Cameroon into the virtual metropolis of the country, with its resultant effects of wholesale alienation of land previously belonging to local peoples, their pauperisation and marginalisation, the rising congestion with the influx of migrant labour, and the development of unplanned urbanisation coupled with the absence of a viable policy of national integration – all exacerbated by the abandonment of social and welfare policies. To have a full understanding of the problem let us examine the situation of the local peoples in its real perspective. This pertains to the land question and the survival of local peoples in the context of an overbearing modernisation. The present crisis is the logical conclusion of the predicament of a people dispossessed of their living space by two colonial instruments, one purportedly a voluntary agreement between an imperial colonial power and local chieftains of a small people, and another supposed to be peace terms imposing reparations consequent on an armistice after a colonial pacification war between the colonial power and local peoples. Clause one of the German-Duala treaty of 12 July 1884, which led to the German annexation of Cameroon, stated that the chiefs of what was then referred to in German as Kamerun or was later to become Kamerunstadt, situated along the Cameroon River (i.e. Wouri) and extending to the River Bimbia to the North and the Kwakwa to the South, an area covering the Duala and Mongo country, had surrendered total sovereignty including matters of legislation and administration to German firms acting on behalf of the German Imperial government. This has been naively presented and was in fact naively perceived at the time as the result of a consensual agreement between the colonists and the local chiefs. As we will see later the reality of this apparently harmless treaty was to constitute a perennial predicament for a people. This would be the same fate for the Bakweri after a bloody resistance during a punitive expedition. Between 1891 and 1894 the Germans staged a series of attacks on the Bakweri of Buea over what has been presented by an informant of the late Dr S.J. Epale as an attempt to stamp out barbaric customs among the latter. At the end of the expedition the first clause of the armistice imposed on the Bakweri was the loss of sovereignty over land formerly inhabited and cultivated by the latter and the displacement of the people to a new site. Other clauses bordered on the enslavement of a once dynamic people: payment of reparations, loss of rights to legislation and freedom to involve in interethnic disputes, provision of 100 labourers and an undertaking to obey all orders of the imperial colonial government. Although operating under two different imperatives, these two colonial instruments have had the same type of impact in recent times.

The Duala Land Crisis

While the Duala treaty and its critical aftermath has been the source of extensive studies (Nyounae-Libam 1970; Brutsch 1955; 1956; Kala-Lobe 1977; Austen and Derrick 1999; Derrick 1989), the Bakweri predicament has received almost no attention in serious academic discussions except for occasional references to the land question, although the Bakweri people had for a long time petitioned for redress to the predicament caused by the expropriation of their lands. I will start with a summary of the Duala situation and then move on to examine the Bakweri question more extensively. Nyounae-Libam (1970:32) informs us that the first clause of the German-Duala treaty was used in deciding on the expropriation of 280 hectares decided in 1910 for the purposes of establishing colonial administrative services and a residential area on land formally occupied by the Bonanjo segment of the Duala. Brutsch (1956) reports that a formal decree deciding on the expropriation of 903 hectares was ordered on 15 January 1913. What one has to note is that despite the initial protests against the 1884 treaty and the subsequent protests against the expropriation of land, the German colonial administration went about forcefully in implementing its design of remodelling the area once occupied by the Duala and creating a problem successive regimes were unable to solve. The German solution to the protests was repression, either in its naked military form or a travesty of justice in its colonial form (witness the case of Duala Manga Bell). The French administration, acting on the logic of the German-imposed terms of the 1884 treaty, went about its scheme of urban modernisation (Austen and Derrick 1999:138–175) despite continued Duala protests.

Requests for the return of land expropriated by the German colonial administration were turned down by the successor French colonial regime on the grounds that 'it had inherited what had (so it said) legally become German government property' (Derrick 1989:107). Only cosmetic redress was provided when in 1926 the French agreed to provide free plots to the Bell clan who had been moved to New Bell after the German expropriation. Although they initially turned it down, the Bonadoo (traditional name of the Bell clan) agreed to take the land. According to Derrick (1989) the opposition to colonial expropriation of land broke down by mid-1931 and then set in a period of not only of the elitism of the Duala as a westernised peoples but also one of accelerated urbanisation controlled in colonial style by the French. The benefits of modernisation enjoyed in elite life and position vis-à-vis other local peoples seem to have cast a veil that occasioned a relapse in collective self-consciousness. Coupled with the repression that accompanied the decolonisation process and the early post-colonial period this relapse seems to have given way only with the spate of democratisation that has characterised the neo-liberal drive. The Duala increasingly became a minority in Douala town as from the 1930s (Derrick ibid: 132). The town became the leading urban centre and concentrated enormous services and industrial activities. So also did the development of elitism (Derrick ibid: 132). The town has eventually grown into a gigantic metropolis (planned in some areas, unplanned in others) (Fombe and Fogwe 2001; Mainet 1985) where the Duala population and their voice appealing for recognition have been engulfed and go virtually unnoticed. The decline of the Duala as a privileged group (which privileged position was however short lived) seemed to have been profitable predominantly to elite persons from other ethnies that had taken over the country. The management of diversity and its problematics inherited from the colonial administration and the way decolonisation was managed would account for the style of crisis management in the post-colonial state.

The Land Question in the Mount Cameroon Region

Both the armistice terms subsequent on the German-Bakweri war and the independent activities of German colonial businessmen led to the large-scale appropriation of land around the eastern slopes of Mt Cameroon, Mongo country and some parts of the Meme and Kupe-Manenguba Divisions of Cameroon. We will limit ourselves to the expropriation of land around Mt Cameroon, although occasional references will be made to the situation in the other areas. While the armistice terms expropriated native land principally in Buea for administrative purposes, the individual businessmen went about expropriating land in various parts of the present Fako, Meme and Kupe-Manenguba Divisions. It is reported that the total land area alienated in transactions involving principally the German colonial administration and capitalists – leading to the forceful expropriation of natives - amounted to 115,000 hectares (Epale 1975:49). Under the governorship of Jesco Von Puttkamer alone, over 400 sq.miles of this area was alienated to individual Europeans and companies for various purposes, including plantations (Petition of 24 August 1946). The effect of this expropriation of native land was to move villages from 'lands considered suitable for plantation agriculture, to prevent their inhabitants from continuing their use of these properties for their purposes, mainly the grazing of their livestock. In the process the Bakweri were deprived of their homes and left with a very small amount of land for their personal use' (Delancey 1974:184). The situation constituted a perennial problem to which neither the German and British colonial governments nor the post-colonial regimes found lasting solutions.

Firstly, a 'policy of creating native reserves around the plantations was introduced' as the plantation capitalists were intent on creating 'rectangular blocks in order to show them on the map as undivided units' (Epale 1975:62). The displaced communities were relocated into crowded reserves which were for the most part barren upland located at high altitudes on the mountain slopes or in swampy areas. When the problem of congestion in the reserves immediately became acute, cosmetic amends were made when the German colonial government convinced one of the plantation companies, WAPV, to cede 6,000 hectares for the extension of the reserves.

During the First World War, when the German plantation owners had abandoned the plantations, the inhabitants of the crowded reserves had no alternative than to encroach on the plantation lands. However, when the plantations were resold to their former owners in 1925, the land problem which had become an essential component of the capitalist development in this area was as alive as ever. By 1926, 34 villages were hemmed in by plantations, as companies were reluctant to surrender alienated land. The British colonial government could only purchase 5,250 hectares of land in the years 1931–1933 to return to the natives as a palliative. By 1938, of 800 square miles declared native land in the then Victoria Division,[3] 600 sq. miles 'consisted of mangrove swamps and mountain uplands that [could] not be cultivated', the 'remaining 200 square miles' (Epale 1975:110) supporting the native population as opposed to 381.6 square miles of fertile land alienated for plantation use. The situation in the area made up today of Meme and Kupe-Manenguba divisions was less acute but similar as 15,744 sq. miles were in the hands of non-native Europeans.

The British presented conflicting signals in providing solutions to the land question during the Second World War, although it adopted an attitude born of self-interest when it came to deciding the fate of the plantations as capitalist concerns. The colonial government argued simultaneously that on the one hand any policy selling the plantations expropriated from the German plantation owners would be 'detrimental to the aspirations of the local inhabitants from whom the plantation lands were originally expropriated', and on the other, that it would be foolhardy to return the plantations to the Bakweri natives 'as this would have spelt chaos' (Epale 1975: 159). Such chaos would result from the fact that the natives were lacking in managerial and technological expertise and the financial resources needed to keep the companies afloat. In the end it was the strategic interests of the British that the proceeds (rubber, palm oil) were to serve that played a much more important role in the decision not to turn over the lands to the natives (Epale 1975: 160).

When it became clear that the land, alienated by the Germans and restored to them by repurchase when they had lost it in the First World War, was going to change hands definitely and become British colonial property, the local peoples constituted themselves into a Bakweri Land Committee. Despite initial appeals for redress, the process of acquisition by the British went on in total disregard of requests that the land should be returned to the original native owners. In a petition dated 24 August 1946, the Bakweri enumerated the economic, social and psychological impact of the establishment of the plantations through some of the most forceful and inhumane means. They complained that their alienation from fertile plains and relocation to barren mountain slopes of between 6000 and 8000 feet above sea level changed their farming habits, as native staples could not thrive in such altitudes, and that malnutrition had become a common feature as a new staple (the cocoyam) was introduced. There was hardship and a breakdown in the health of women, since working at high altitudes had placed too great a demand on them. All these coupled with plantation demands on male labour were reported by petitioners to lead to a 'decrease in population and deterioration of a people'. The petition argued that 'since these lands were not acquired in a justifiable way they were... misappropriated property and therefore should be returned to us the rightful owners'. They could then manage such under the Native Administration system and on a cooperative basis, 'after enough of the cultivated and uncultivated areas had been given to natives for growing local and other crops for consumption and economic purposes'. The petition also requested compensation for the period of exploitation of the lands and a return of unused land held by Christian missionary bodies.

The British colonial secretary's proposals on the matter were vague. They promised to make reparation for the ills of the past, but only by adjusting the boundaries of native lands, co-opting Cameroonians (not necessarily the original land owners) into management, providing welfare facilities and improved housing on the estates and using the proceeds to improve the lot of all Cameroonians. A bill to incorporate a company, the Cameroons Development Corporation (CDC), out of the ex-German plantations was passed in the British legislative council of 9–12 December 1946 but was totally misconstrued by the local peoples to mean that their land had been returned or would be returned to them later (Epale 1975: 117). Discussions between colonial officers and local chiefs also gave the former the impression that the local people had accepted the terms of incorporation of the company, a misconception nurtured by the attitude of some of the chiefs that bordered on complicity as protests and violent criticisms by some of the chiefs did not see a change in the situation.

The Land Committee continued to petition for redress. In a memorandum dated 3/11/1949 presented to a UN visiting mission the Bakweri were described as '... a race living in the declining graph of the imminence of extermination...' and described British colonial attitudes to the perennial land/human existence question as 'luring theories and promises'. The petition openly accused the British administration of trying to perpetuate the same inhuman policies of the Germans and pointed to the decline in the population of the Bakweri, leading to pauperisation with a 'death rate bordering on extinction'. It did not end without highlighting the complicity of the Christian Missions in the expropriation and exploitation of extensive lands as they made 'high profits from these lands' by receiving rents on them.

The reply of the colonial Governor, A.F. Richards, was rather situated within the logic of capitalist imperialistic interests. He argued that the British government had acquired title to the land by conquest, implying that the British had endorsed German methods of land acquisition (as the French had done in Douala) and so was not intent on resolving the crisis of expropriation but rather disposed to building on it. By arguing that plantations were enemy property and as such were war reparations, which could not be returned to third parties, the colonial administrator was asserting that the land question had become situated within a wider logic of competing imperialist interests. In the same vein, this governor endorsed the acquisition of lands by the Christian missions and offered only vague promises of investigating how the scarcity of land for natives could be alleviated. As with the Duala case we could find a successor colonial administration endorsing and even exploiting its predecessor's abuses in a perverted logic of the continuity of the state. A 1950 proposal by the colonial government to return 25,000 hectares to the natives was turned down because this would have implied an endorsement of the original forceful alienation of land.

Studies to find solutions to the problem did not produce any viable proposals. Even those proposed could not be implemented to the extent that 'until the time of the departure of the British from the Trust Territory neither the Bakweri land problem nor the settlement scheme proposed by the Government had been resolved' (Epale 1975:183). The Bakweri continued the petitions which went unheeded, as the plantations and the land with it continued to change hands from one state structure to another (Britain to Southern Cameroons, Southern Cameroons to Cameroon via West Cameroon). The overriding concern was the capital and the proceeds in profits accruing from investments to the entrepreneurs (state or private) and rents going to the state, and not the welfare of the local peoples. Even the lever provided in the following proviso of the Deed of Incorporation was rather lame and meant to lure local peoples than to provide lasting solutions to a problem which was acute. The proviso compelled the Cameroons Development Corporation:

> Not to refuse unreasonably any request made by the lessor [now the state] for the surrender and delivery up to the lessor (after reasonable notice and subject to fair compensation in request of cultivation and of any buildings and fixtures which cannot reasonably be removed from the land) any part of the said lands in the vicinity of a hamlet, village or township existing on 31st December 1959, which is required to enable desirable expan-

> sion of any such hamlet, villages, or townships to take place (in Epale 1975:211).

Some lands have occasionally been released. But the lands are never specifically released to specific indigenous communities, most of them having been engulfed by urbanisation, or fall into the hands of local land speculators. The demand for labour and the growth of the area into a cosmopolitan settlement, the growth being natural at times and chaotic at others, has transformed the area into a gigantic economic growth pole. The development of an oil refinery in the neighbourhood of Limbe, the establishment of a mini-industrial zone in Ombe, and the establishment of a University in Buea have compounded the social crisis resulting from the land problem. Let us look at this problem in detail, and see how a social crisis has developed from these changes.

From Land to Social Crisis and Management by the Creation of Elites

The land question has been the central crisis of the local coastal peoples since colonial times. It has generated a social crisis of great dimensions. As the area developed from the use of forced or near-forced labour, and the voluntary migration of labour in search of jobs in the English and French mandates, there arose a new problem, that of the coexistence of the local peoples with immigrants from other parts of the country and even beyond. Austen and Derrick (1999:141) suggest that Duala ethnicity or feeling of ethnic consciousness in relation to other groups developed in the French Mandate at a period when they had become an 'ethnic minority in their city'. The development of Douala town into a metropolitan area brought with it peculiar problems of cohabitation and integration which expressed themselves in the 1996 protests.

The protests also had an appeal in the Bakweri community who had had a long and protracted history of an unsolved land crisis. The plantations in the German period had thrived on near-forced labour conscripted in some of the most inhuman methods in the interior – especially the Grassfields. Later on, free labour was attracted from the Ewondo and Bakoko countries that at the beginning of the British mandate outnumbered all other groups as wage earners. Forced labour on the extension of the German-initiated railway project in the French mandated territory led to further immigration to the plantations. But when French administrative restrictions led to a decline in these population movements, Nigerians filled the vacuum so created. These two categories of people were to add to persons originating in the Grassfields who constituted 28 percent of the wage earners on the plantations (Epale 1975:116), and another small contingent of indigenous labourers. Part of this wage labour lived in the camps but many non-natives were also settling on the so-called native reserves. The British colonial administrator, Bridges, describes this situation in the following terms:

> Since the inception of plantation work, an increasing number of *native strangers* have found their way to this country. Some remain continually at work on the plantations and do not affect the local native organisation. Many others give up their plantation work and settle down in their various villages (in Mbake 1975:75). (Emphasis mine).

The crisis of cohabitation between natives and non-natives was evident in the friction between these two categories of people as early as 1935. Such a crisis was at the basis of the further delineation of the remaining land constituted as reserves into native land and stranger quarters. It has to be noted that the concepts of native and stranger as in use today to designate indigenes and other Cameroonians have their origins in colonial discourses and practices: note the use of the term of *native stranger* to refer to immigrants from other areas of Cameroon. As such Fako division is the only place in Cameroon where the concepts of *native, stranger, reserve, native land, stranger quarters* still persist in popular imagination and are pregnant with meanings that are not obvious to persons unfamiliar with the historical dimensions of the reality. Of recent the category of persons that went under the label of stranger have been styled *come-no-go.*

The growth of the Fako area into a cosmopolitan administrative, commercial, agro-industrial pole and later on the seat of a university has hardly helped to alleviate the crisis. Not only did the population in the camps grow and spill over into the local population to create its own army of job seekers, business operators, craftsmen and farmers among others, problems of a different kind and magnitude began to make themselves felt as formal economic and administrative action came to concentrate in the area. The establishment of the national refinery in the neighbourhood of Limbe has transformed the human and physical landscape of the area. The carving up of land into a Government Residential Area, Bota and New Town had only gone to show that it no longer belonging to natives. The recent resettlement of natives to give way for the establishment of an industrial shipyard company generated protests in the tradition of the Bakweri land question and received almost the same response as the colonial solution to this perennial problem. The colonisation of the West Coast extending from the Sonara to Bakingili by resorts and hotel establishments also goes to emphasise the rate at which capitalist developments are displacing largely weak local interest groups. Buea, for its part, has also witnessed chaotic growth since 1970, a situation which has led to the government occupying 54.3 percent of the land (with 10.9 percent being in CDC hands and 13.8 percent held by the University of Buea (Forba Fru 1999). The establishment of the latter has also meant an increase in pressure on the land for construction of dependent services (private student hostels, private business services, and living apartments).

Initially, the spate of developments occurring during the colonial era, either in the British or French spheres, gave a semblance of meeting the needs of a local peoples who had lost their landed property but who could replace it with some cultural capital (western schooling) and advantaged positions (employment in subordinate clerical positions in the colonial administration). Derrick (1989) has analysed the growth of Duala elitism at this time but it was also the end of an epoch as the decolonisation movement and the development of a post-colonial state was going to overtake and have an overbearing influence on the space once occupied by local peoples. The same is true of the Bakweri, but to a lesser degree. It appears that it was the appointment of prominent elites to serve on the Board and the recruitment of other natives to work in the administration of the CDC, as well as initial domination of the modern civil service and political life in colonial times by coastal peoples, that pushed the movement for redress into relapse. The political developments surrounding the decolonisation of Southern Cameroons were thus fraught with bitterness, rancour and the manipulation of ethno-regional cleavages. It has also further served to divert attention from the land question and its attendant ills. The preoccupation with the question of the ethnic origins of political leaders overshadowed and cast a veil on problems that were real. The policies of the Kamerun National Democratic Party (KNDP) government, largely characterised by partisan victimisation and a propensity rather to manage the profits of the Corporation than solve the crisis of the structural location of the plantations, only confirmed the native conception of their problem as one caused by the 'stranger'. The new stranger had succeeded the old stranger to continue with the same policies by treating the *status quo* as a *fait accompli*, which could not be revisited. It is the political dimension that has resurfaced, and not the real objective question of human existence. The calls for solutions are only reminiscent of the cosmetic palliatives of the colonial period. Just as the Duala had secured a privileged position in the colonial era (even in a subordinate manner) and the Bakweri had secured privileged positions in the CDC, they were requesting a similar 'protection' or privilege' as a solution to their predicament in the face of a current neo-liberal drive characterised by individualism (either in the vote or in entrepreneurship). At this point it was the communitarian/identity vision of society represented by Sawa claims against an individualistic vision represented by the neo-liberal modernity of individualistic democracy (universal suffrage, secret ballot, political party programmes) and unbridled capitalism (liberalisation, state withdrawal from social sector, privatisation of public corporations, rule of the market and domination of transnational financial institutions).

The Multiple Social Crises

Beyond the land question and its fallouts there is a veritable social crisis that rocks the very basis of the state and particularly affects the area in question. The first manifestation of this crisis is uncontrolled urban growth and the absence of a settlement policy as well as adequate legislation on land. This results from the chaotic development of the seat of colonial administration into virtually natural growth poles as other functions (industrial, commercial) are added to the already cumbrous one imposed by colonial regimes. This has led to the growth of certain towns beyond their natural limits generating in its wake social problems that governments either overlook or are unable to tackle. One will observe inter-ethnic bitterness in most of the urban agglomerations of Cameroon (Yaoundé, Douala, Kumba, Bamenda, Bafoussam). Although one could say that it is in the urban areas that the notion of a Cameroonian nation is lived as people come face-to-face with people from areas or ethnies different from theirs, it is also there that the crisis of co-existence is most felt. It is also the urban area that attracts the army of unemployed from the rural areas at the same time as it generates its own unemployed. It is here we have rising crime as a consequence of unemployment. There is also the crisis of anarchical occupation of land in the urban space and the absence of an urban housing policy.

The second crisis is that of the commoditisation/alienation of once tribal land. This problem, which started in the colonial period, has reached dramatic proportions, as it is promoted and actively championed by local clan/family heads and tribal chiefs. While the majority of local peoples and the younger elites are clamouring for the return of once tribal land, the chiefs or the heads of the kinship groups are busy either negotiating for compensation to be paid to them by the state, or continue to sell out what is left or re-sell land returned to local communities by the CDC. The case is reported in the Muea (Lysoka) neighbourhood of a chief who is selling out land returned to the community by the CDC. The paramount chief of Buea has also questioned the right of some Bakweri elite in the USA to constitute themselves into a Bakweri Land Committee (not to be confused with its predecessor of 1946). Moreover, the role of the chiefs in the eventual privatisation of the plantations (corporation) has been far from desirable and at worst ambiguous. As such, there is a failure on the part of the chiefs to represent the tribal landed interests to the extent that one would not be wrong in talking of a crisis of representation.

Third, the crisis of overpopulated cosmopolitan area in the coastal area of Cameroon also manifests itself in the problem of political participation and representation, in short, a crisis of democracy. It is my observation, as has been ably demonstrated before me by Samir Amin, that the overbearing impact of capitalist development in the area subverts any notion of democratic participation, whether native or immigrant. What can a vote do to change the fate of a labourer on a fixed paltry salary living in overcrowded bidonvilles in the urban areas where a bourgeois capitalist class is in control? It was just natural that the people living in this area would massively adhere to a left wing populist political party, the Social Democratic Front, as an alternative to the socio-political and economic system. Coincidentally this impoverished lot living on the fringes of modernity was composed as it were of 'stranger'/immigrant origins, that is, from areas beyond those under study. The implication of this assertion is that the political vote of the 1990s up till 1996 was a protest vote and an expression of a reaction to a situation of deprivation which political monolithism had succeeded in obscuring. The reactions of the Sawa elite went to underscore their opposition to a modification of privileges, which had been obtained at the expense of popular interests. The success of these elites in reconverting at least the 'natives' into militants of the incumbent CPDM party, although an insignificant following because of its minority status, and progressively disenfranchising the 'strangers', has not succeeded in solving the crisis. The situation has moved from one of a crisis of belonging/marginalisation to one of lack of representation that has gone on unattended, a situation that is favourable to the incumbent regime. That is why I liken this to a predator strategy where the regime is feeding on the ethnic cleavages and the social crisis born of a violent and insensitive modernity.

Last, an important issue that is central to the question under study is the psychosocial and socio-cultural identity dimensions of the crisis and how it can be resolved. From the very early contact of the British colonial administration with the human side of the plantations, the impact of the agro-industrial complex on local peoples has been far from positive. E. C. Duff's *Annual Report on the Cameroons Province* for the year 1916 indicated that 'the result of European enterprise on the coast seems to have been far more a curse than a blessing to the country' (in Epale 1975:1). The British colonial administrator W.M. Bridges also remarked in an intelligence report that, affected by the expropriation, the Bakweri people 'were deprived of all incentive and relapsed into what is still an indolent state of mind' (in Epale 1975:62). Epale, although making technocratic arguments in favour of the plantations, is however correct in asserting that:

> Uprooted from the homes of their forebears and settled willy-nilly on strange sites in order to make way for the plantations and deprived of old-time hunting ground, the Bakweri somewhat lost ethnic cohesion and group unity and it was not long before the Germans realised that the land acquisition was dealing a fatal bow to the Bakweri (Ibid:61).

He goes on to assert that:

> the introduction of large scale agro-industrial estates in an area which was and still in sparsely populated, and where a large section of the population appears to have lost its will owing, in part, to the hard terms imposed on them... left the natives with a certain amount of the lethargy which was further accentuated by the forcible alienation of their land by the Germans and reinforced by the disappointment that the lands now leased to the Cameroon Development Corporation did not, contrary to the expectations, return to their original owners (ibid: 251).

Epale (ibid: 252) reports the following side effects of the establishment of the plantations: prostitution involving both married and unmarried women, the instability of family life consequent on this, and a variety of social problems. Needless to return to the substance of the memorandum of 1936 which had highlighted some of these problems impinging on psychosocial and socio-cultural crisis, in other words, a crisis of collective life and identity. This analysis of the identity of the predicament of the Bakweri is buttressed by the remark of Kuezniski in the 1936 petition to the effect that '... there is no doubt that [Bakweri] relegation to reserves has to a large extent made them lose their interest in life...' Van Slageren confirms this point when he notes that the punitive expeditions ended in breaking up the community spirit of the Bakweri and reduced them to 'slavery' in a process of expropriation during which even villages not in revolt were deprived of their land and crowded into reserves too small to contain them and their livestock.

The preceding references bring to focus an imagery of the disappearance of identities and communities as their environment and community resources are alienated. This crucial problem is one that has not been attended to, other than in terms of the creation of a participating bureaucratic bourgeoisie. The crisis of identity is one that spares no primordial historic community that has come into contact with modernity, and its imposition of change in the direction of acquiescence and subordination to the capitalist trends towards polarisation (Amin 1993; 1998). The problem is just one of degree. The classical solution has been to split the local peoples along the polar lines of a co-opted bourgeoisie and a mass of marginalised, pauperised, and alienated peoples. This was the solution when the colonial administration opted to include local elites in the management of the CDC in lieu of a viable solution to the land question. It was the same solution in the Duala land crisis when colonial elite were sponsored by the French colonial administration that had endorsed German expropriation plans (cf. Derrick 1989). The promotion by the colonial administration of intermediary traditional chiefs as a new and independent social class cut off from the ethnic groups which they represented was in direct line with this policy of seeking for local relays in the capitalist network in the making (see also Yenshu and Ngwa 2001). As Claude Ake (2000: 98) points out, colonial rule was cheap rule with no commitment to social welfare. The current institution of chiefs as auxiliaries of the post-colonial administration and the struggle by several categories of chiefs to position themselves as a social appendage to government in opposition to local interests, operates according to the same logic and rids the chieftaincy institution of any semblance of legitimacy it might have enjoyed as an indigenous institution rooted in local customs. It is the same policy that was used in a response to the 1996 protests as local elites were compensated with political appointments and the role of chiefs enhanced to the detriment of the local peoples.[4]

This is in line with a warped style of managing ethnic diversity based on arguments to the effect that:

> Every ethnic group wishes to see its sons and daughters employed so that they bring something back home. No ethnic group wishes to be absent at the national dining table where the national cake is shared. Employment in the public service is a source of pride for those whom ethnicity is a highly sentimental affair. Positions in the public service are seen as symbols of ethnic power and superiority or at least equality to other ethnic groups... Ethnic groups have a belief... that if they are not represented in the process of public policy-making, they will lose out in the services they receive and development opportunities, programmes and projects coming to them... (Kauzya 2001:113).

Beyond the oft-quoted metaphor of national cake sharing, one can pose the question of the viability of the capitalist solution of polarising people between a bourgeoisie participating at some levels within the peripheral capitalist structure, and disadvantaged masses that the former are supposed to represent. To the question of how representative any bourgeoisie are, we will answer by saying that they represent only their interests and that elements of local peoples co-opted by the dominant structures rather end up operating according to the laws of the system than articulating local interests in any democratic way. Neither will they, in any way, replace a viable social democracy capable of meeting the needs of local peoples or rehabilitating them in the process of accelerated disintegration/loss of identity. The co-opted bourgeoisie often operate as the internal guarantors of the efficiency of the system, the local relay that ensures the universal character of the system by presenting it as trans-ethnic, the local operatives that provide a semblance of participation, the ideological smokescreen behind which the system finds operational efficiency, the system's man-eaters from within. Popular imagination has for long assimilated capitalism to cannibalism in the phenomenon of *famla/nyongo* where the rich only grow by contributing to a *nchua* or rotating association of man-eaters. In the case of the witches, man-eating operates by way of eating of souls or the transubstantiated bodies of the sacrificed. In the present case, the person is eaten in advance as his resources are taken away from him and he is left to pine away in penury. While the *famla/nyongo* businessman eats the live person's double and destroys him by weakening a spiritual side concurrently, the modern capitalist kills in advance by alienating the vital space and looking for collaborators from within. It is a slow, hardly perceptible genocide that thrives by way of a technical rationality that both subjugates, thus alienating, labour and drives to the fringes of existence and extinction what cannot be labour.

This is one of the universal trend laws of the system that creates the bourgeoisie and its support elements, labour, and the rest of social misfits (work in the informal sector, crime, the underground economy, parallel forms of economic activity). In social terms one would have the man-eaters and the rest they feed on in different ways by a monopoly over resources (cf. Amin's concept of five monopolies of the current phase of capitalism). This is reflected in settlement patterns and the occupation of space: the senior service and mid-senior service quarters, the Government Residential Areas (residential quarters), the labour camps, clerks quarters and the new towns (Limbe), popular quarters such as Great Soppo, Small Soppo, and Buea Town. In Douala one would have the central business district and upper class residential areas (Bonanjo, Bonapriso, Bali, parts of Akwa, Makepe), and the sprawling bidonvilles and suburbs that combine intermediate and lower class residential areas. It is in these areas that one would find relatively rich traders and lower middle class wage earners and craftsmen living side-by-side with lower class and very poor groups. The intermediate class of traders and craftsmen (when constituted into an entrepreneurial category) becomes an exploiting segment playing the relay and cannibal function.

That is why we are right in situating the failure of the coastal people's petitions for redress at the period when the colonial capitalist interests has succeeded in creating this class. This has been the classical capitalist solution to the ethnic question at all levels (micro-level to the transnational) wherever the ethnic question is coupled with a strong social crisis. As history has shown, the minority status of this fragment of the bourgeoisie rids them of any capacity for meaningful initiative to redress the ills suffered by any supposed community of origin taken as constituency. Their assimilation, on the contrary, serves a legitimating function for the system by giving the impression that all that matters is for a people to have its own kind in the sun of the system. In this way the present peripheral capitalist modernity operating through the state succeeds in circumventing the social crisis of pauperisation, misery, and dehumanisation that it generates. The response of the state structure to the social question thus takes the form of an insensitive process of dehumanisation that offers hope only to a select few as its own 'representatives of the majority'.

Conclusions

The general tendency in ethnicity studies has often been to observe the crisis of inter-ethnic co-existence as the problem of amalgamating aggregates of virtually antagonistic peoples into one single space irrespective of historical circumstances. This attitude, transposed from ideological/political perceptions of what is essentially a complex anthropo-social reality, is largely deficient in scientific reasoning. What we have shown here is that the crisis of co-existence is the product of a specific historical situation, in this case, the development of agrarian capitalism within the colonial setting. We have demonstrated that the dimension that this crisis has taken on can be attributed largely to colonial policies ranging from violent pacification through high handed insensitivity to the social crisis, to the creation/cooptation of a participating subordinate bourgeoisie.

We have shown that these developments fashioned the responses of succeeding elites to the social crisis of marginalisation by providing a frame of reference in which immigrants and not chaotic urban, commercial, industrial and agro-industrial developments, were to blame for the social ills affecting a peoples in a perennial manner. We have qualified the response of the successive regimes in the post-colonial period as lacking in creativity as they have either never examined the background to the social crisis, or have exploited this crisis as they have endorsed the colonial heritage without any critical examination. One would be right in treating these regimes as essentially lacking in nationalist orientation as one would have expected a critical examination of the social crises arising out of the colonial experience and an autonomous search for solutions. In place of such solutions one only finds vague romantic references to the need for Cameroonians to display fraternity in the manner of the 'national unity' and 'national integration' projects.

While it has became increasingly evident that it is important to manage the crisis of diversity that the creation of the nation-state has ushered in, the solutions proposed have been vague. Transcending the unfounded belief in an ethnic reality's propensity to divisiveness, a view now largely discredited (Ake 2000:92-115), there have been calls for a sane democracy, which respects not only minorities (as the 1996 protesters were calling for) but diversity. Alain Touraine (1994:25-30), for instance, posits that the lessons to be learnt from the tragic events of Bosnia-Herzegovina are the need to respect liberties and diversity and not only the focus on the concepts of participation and consensus. He is categorical when he states that:

> Ce qui définit la démocratie, ce n'est donc pas seulement un ensemble de garanties institutionnelles ou le règne de la majorité mais avant tout le respect de projets individuels et collectives, qui combinent l'affirmation d'une liberté personnelle avec le droit de s'identifier à une collectivité sociale, nationale ou religieuse particulière (Touraine ibid: 26).

> La démocratie ne réduit pas l'être humain à être seulement un citoyen; elle le reconnaît comme un individu libre mais qui appartient aussi à des collectivités économiques et culturelles. (ibid. p. 30).

Touraine (1994: 228) is however cautious when proposing general solutions to the problem of diversity as he states that it is not sufficient to say that it is necessary to strike a balance between the diversity of cultures that makes up the nation-state and the universalising tendency of the nation-state. He feels that one has to look for practical ways of how this balance will be achieved. Institutional guarantees such as constitutional provisions have been the earliest but most vague solutions that have been proffered (Touraine ibid: 229). More recently, diversity issues have become part of the research into public management. Kauzya (2000:117) proposes a holistic model whose aim is 'to build a representative civil service that respects the core values of responsiveness to ethnic diversity, inclusiveness of all ethnic groups in the country and high quality service delivery'. Balogun (2000:43) argues in the same vein when he says that 'diversity may be perceived as a minimum condition for the safeguard of the rights and autonomy of groups constituting a nation-state'. This is crucial to a lively debate on the future of the nation-state if it is to develop into a viable framework for social existence. What remains now is how these prescriptions have to become reality. Moreover, this is restricted to the domain of the public service, whose propensity, we have seen, is to treat the social crisis by substituting a social policy which misses the point in the management of social questions.

Our analysis of the specific context where the crisis of diversity arose out of the development of an economic system dictates that each solution should be adapted to the specific problems that generate it. This study has shown, as others before it, that at times ethnicity or the diversity crisis is rather a misplaced interpretation of other deep social crises with which it coincides or onto which it is grafted in popular imagination. What we have here is a crisis that combines problems of the capitalist mode of production and the polarisation that it breeds, and the grafting of social problems to political discourses and practices. The only viable solution to this crisis would be a viable national development policy which does not only seek to decongest already overcrowded growth poles but also returns to a balanced development which is people-centred without simply talking of protecting minorities that are difficult to define. The simple management of diversity in pure colonial style is not sufficient. In examining the possibility of balanced rural development in a democratic context I had indicated that this would be largely affected by the inequality between regions as they were shaped by the post-colonial experience within a centralised state which ushered in 'the development of a unique metropolis at the coast with a vast periphery at the hinterland' (Yenshu 1997: 135). The solution I proposed then was that of developing new growth poles out of the regions. Our analysis makes this position as tenable today as it was six years ago. I will go on to add that this will become the more responsive to social needs if it is inscribed in a logic of redressing the distortions inherited from colonial urbanisation and capitalist development policies – rather than building on them.

Notes

1. The same facts are related in Yenshu (1998) almost verbatim. The repetition is meant to refresh the minds of the reader with the events which we intend to reinterpret.
2. The city of Douala currently numbers more than two million inhabitants.
3. This area covered the administrative unit designated today as Fako Division.
4. Quite a number of Bakweri and Duala were appointed in prominent places in government after the 1996 protests, starting with a Prime Minister, a Minister of Defence, Assistant Secretary General at the presidency, the Government Delegates to the Urban Councils of Limbe, Douala and Kumba, the headship of University institutions in the Coastal region, Director General positions in state corporations, and several mid-level managerial positions in governmental and parastatal organisations disproportionately in relation to their demographic strength within the country.

References

Ake, C., 2000, *The Feasibility of Democracy in Africa*, Dakar: CODESRIA.

Amin, S., 1998, *Africa and the Challenge of Development. Essays by Samir Amin.* Edited by Chris Uroh, Ibadan: Hope Publications.

Amin, S., 1993, '1492 : la polarisation des mondes : entretien avec Samir Amin', *Cahiers des Sciences Humaines*, Num. hors série, p. 20-23.

Austen, R. A. and Jonathan, D., 1999, *Middlemen of the Cameroons River. The Duala and their Hinterland, c.1600-c.1960*, Cambridge: Cambridge University Press.

Balogun, J., 2001, 'Diversity Issues Facing the Public Service in Sub-Saharan Africa', in UNDESA-IIAS, *Managing Diversity in the Civil Service*, Amsterdam, Berlin, Oxford, Tokyo, Washington D.C.: IOS Press.

Brutsch, J.R., 1956, 'Autour du Procès de Rudolf Duala Manga', *Etudes Camerounaises*, Institut Français d'Afrique Noire, Centre Cameroun, Mars.

Brutsch, J.R., 1955, 'Les Traités Camerounaise. Recueillis, Traduits et commentés', *Etudes Camerounaises* (Institut Français d'Afrique Noire, Centre Cameroun), Mars-Juin.

Delancey, M.W., 1972, 'Plantation and Migration in the Mount Cameroon Region', in Heransgegeben Vou Hans F. Illy (ed.), *Kamerun: Structuren und Probleme der Sozio-ökonominschen entwicklung*, Mainz: v. Hase and Koehler Verlag, Institut für Internationale Solidarität, Der Konrad-Ardenauer-Stiftung, Schriftenreiche BD.12.

Derrick, J., 1989, 'Colonial elitism in Cameroon: The Case of the Duala in the 1930s', in M. Njeuma (ed.) *Introduction to the History of Cameroon: Nineteenth and Twentieth Centuries*, London: Macmillan.

Epale, S. J., 1975, *Agrarian Capitalism in Western Cameroon, 1885–1975: A Case Study in the Modernisation of a Backward Economy*, unpublished mimeograph.

Fombe, L.F. and Fogwe, Z.N., 2001, 'Urban Housing Infrastructure and Implications in the Bonaberi Suburban area, Douala', in C. M. Lambi and E. B. Eze (eds.),

Readings in Geography, Buea, Research Group in Geography and Environmental Sciences.

Forba Fru, C., 1999, *Urbanisation in Buea: Process and Problems*, unpublished M.Sc. Thesis, University of Buea.

Kala Lobe, I., 1977, *Douala Manga Bell: Héros de la Résistance Duala*, Paris: Editions ABC.

Kauzya, J.M., 2001, 'A Holistic Model for managing Ethnic Diversity in the Public Service in Africa', in UNDESA-IIAS, *Managing Diversity in the Civil Service*, Amsterdam, Berlin, Oxford, Tokyo, Washington D.C.: IOS Press.

Levine, V.T.,1964, *The Cameroons from Mandate to Independence*, Berkeley and Los Angeles: University of California Press.

Matute, D.L., 1990, *Facing Mount Fako: An ethnographic study of the Bakweri of Cameroon*, Milwaukee: Omnipress.

Mainet, G., 1985, *Douala: Croissance et Servitudes*, Paris: L'Harmattan, Villes et Entreprises.

Mbake, S. N., 1975, 'Traditional Authority among the Bakweri. An Historical Survey from Precolonial Times', unpublished DES dissertation, University of Yaoundé.

Nyounae-Libam, J.P., 1970, *Le traité Douala-allemand du 12 Juillet 1884. Historique, texte, exposé critique*, Paris: CNRS.

Slageren, Jaapvan, 1972, *Les origines de l'église évangélique du Cameroun. Missions européens et christianisme autochtone.* Leiden: J. Brill.

Touraine, A., 1994, *Qu'este-ce que la Démocratie?*, Paris: Fayard.

Yenshu, Vubo E., 2001, 'Changing inter-community relations and the Politics of identity in the Northern Mezam Area', *Cahiers d'Etudes Africaines*, 161, XLI-1:163-190.

Yenshu, Vubo, E., 1998, 'The Discourse and Politics of Indigenous/Minority Peoples' Rights in some Metropolitan Areas of Cameroon', *Journal of Applied Social Sciences*, Multidisciplinary Journal of the Faculty of Social and Management Sciences, University of Buea,Vol. 1, No. 1, October.

Yenshu, Vubo, E., 1997, 'Balanced Rural Development in Cameroon within a Democratic Context', in P.N. Nkwi and F. B. Nyamnjoh, *Regional Balance and National Integration in Cameroon: Lessons Learnt and the Uncertain Future*, Leiden, African Studies Centre/Yaoundé, International Centre for Applied Social Science and Training (ICASSRT) Monograph No. 1.

4

Effects of the Foreign Debt Burden on Saving Ratios in the CEMAC Zone

George Ndoh Mbanga

Introduction and Background

Empirical studies often find that saving is highly correlated with foreign debt. The poor saving performance in Sub-Saharan Africa over the past three decades is a matter of concern given the increasing scarcity of foreign aid. Private saving ratios declined from an already low level of 11 percent in the 1970s to 8 percent in the 1980s (Loayza et al. 2000). The Central African Sub-region (the CEMAC[1] Zone) has been no exception to this poor saving trend. The experience of the negative real institutional interest rates is manifested through reduced national saving, more capital flight, worse misallocation of resources, excessive lending to prime borrowers, resurgence of non-institutional money markets, increased used of foreign financial institutions, and increased problems of monetary control (Fry 1995).

National saving flows via domestic investment in three ways: government appropriation, self-finance, and financial intermediation (Idem, p.56). The level of development influences enormously the relative importance of each channel.

The economic and financial situation of Central Africa deteriorated steadily from the late 1980s, when large external shocks, coupled with poor economic and financial management, led to a fall in the economic performance of the zone. All these countries suffer from the basic and prolonged imbalance in the demand for and the availability of resources, that is, a resource gap. It was only after the 1994 devaluation of the CFA franc that growth sluggishly picked up in this sub-region with positive growth rates recorded during the late 1990s (see Table 1).

Table 1: GDP and GDP Growth Rates of the CEMAC Zone

Country	Value ($ Millions)		Share of Africa's Total (%)		Growth Rate (%)	
	1998	1999	1998	1999	1998	1999
Cameroon	13,852	14,516	2.59	2.63	5.2	4.8
CAR	1,600	1,680	0.30	0.30	5.5	5.5
Chad	1,599	1,618	0.30	0.29	6.0	1.2
Congo, Rep.	3,111	3,267	0.58	0.59	8.1	5.0
Equat Guinea	390	429	0.07	0.08	14.7	10.0
Gabon	63	65	0.01	0.01	2.6	2.8
CEMAC	27,435	28,654	5.13	5.19	5.0	4.5

Source: Economic Commission for Africa 2001.

With growth rates of 5.0 percent and 4.5 percent for 1998 and 1999, respectively, the Central African sub-region was the best performer in Africa during this period, compared with 4.4 percent and 3.6 percent for North Africa; 3.6 percent and 3.3 percent for West Africa; 2.6 percent and 4.1 percent for East Africa and 1.7 percent and 2.2 percent for Southern Africa. Equatorial Guinea remains the highest growing country in the CEMAC zone; unfortunately, it has not used its incredible growth in GDP to reduce poverty (ECA 2001).

Statement of the Problem

The external debt stock of countries of the CEMAC zone has impacted negatively on their saving rates. This is because investment resources for productive pursuits have been consistently used to meet external debt service obligations. Thus, the excessive external debt stock is impairing growth and compromising the socio-economic development of the CEMAC countries, and therefore crowding out saving. Thus, the debt burden has now painted a new vicious circle in the analysis of development problems of the zone.

Of the six countries that make up the sub-region, five have been classified as heavily indebted poor countries (HIPCs). Only Gabon stands out of this classification. The foreign indicators of the HIPCs of the CEMAC zone are presented in Table 2.

Table 2: External Debt Indicators of the CEMAC zone HIPCs

	Total Debt Stock ($Mns)		Debt/GDP (%)		Distribution of Long-term Debt (%)					
					Multilateral		Bilateral		Private	
Country	1992	1997	1992	1997	1992	1997	1992	1997	1992	1997
Cameroon	7415	9293	69	109	22	19	54	72	23	10
CAR	814	885	57	88	69	75	28	23	3	2
Chad	723	1027	41	65	76	80	23	80	1	2
Congo	4770	5071	187	232	14	14	63	66	23	19
Equ Guin.	255	283	172	165	37	45	55	48	7	7

Source: World Bank, *Global Development Finance* 1999.

From Table 2, the debt ratios (debt/GDP) are very high, and have had a deleterious effect on the saving ratios in the sub-region. This is because residents (be they nationals or foreigners) have been scared by the heavy debt burden from saving, as they expect the policy makers could raise taxes or use their savings ratios for debt service payments (for instance, the disappearance of some commercial banks with the savings of people in this sub-region has helped in reducing savings). On the other hand, a large amount of foreign earning is needed to service foreign debt, thereby diverting foreign exchange earnings from investment and reducing potential capital formation, though low savings. Thus, the causality between foreign debt burden and savings ratios can be traced through the impact on investment of the *debt overhang* and *crowding out* effects, and the increased level of uncertainty in the economy due to a large stock of debt (Ajayi 2000; Elbadawi et al. 1996; Elbadawi and Mwega 2000; Fosu 1996 and 1999; Mbanga 1994, and Mbanga and Sikod 2001).

The high debt-burden (measured either as the debt-GDP ratio or debt-exports ratios) is of great importance because of its negative impact on investment and saving. According to Ajayi (2000), an important aspect of the high debt burden (debt-exports) is that the large stock of foreign debt can be associated with lower investment. Hence, the payment of the foreign debt reduces the funds available for investment and saving in the debtor economy. In the second instance, the economy loses the amount of money that if invested domestically would have had a multiplier effect and a stimulus on future investment and saving. In short, the debt burden encourages capital flight from the debtor economy, which is a diversion of domestic savings away from domestic real investment (Ajayi 2000).

The case of the CEMAC zone is really surprising because the sub-region is endowed with enormous oil and forest resources, and favourable agricultural conditions, with one of the best-endowed primary commodity economies in Sub-Saharan Africa. Yet it faces many of the serious development problems other developing regions encounter, due to the high debt burden.

Objectives and Hypothesis of the Study

The main objective of this study has been to empirically investigate the relationship between the foreign debt and the saving ratios in the CEMAC zone. That is, the bottom line of the paper is to estimate *aggregate savings functions* for the countries in the CEMAC zone, and test the presence of *non-linear effect* of external debt burden on savings rates. The hypothesis to guide this study has been that the debt burden of the CEMAC zone is one of the factors behind the poor saving rates and poor economic performance in general. This is because the size of the foreign debt has acted as a deterrent to saving, thus painting a negative relationship between debt burden and the saving ratios.

The Debt Status of the Sub-region

The alarming burden of external debt in the sub-region can be explained simply by the fact that five of the six countries are classified as heavily indebted poor countries (HIPCs). By 1999, the ratio of debt-to-export in the sub-region stood as follows: Cameroon – 219 percent, Central African Republic – 175 percent, Chad – 218 percent, and Congo Republic – 187 percent. Also, the ratio of debt-to-revenue during the same period was alarming with Cameroon having 278 percent, Central African Republic 288 percent, Chad 308 percent and Congo Republic 410 percent. The debt burden of the CEMAC zone is further demonstrated in Table 3.

It is evident that the debt burden has kept growing more rapidly in the CEMAC zone, despite the debt relief strategies that preceded the HIPC initiative. The ratios of the debt-to-exports and debt-to-GNP have grown seriously for all countries, except Equatorial-Guinea. This means that the growth rate of debt has by far exceeded that of the GNP and exports, thus impairing the possibility of increasing saving rates in the sub-region.

Another noteworthy disturbing feature is the debt-service burden of the sub-region. This means that debt-servicing has continued to absorb the financial resources destined for investment in the zone. Thus, large outward net transfers to creditors have been financed from inward multilateral and bilateral grants. The largest outflows and debt service burden are accounted for by long term debt.

Table 3: External Debt Variables (Millions of Dollars) – 1998

	Cameroon	CAR	Congo	Gabon	E. Guinea	Chad
Short & Long Term debt	9829	921	5118	4424	306	1092
Long term debt	8275	830	4250	3833	217	1005
IMF credit	156	18	34	113	11	64
Long term debt-service	1398	74	834	478	79	23
Long term Principal	528	95	1473	85	97	38
Arrears Export Credits	2603	55	1678	2223	56	78
External Debt Ratios (%)						
Debt/Exports of goods & services	411.4	633.4	407.2	173.1	73.3	326.9
Debt/GNP	119.0	88.8	306.9	90.7	75.5	65.5
Debt Service/exports of goods & ser	22.3	20.9	3.3	12.0	1.4	10.6
Interest Payments/exports of gds & ser	9.9	5.5	1.9	6.7	0.6	3.7
Multilateral debt/debt total	15.1	67.7	12.2	12.5	32.0	74.6

Source: World Bank, *Global Development Finance*, 1999.

Review of Related Works

Several studies exist in the literature on the relationship between capital inflows and saving. Weisskopf (1972) posits an ax-ante relationship between the saving rate and capital inflows and exports. He pooled time-series and cross section data on seventeen countries, found a highly significant impact of capital inflow on saving and estimated that about 23 percent of foreign inflows were offset by declines in domestic saving. Other authors such as Bhagwati and Srinivasan (1976), Gupta (1990), and Papenek (1972) have come out with different results, but suggesting a positive marginal propensity to save, resulting from capital inflow in the short run. Graham (1989) insinuates that borrowing may be viewed as a way of closing the domestic gap, i.e. the gap between savings required to finance the investment which is itself needed to achieve a target growth rate, and the actual amount of domestic saving. If borrowing is necessitated by a deficiency of domestic saving, it follows that to service and repay debt, there has to be an excess of domestic saving over and above that for financing domestic investment. A crucial factor here is what is happening to the domestic saving ratio. If the marginal propensity to save exceeds the average propensity to save, the saving ratio will rise. Thus, following economic theory it implies that a rising saving ratio will offer a better prospect that the debtor will be able to meet its obligations than if the ratio were falling.

For Fry (1995), the effects of the real deposit rate on national saving is ambiguous, given possible counteracting income and substitution effects. After some of the negative consequences of excessive foreign debt accumulation emerged in the early 1980s, many developing countries took a fresh look at their policies towards foreign direct investment. Fry adds that capital inflow allows domestic investment to exceed national saving when they finance a current account deficit. Domestic investment equals national saving, as shown by the national saving definition of the balance of payments on current account IY = SNY + SFY, where SFY is foreign saving, which equals the current account deficit as a proportion of GNP (CAY), SNY is national saving as a ratio of GNP, and IY is domestic investment divided by GNP. Therefore, capital inflows that finance the current account deficit can increase investment and the rate of economic growth.

Thus far, the literature has focused on the positive relationship between capital inflows and saving. That is, showing how foreign debt and other inflows have enhanced savings in the developing debtor countries. This means that in the short term, the inheritance of foreign debt crowds in savings, but in the long term this relationship changes to one of a crowd out.

Attention will now be focused on the literature that demonstrates the negative relationship between foreign debt and the saving rates.

Fry (1995) holds that capital outflows from a debtor country reduce national saving, even in the unlikely event that the true level of saving remains constant. Hence, one might expect a higher value of foreign debt to reduce measured national saving, implying leftward shifts in the national saving function. He goes further to say that an increase in foreign debt can worsen the current account by destabilising fiscal effects that outweigh the stabilising financial effect of foreign debt accumulation discussed above. The magnitude of capital flight caused by a buildup of foreign debt can be, and in several developing countries has been, destabilising (Ajayi 1991 and 2000). Instead of increase in foreign debt reducing domestic investment and increasing national saving, the foreign debt accumulation shifts the national saving function to the left, therefore increasing the current account deficit.

Empirical results reported in the last decade show that in countries with increasing external debt, the debt burden (debt/GNP or debt/exports) has actually reduced saving by more than it reduces investment (Aghevli et al. 1990; Ajayi 1991 and 2000; Cohen 1993; Collier and Gunning 1999; Fry 1995; Mbanga 1994; Khan and Villanueva 1991; Ghura 1997; and Geiger 1990). Thus, when foreign indebtedness reaches some critical levels, additional capital inflows seem to be more harmful than good. Most of these studies suggest that the tendency to over-borrow can be countered by macroeconomic policies designed to stimulate saving (or to depress investment). Higher saving (or reduced investment) depreciates the real exchange rate, which in turn, increases exports and reduces imports, thus, fostering the competitiveness of the economy.

In the case of Africa, economic literature has grown on the depressive effect that external debt can have on the formation of domestic saving. Mbire and Atingi (1997) have shown the impact of capital imports on aggregate performance in Uganda. They used the two-gap theory which suggests that growth is limited by two constraints: the saving gap, which contains the country's ability to save and invest, and the foreign exchange gap accruing from limited export revenues and the target growth rate of the economy causing imports to exceed the economy's ability to finance them. Mbanga (1994) uses time series data to prove a negative and significant relation between external debt and the rate of saving in Cameroon. Elbadawi and Mwega (2000) in their study on saving and investment in Sub-Saharan Africa concluded that causality runs from growth to investment (and perhaps to private saving), whereas a rise in the saving rate causes an increase in investment. Foreign aid causes a reduction in both saving and investment, and investment also causes an increase in foreign aid.

Finally, given that investment and saving are two sides of the same coin, all studies on Africa that have proven a negative relationship between external debt accumulation and investment, have to an extent implied the same for saving (Ajayi 1991 and 2000; Elbadawi et al. 1996; Defege 1992; Fuso 1996 and 1999; Iyoha 2000; Mbanga and Sikod 2001; Mjema 1996; and Osei 2000) To the best of our knowledge, no study has been carried out on the relationship between external debt and the saving ratios in the Central African sub-region, thus the present study is an effort to fill this geographical gap in the literature.

Methodological Issues

In order to meet the objectives and verify the hypothesis of this study, the methodology has been divided into two parts: model specification (data analysis) and data issues.

Model Specification

We have used a multiple regression model for this study, adopted from the works of Fry M. (1989 and 1995). The model sets out by identifying the role of the saving component in the traditional macroeconomic identity in an open economy.

$Y_t = C_t + I_t + X_t - M_t$ .... (1)

$Y_t - (C_t - I_t) = X_t - M_t$ .... (1a)

and $Y_t = Ct + Sd_t + INT_t$ .... (1b)

Where:

Y_t stands for real GDP; C_t is the real consumption; I_t is the real investment; X_t and M_t stand for the real exports and imports, respectively; Sd_t is the domestic saving; and INT_t stands for interest payment on external debt.

In equation (1a), the left hand side constitutes the domestic resource surplus (deficit) while the right hand side is the external or current account surplus (deficit).

The interest payment (INT_t) in equation (1b), using the disbursed debt stock (D_{t-1}) and the interest rate (r) as repressor is as follows:

$$INT_t = rD_{t-1} \qquad (2)$$

Substituting equations (1a), (1b), and (2) into equation (1), and rearranging, we can derive an equation of investment as follows:

$$I_t = Sd_t + (M_t - X_t) + r\,D_{t-1} \qquad (3)$$

If we now set Sf_t as the required foreign saving to finance the current account deficit (M_t-X_t) and the interest payments r D_{t-1}, which is actually the gap between domestic saving (Sd_t) and required investment (I_t) to ensure GDP growth (g), equation (1) becomes:

$$I_t = Sd_t + Sf_t \qquad (3a)$$

The equation of the saving component of equation (3a) is:

$$Sd_t = (M_t - X_t) + r\,D_{t-1} \qquad (4)$$

Having now confirmed the role of the saving component in the traditional macroeconomic variables in equation (4), which is an identity, it would be worthwhile to present the determinants of the saving ratio in a behavioural equation by borrowing from the works of Fry (1989 and 1995). According to this author, the saving ratio is influenced by conventional variables (such as: growth rate of real GNP, growth in the terms of trade, World real interest rate, net government credit to total domestic credit), and a policy variable-foreign debt burden.

Thus, the saving function estimated was specified as follows:

$$SNY = a_0 + a_1YG + a_2TTG + a_3RW + a_4DCGR + a_5DETY + a_6(DETY)^2 + a_7SNY_{t-1} \qquad (5)$$

Where:

SNY = Ratio of national saving/GNP,

YG = Growth rate of Real GNP,

TTG =Growth in the terms of trade,

RW = world real interest rate,

DCGR = Ratio of net government credit to total domestic credit,

DETY = ratio of external debt to GNP

The growth of real GNP and the terms of trade are endogenous explanatory variables. The national saving ratio (SNY) is expected to be increased by higher growth in real GNP (YG), and by an improvement in the terms of trade (TTG). Thus, the coefficients of these variables are expected to be positive.

The variable world real interest rate (RW) is expected to have an adverse effect on the national saving ratio. The effect of the ratio of net government credit to total domestic credit (DCGR) on national saving ratio is supposed to be negative.

The main policy variable of this study - the ratio of external debt to GNP (DETY) – is supposed to be positively related to the national saving ratio in its linear form, but negatively related to national saving in its non-linear (quadratic) form (DETY). That is, the ratio of external debt to GNP squared is expected to exert an adverse effect on the national saving. As seen in the literature review, at a low level, the stock of foreign debt increases national saving, but as more foreign debt is accumulated over time, this stimulates capital flight, which leads to a negative net transfer of resources abroad and discourages national saving (Ajayi 2000).

Finally, the lagged value of the national saving ratio $(SNY)_{t-1}$ is included in the model to capture the good savings climate. That is, previous levels of savings could induce more saving.

Data Issues

This study has used secondary data. These were aggregate time-series data for the six countries of the Sub-region, running from 1970 to 2001. The data were collected from documents such as: *Global Development Finance*, *African Development Indicators,* and the *World Debt Tables* (all publications of the World Bank); International Financial Statistics and the World Economic Outlook (all publications of the IMF). Also, the Bank of Central African States (BEAC), which is the central bank of the CEMAC countries, served as another useful source of data for this study, as information was extracted from its annual reports. These data were complemented by information from the Offices of Statistics and National Accounting in Cameroon contained in 'La Loi de Finance'. For the world interest rate, we have used data for the *London Interbank offered Rate (LIBOR).*

Presentation of Results of the Model

The estimation results are on pooled ordinary least squares regressions. The estimated results are presented in Table 4 which shows positive and significant results between the growth rate of real GDP and the ratio of national saving. Several studies of saving have found that the growth rate real GDP positively affects saving rates (Loayza, et al. 2000; Bosworth 1993; Carroll and Weil 1994).

Table 4: CEMAC National Saving Ratio Regression Results

Variable	Coefficient
Constant	0.079
	(0.68)
YG	0.245*
	(2.02)
TTG	0.078*
	(2.14)
RW	-0.665**
	(-1.96)
DCGR	-0.111***
	(-0.51)
DETY	0.282*
	(2.22)
$DETY^2$	-0.455***
	(0.26)
SNY_{-1}	3.651
(2.28)	
Standard error	0.091
R^2	0.987
Adjusted R^2	0.976
LM1	0.32
LM2	0.23

*** Significant at 1 percent, ** Significant at 5 percent, and * Significant at 10 percent. T-ratios in parenthesis.

The relationship between the ratio of national saving and the ratio of external debt to GDP is as predicted by the theory. That is, in the short run, foreign

Dependent Variable: SNY

saving crowds in national saving, in the long run foreign saving crowds out national saving. This means that foreign debt has acted as a substitute for national saving by lessening the liquidity constraints or by inducing Dutch-disease effects in the economy (Elbadawi and Mwega 2000). This is the reason five out of the six countries of the zone have been classified as heavily indebted poor countries (HIPC), by the World Bank and the International Monetary Fund.

The results have also confirmed the positive link between the national saving ratio and improvements in the terms of trade. This is because an improvement in the terms of trade increases income and therefore the level of national saving. This is more likely to happen when the improvement in the terms of trade is expected to be transitory. In the CEMAC zone, this effect is of crucial importance since the CEMAC countries rely only a few commodities for export earnings, which are sold in highly volatile markets. This result is corroborated by other empirical results such as Elbadawi and Mwega (2000).

When we turn to the world interest rate, the result shows that the coefficient is negative as predicted. This variable measures the absence of financial repression in the economy of the CEMAC zone. Its negative sign means that increases in the major international rates such as the London Interbank Offered Rate (*LIBOR*) help in destroying national saving in the sub-region, since this renders the economy less competitive.

Also, the results confirmed a negative and significant relationship between the ratio of net government credit to total domestic credit and the national saving ratio. Thus, as the government grants more credit to the private sector, this reduces the amount of national savings.

Finally, the positive relationship between the lagged value of the ratio of national saving and the current ratio of national saving portrays a good saving climate. The implication here is that past levels of national saving help in fostering the level of national saving, although the coefficient is insignificant.

Conclusion

The main objective of this study has been to empirically investigate the relationship between the saving ratio and the debt burden. The size of the foreign debt and debt service payments of the CEMAC countries is compounded by poverty and the structural weakness of the economies of these countries. They produce and export the same exports (primary products) and so have not been able to diversify their export base (even before the devaluation of 1994) to take care of the changing world economic conditions.

The paper has arrived at the inescapable conclusion that debt overhang is a reality in the Central African sub-region Thus, this heavy debt burden has militated against any rapid economic growth and development. Analysts and international policy makers appear to have agreed that a satisfactory recovery of investment and output growth in the zone will remain a distant dream as long as the debt burden, that requires the transfer of enormous resources abroad and impairs saving, remains in place. Hence, many now believe that a necessary condition for economic growth and development is debt relief that goes beyond reschedulings. But to effectively effect such a relief, it would be wise to know to what extent the debt burden has been deleterious to economic variables in the zone.

This study being the first of its kind for the CEMAC zone has established a causal relationship between the foreign debt burden and the saving ratio (one of the key variables to growth). This has provided an insight to the impact of the debt burden on the economic performance of the zone. Given also, that in the CEMAC zone five of the six countries (Cameroon, Central African Republic, Chad, Congo, and Equatorial Guinea) are classified as heavily indebted poor countries (HIPCs), the results of the regression model have shown how the continuous accumulation of debt over time has pushed these countries to reach this stage. Debt has been seen as one of the causes of the development problems of the sub-region, but debt is an integral component in intensifying the vicious circle of the sub-region's decreasing performance and increasing marginalisation.

Note

1. CEMAC means the Economic and Monetary Community of Central Africa, formed in 1994. It was formerly called 'Union Douanière et Economique de l'Afrique Centrale (UDEAC)', created in 1966. During its creation in 1966, the UDEAC zone was made up of Cameroon, Central African Republic, Chad, Congo and Gabon. Equatorial Guinea joined the Union later in 1989.

References

Ajayi, I., 2000, 'Macroeconomic Approach to External Debt: The Case of Nigeria' in Ajayi, I and Moshin Khan (eds.) *External debt and capital flight in Sub-Saharan Africa*, Washington: International Monetary Fund.

Aghevli, B., Boughton, M. Montiel, P., Villanueva, D., and Woglom, G., 1990, 'The Role of National Saving in the World Economy, Recent Trends and Prospects', IMF, Occasional Paper 67, Washington D.C

Azam, J.P., 1996, 'Saving and Interest Rates: The Case of Kenya', *Saving and Development*, Vol. 20, No. 2, pp 33-44.

BEAC, 2001, Conjoncture Economiques et Monétaire de la CEMAC.

BEAC, 2001, Rapport d'Activités de la BEAC, 1999-2001.

Bhagwati, J. and Srinivasan, T.N., 1976, *Foreign Trade Regimes and Economic Development*, New York: Columbia University press for NBER.

Blejer, M. and Khan, M., 1984, 'Private Investment in Developing Countries', *Finance and Development,* Vol. 31, N°. 2, pp.26-29.

Bohoun, B. and Kouassy, O., 1997, 'External Debt and Growth in Côte d'Ivoire, Financial Constraints to Sustainable Growth', Final Report submitted to AERC, Nairobi.

Borenzstein, E., 1991, 'Debt Overhang, Credit Rationing and Investment', *Journal of Development Economics*, N°. 32, pp. 315-35.

Bosworth, B.P., 1993, 'Saving and Investment in a Global Economy', Washington, D.C.: Brookings Institutions.

Carroll, C. and Weil, D.N., 1994, 'Saving and Growth: A Reinterpretation', Carnegie-Rochester Conference series in Public Policy 40, pp 133-92.

Cohen, D., 1993, 'Low Investment and Large Debt in the 1980s', The *American Economic Review*, Vol. 83, N°. 3.

Collier, P. and Gunning, W., 1999, 'Explaining African Economic Performance', *Journal of Economic Literature*, Vol. XXXVII, March.

Collins, C., 1999, 'Breaking the Chains of Debt', *UN Africa Recovery*, Vol. 13, N°. 2-3, September.

Defege, B., 1992, 'Growth and Foreign Debt: The Ethiopia Experience, 1964-86', AERC Research Paper, N°. 13, Nairobi: AERC.

ECA, 2001, 'Transforming Africa's Economies: Overview', Economic Commission for Africa, Addis Ababa, Ethiopia.

Elbadawi, I. and Mwega, F., 2000, 'Can Africa's saving collapse be reversed?' *The World Bank Economic Review*, Vol. 14, N°. 3, September, pp. 445-56

Elbadawi, I., Ndulu, B. and Ndung'u, N., 1997, 'Debt Overhang and Economic Growth in Sub-Saharan Africa', in I. Zubair and R. Kanbur (eds.), *External Finance for Low-Income Countries*, Washington D.C.: IMF.

Fosu, A., 1999, 'The External Debt and Economic Growth in the 1980s: Evidence from Sub-Saharan Africa', *Canadian Journal of Development* Studies, Vol. XX, N°. 2, pp. 307-18.

Fosu, A., 1996, 'The Impact of External Debt on Economic Growth in Sub-Saharan Africa', *Journal of economic Development*, Vol. 21, N°. 1, pp. 93-118.

Fry, M.J., 1995, *Money, Interest and Banking in Economic Development*, Baltimore: The Johns Hopkins University Press.

Fry, M.J., 1989, 'Foreign Debt Instability: An Analysis of National Saving and Domestic Investment Responses to Debt Accumulation in 28 Developing Countries'. *Journal of International Money and Finance*, Vol. 8, N°. 3, September, pp. 315-344.

Geiger, L., 1990, 'Debt and Economic Development in Latin America', *Journal of Development Areas*, Vol. 24, N°. 2, pp.181-195.

Graham, B., 1989, *Third World Debt*, Worcester: Billing and Sons.

Ghura, D., 1997, Private Investment and Endogenous Growth, Evidence from Cameroon', IMF working papers WP/97/165, International Monetary Fund, Washington D.C.

Greene, J. and Khan, M., 1990, 'The African Debt Crisis', Special Paper 3, Nairobi: AERC.

Gupta, K.L., 1990, 'Foreign Capital and Domestic Saving: A Test of Haavelemon's Hypothesis with Cross-Country data', *Review of Economics and Statistics*, Vol. 52, May, pp. 214-16.

IMF, 1999, *Cameroon: Selected Issues and Statistical Appendix*, Washington D.C.:IMF

Iyoha, M., 2000, 'External debt and Economic growth in Sub-Saharan African Countries: An Econometric Study', in Ajayi, I. and M. Khan (eds.), *External Debt and Capital Flight in Sub-Saharan Africa*, Washington D.C.: International Monetary Fund.

Khan, M. and Villanueva, D., 1991, 'Macroeconomic Policies and Long-term Growth', AERC special paper 13, Nairobi: AERC.

Krueger, A., 1987, 'Debt, Capital Flows, and LDC Growth', *American Economic Review* Vol. 77, N°.2, May.

Loayza, N., Schmidt-Hebbel, K. and Serven, L., 2000, 'Saving in Developing Countries: An Overview', *The World Bank Economic Review*, Vol. 14, N° 3, September.

Mbanga, G., 1996, 'The External Debt and the Future of Africa', *African Journal of Economic Policy*, Vol.3, N°.2, December.

Mbanga, G., 1994, 'The External Debt Situation of Cameroon: Review and Analysis', Unpublished Doctorate Thesis at the University of Yaounde II, Yaounde.

Mbanga, G., and Sikod, F., 2001, 'The Impact of Debt and Debt-Service Payments on Investment in Cameroon', Final Report submitted to AERC, Nairobi, May.

Mbire, B. and Atinge, M., 1997, 'Growth and Foreign Debt: The Ugandan Experience'. AERC, Research Paper 66, Nairobi: AERC.

Mjema, G.D., 1996, "The Impact of Debt and Debt-Servicing in the Economy of Tanzania: A Simultaneous Equation Approach", *African Journal of Economic Policy*, Vol.3 N°. 1, June.

Mwega, F.M., 1997, 'Saving in Sub-Saharan Africa: A Comparative Analysis, *Journal of African Economies*, Supplement to Vol. 6, N°. 3, pp. 199-228.

Osei, B., 2000, 'Ghana: The Burden of Debt-Service Payment Under Structural Adjustment', in I. Ajayi and M. Khan (eds.) *External Debt and Capital Flight in Sub-Saharan Africa*, Washington D.C.: International Monetary Fund.

Papenek, G., 1992, 'The Effect of Aids and other Resource Transfers on Saving and Growth in the Less Developed Countries', *Economic Journal*, Vol. 28, September, pp. 934-40.

Thirlwall, M., 1999, *Growth and Development with Reference to Developing Countries*, London: Macmillan Press Limited.

Touna, M. and Mbanga, G., 2001, 'The African Debt Crisis: A Critical Examination of Debt Relief Strategies', *Revue Africaine des Sciences Economiques*, Vol. III, N°.2, Juillet-Decembre.

Van Wijnbergen, S., 1991, 'Debt Relief and Economic Growth in Mexico', *The World Bank Economic Review*, Vol.5. N° 3, pp 430-455.

World Bank (various issues), *World Development Report*, Oxford: Oxford University Press.

World Bank (various Issues), *Global Development Finance*, Washington D. C.: World Bank.

World Bank (various Issues), *World Debt Tables*, Washington D.C.: World Bank.

Annex Tables

Table A1: Economic Indicators of CEMAC Member Countries (% of GDP)

Country	1987	1990	1994	1995	1996	1997	1998	1999	2000	2001
Exports of nonfactor goods & services										
Cameroon			23.8	25.8	24.2	25.0	25.3	21.7	25.0	26.2
CAR			24.0	22.2	21.8	25.3	20.0	18.4	18.8	18.7
Congo			57.8	64.7	68.8	74.1	76.2	72.1	89.5	87.0
Gabon			62.3	59.4	62.7	61.3	47.4	60.3	66.0	60.3
Eq.Guinea			57.3	56.9	80.0	91.4	93.5	95.1	102.0	101.3
Chad			15.7	22.1	17.4	18.8	19.5	19.1	19.9	17.1
CEMAC			38.5	38.7	40.5	42.0	35.7	39.6	48.6	45.3
Imports of nonfactor goods and Services										
Cameroon			20.0	20.1	20.0	20.3	23.5	21.8	21.7	24.8
CAR			29.8	28.2	25.1	27.8	27.2	23.2	22.4	24.9
Congo			90.5	63.1	59.9	57.2	72.6	66.5	52.7	58.4
Gabon			-34.9	-35.7	-33.0	-37.2	-48.0	-38.5	-32.7	-34.2
Eq.Guinea			-64.5	-90.9	-160	-110	-151	-115	-69.9	-88.9
Chad			32.9	34.0	28.8	31.2	30.7	31.8	36.6	61.8
CEMAC			34.5	31.4	31.4	33.7	37.7	35.2	35.1	38.3
Investment rates										
Cameroon	15.7	16.5	12.7	14.2	13.6	16.4	15.2	14.6	20.0	20.4
Public	-	-	3.4	1.2	1.1	1.7	1.9	1.9	2.3	4.0
CAR	13.7	11.1	14.8	17.8	5.1	9.2	14.3	14.4	9.2	11.7
Public	-	-	10.3	10.4	2.5	7.1	11.7	11.8	6.1	8.1
Congo	18.6	15.9	55.9	50.6	29.1	30.0	40.1	50.4	30.9	37.9
Public	-	-	2.8	3.0	8.0	4.1	4.4	5.5	7.3	9.3
Gabon	28.2	22.4	21.6	23.3	19.7	31.5	39.1	24.9	21.3	24.3
Public	3.2	4.2	5.6	5.5	5.0	11.2	13.7	4.2	3.1	3.6
Eq. Guinea	24.2	24.3	54.2	54.6	102	59.7	77.6	64.0	56.2	51.1
Public	16.8	17.2	9.5	4.4	5.8	5.4	11.1	6.6	6.4	6.3
Chad	12.3	10.3	20.8	13.5	20.2	17.8	15.5	18.4	25.1	49.7
Public	11.8	9.8	9.0	9.1	9.0	9.6	7.9	7.7	9.2	16.0
CEMAC	-	-	22.5	21.7	20.0	23.9	26.9	25.7	24.2	28.1
Public	-	-	4.3	3.7	3.9	5.6	6.2	4.1	4.5	5.7

Source: BEAC (2001), p.8 and World Bank (1992) African Development Indicators, p.31

Table A2: Economic Performance in the CEMAC Zone

Country	1993	1994	1995	1996	1997	1998	1999
Real Growth Rate of GDP							
Cameroon	-3.0	-3.0	3.3	5.0	5.1	5.0	4.4
Central African Republic	4.9	4.9	6.4	-3.1	4.2	5.5	3.5
Congo	-4.5	-4.5	2.6	6.4	-2.4	4.5	-4.3
Gabon	3.7	3.7	5.0	3.6	5.7	2.6	-9.7
Equatorial Guinea	11.5	4.3	12.9	37.4	93.8	18.5	23.2
Chad	5.7	5.7	0.9	3.2	4.4	6.4	0.3
CEMAC	1.2	1.1	4.2	4.5	5.2	4.6	-0.1
Average Annual Inflation rate							
Cameroon	-1.0	32.5	9.1	3.9	4.7	3.2	0.9
Central African Republic	-2.9	24.6	19.2	3.7	1.6	-1.9	-1.5
Congo	4.9	42.4	9.4	7.5	16.6	-1.6	3.6
Gabon	-8.9	36.2	9.5	1.8	4.1	2.3	-0.7
Equatorial Guinea	3.9	38.8	11.7	6.7	8.4	7.8	1.1
Chad	-6.9	43.7	9.3	11.3	5.6	4.3	-8.0
CEMAC	-2.6	35.2	9.9	4.4	6.0	2.4	0.5
Global Budget Balance as % of GDP							
Cameroon	-6.4	-9.2	-3.2	-1.8	-1.2	-0.7	-1.9
Central African Republic	-13.8	-14.8	-11.5	-5.2	-8.2	-10.8	-10.5
Congo	-20.4	-14.2	-9.3	-5.4	-7.7	-12.7	-2.9
Gabon	-6.1	-2.0	3.2	3.7	1.6	-14.0	-0.2
Equatorial Guinea	-32.4	-11.8	-8.2	-7.1	-1.1	-1.9	-1.8
Chad	-10.5	-14.0	-11.9	-11.1	-10.2	-8.6	-8.9
CEMAC	-9.7	-7.0	-3.1	-1.5	-2.0	-6.4	-1.8
Real Exchange Rate Variation							
Cameroon	2.4	2.6	7.0	-1.6	12.2	2.5	-4.6
Central African Republic	16.4	19.1	13.0	-4.5	5.3	-8.1	-3.4
Congo	7.6	9.8	6.4	15.9	0.5	-2.8	-1.4
Gabon	-1.3	-1.8	9.6	-2.8	13.8	-6.5	-4.1
Equatorial Guinea	-1.7	-1.4	3.1	-4.2	24.2	-8.2	-1.9
Chad	6.7	5.8	8.7	0.8	5.0	-6.5	-2.3
CEMAC	2.9	3.6	9.0	2.5	8.2	-2.1	-3.2

Source: Rapport d'Activité de la BEAC, 1999–2000.

5

The NEPAD Initiative: A Basis for Fostering Economic Recovery in the CEMAC Zone

Ntangsi Max Memfih

Background

After many years of intense colonial activities in the African continent, a majority of countries gained independence during the late 1950s and early 1960s. The immediate post-independence era was marked by a continuation of colonial policies, structures and institutions. The determination of colonial powers to safeguard their interests and influence in the continent was manifested in various neo-colonial practices like the promotion of the divide-and-rule tactics, and political authoritarianism. The policy-making environment was therefore characterised by the complexity of competing domestic and external interests. These contestations had the consequence of weakening state and governmental capacity over time. Within this context, the project of nation building that was the focal point of Pan-Africanists at independence suffered so many setbacks. The challenge of effectively managing the multi-ethnic societies was compounded by the failure of the political society to evolve adequate rules for governing itself and offering transparency and accountability for its people.

On the international front, the hope for a New International Economic Order (NIEO) arising from various international socio-economic and political negotiations became largely misplaced due to the lopsided socio-economic development pattern that accompanied such negotiations. The worsening terms of trade for primary products and the improvements for manufactured goods was a glaring example. Against this background, the progress of African countries that adopted the 'isolationist' development approach to their respective national development programmes was jeopardised. The emerging undesirable trends of socio-economic and political developments in both the pre- and post-colonial periods in Africa made it clear, especially within the first decade of independence, that the development gap between them and the developed countries would continuously widen over time in the absence of any determined effort to reverse the trend. Given the positive impacts of regional groupings on the Latin American and European economies, economic integration provided the basis for the attainment of the objective of 'collective self-reliance and self-sustenance' under a regional economic framework. Against this background, regional and sub-regional groupings couched as a cooperative approach to economic development and focus on collective self-reliance gained impetus in Africa. Currently, there are above ten regional economic groupings in the continent with virtually every country belonging to at least one.

In spite of the numerous regional and sub-regional groupings, which sprang up amidst abundant development potentials, no meaningful development has been recorded. Progress of various Regional Economic Communities (RECs) has been inhibited by increasing problems. Lack of political commitment, overlapping membership, problems of harmonising policies, issues related to compensation and the lack of private sector participation, are some of the constraints. Coupled with these integration difficulties are the routine developmental constraints of poor governance, poor infrastructure, lack of the rule of law, mounting debts, lack of adequate human resources, diseases, conflicts and a host of other factors. It is thus not surprising that the pace and pattern of socio-economic and political development in Africa, particularly since the 1980s, has been catastrophic.

Against this background of economic problems, since 1980 many Sub-Saharan Africa (SSA) economies (this includes CEMAC), adopted economic policy reforms designed to achieve macroeconomic and structural adjustments, as well as economic growth. Unfortunately, these programs designed by the Bretton Woods Institutions (World Bank and International Monetary Fund) have been highly controversial. One of the strongest reasons voiced against the reforms is that they have forced governments to reduce their role as providers of social services. Health and education expenditures for example, have declined seriously. In fact, the reforms have been perceived to be all pain, with no gain.

Thus, poverty and misery continue to be the main challenges facing policy makers on the continent. About 340 million people or half the population of Africa live on less than one US dollar a day. The mortality rate of children under 5 years is as high as 140 per 1000, and life expectancy at birth is only 54 years. The illiteracy rate of people above 15 years is, alarmingly more than 41 percent. Only about 58 percent of the population have access to safe water. There are only 18 mainline telephones per 1000 people in Africa compared with 146 for the world and 567 for developed countries (Nathan et al, 2002). The increased globalisation and liberalisation of the world economy increases the fears that Africa might be marginalised more than ever before.

As a result of these difficult economic realities, several initiatives launched to develop Africa have failed. The dilemma for scholars, policy makers and development specialists now is how to isolate and explain Africa's economic dislocation and disarticulation so as to bridge the gap with other societies and to benefit from globalisation. It is in this light that the New Partnership for Africa's Development (NEPAD) was created in July 2001 by recognising Africa's responsibility to create the conditions for economic recovery and sustainable development. African leaders are seeking the support of the international community to achieve these goals. They are seeking help in ending Africa's acute economic marginalisation with measures including increased resource flows, improved trade access, debt relief, support for infrastructure, conflict resolution, agricultural diversification, human resource development and above all, good governance.

This paper takes its point of departure from this premise and is articulated to assess the possibility of economic recovery taking place in Africa, particularly in the CEMAC zone through the NEPAD initiative. Specific objectives include assessing the performance of the CEMAC zone and pointing out the difficulties encountered; examining briefly NEPAD, particularly its background and objectives; assessing how it can foster economic recovery and sustainable development in the CEMAC sub-region, with a focus on its limitations; and finally making recommendations relating to what could be done to further enhance developmental efforts in the sub-region so as to sustainably fight poverty and exclusion. To achieve the above, a descriptive approach is used with information collected from secondary sources. This approach is biased towards policy makers and as a result requires less sophisticated theories. The rest of the paper is structured as follows: Section two briefly examines the CEMAC region and its development experience both in socio-economic terms and progress in regional integration, and points out the constraints; Section three outlines the raison d'être of NEPAD and points out its usefulness in fostering economic development in the sub-region; Section four discusses the weaknesses of the initiative; and the last Section contains the conclusions and some recommendations.

CEMAC Sub-region

Origin and Objectives

Regional integration initiatives in Africa have a a long history, dating back to the establishment of the South African Customs Union (SACU) in 1910, and the East African Community (EAC) in 1919. Since then, a number of RECs have been formed across the continent. This trend stemmed from the fact that 'isolationist' economic policies by individual countries led to marginalisation on the international scene and also because economic integration experiences elsewhere, particularly in Europe and Latin America, had prove beneficial. The similarities in cultures, geography and developmental problems are some of the factors favouring regional integration.

In this vein, in 1959, four French-speaking countries of the Central African sub-region – Chad, Central African Republic (CAR), Republic of Congo and Gabon – formed a Customs Union. In 1964, Cameroon joined the group to form the Central African Economic and Customs Union better known by its French acronym as UDEAC (Union Douanière et Economique de l'Afrique Centrale). Following this, on 22 and 23 November 1972, these countries signed two conventions relating to monetary cooperation. One was between themselves and the other with France, all relating to a common money: 'le franc de la cooperation financiére en Afrique' (FCFA). On 1 January 1985, the Republic of Equatorial Guinea became the sixth member. Thirty years of cooperation, on two fronts, economic and monetary, functioned perfectly well. Member states, however, faced new challenges from the international scene. These included the globalisation and the liberalisation of the world economy, the reinforcement of regional economic groupings elsewhere, profound economic and political crises characterised by severe macroeconomic disequilibria, economic decline, political instability and above all the increasing scourge of poverty and diseases. These necessitated that the role of UDEAC be redefined to reinforce the integration between economic and monetary cooperation. This led to the birth of CEMAC on 16 March 1994 at N'Djamena, Chad. However, the head of states officially launched the activities of CEMAC on 25 June 1999 in the Malabo declaration. Its headquarters are in Bangui, CAR.

The main objectives of CEMAC include the harmonisation of policies and the elaboration of an economic and legal environment conducive for investments; the realisation of a common market; the establishment of straightforward cooperation between the peoples of member states to reaffirm geographical and human solidarity; the promotion of national and regional markets by eliminating trade barriers; the coordination of development programmes and the harmonisation of industrial projects; and the creation of solidarity among member countries. The mission of promoting harmonious development of member countries is being undertaken within the context of two unions: an Economic Union (Union Economique de l'Afrique Centrale) and a monetary union (Union Monétaire de l'Afrique Centrale).

The functioning of the community is managed by the conference of heads of states which is the supreme organ and determines major orientations of the community and its institutions, the council of ministers (with 3 ministers from each country), the Executive Secretariat, the Inter-state Committee, the Community Court of Justice and Parliament. A number of institutions are associated with UEAC including Ecole Inter-Etats des Douanes (EIED), Institut Sous-régional multisectoriel de Technologie Appliquée de Planification et d' evaluation de projets (ISTA), Institut Sous-régional de Statistiques et d'Economie Appliquée (ISSEA) and Banque de Développement des Etats de l'Afrique Centrale (BDEAC), whereas UMAC is made up of two institutions: La Banque des Etats de l'Afrique Centrale (BEAC) and Commission Bancaire de l'Afrique Centrale (COBAC).

Socio-Economic Performance of CEMAC

This sub-region is richly endowed with abundant natural and human resources, which remain largely unexploited, misused or misdirected. Between 1960 and the early 1980s, economic performance was characterised by mixed results, but on average, a positive growth of 3 percent was recorded. Agriculture and oil were the main sources of growth and foreign exchange earnings. The Gross Domestic Product (GDP) per capita was in the neighbourhood of 750 US dollars on average, ranging from 210 in the republic of Chad to 4960 in Gabon. Various governments concentrated on creating a large public and parastatal sector, which resulted in high expenditures on the civil service, subsidies to inefficient public enterprises and low-return capital-intensive investments.

Three major shocks during the early to mid-1980s exposed some weaknesses in the economic structures and policies of these countries. Firstly, the external terms of trade declined by 60 percent through 1993 as the prices of coffee, cocoa and oil fell sharply. Secondly, oil output began contracting and thirdly, the real exchange rate appreciated by more than 53 percent, resulting in a reduction in competitiveness. By 1993, the economy and its external accounts had deteriorated significantly. Continuous public finance deficits were generated, as falling revenues were not matched by expenditure cuts. The burden on public finance was exacerbated by a large and inefficient public sector. Growing public sector deficits were internalised in the financial sector to the detriment of banks and the private sector. These deficits were largely financed through debt accumulation both from foreign and domestic sources. This led to a debt burden of more than 50 percent of GDP by 1989. This decline in the economy was accompanied by increased poverty, as poor farmers took the brunt of falls in producer prices and various governments cut down drastically on expenditures on social sectors, particularly health and education.

During the period 1986-1989, various governments launched economic recovery programmes supported by the IMF and the World Bank designed to correct major problems across sectors. These programmes included streamlining public finances; restructuring public enterprises and banking sectors, and progressive export crop liberalisations. Internal commerce was to be deregulated; the petroleum sector incentives improved; forestry, health and education policies reoriented; and special programmes established to mitigate the cost of adjustments. The internal adjustment programmes failed, however, and little progress was made in structural reforms. The collapse in terms of trade and the severe appreciation in the real exchange rate, had adverse effects on incentives and income distribution, and were not matched by corresponding policy adjustments. Economic policy and management deteriorated after 1989 reflecting the lack of commitment of political leaders to economic reform and the corrosive effects of political instability. Coincidentally, this period corresponded to that of attempts at political liberalisation. By 1993, the economy of the sub-region had contracted by more than 2 percent.

In January 1994, countries of this sub-region and the others in the CFA zone realigned the parity of their currency from 50 to 100 FCFA to the French franc and the governments began implementing the Central African Customs Union trade and tariff reform. The various governments equally adopted new macroeconomic programs supported by the IMF and the International Development Agency (IDA). These were designed to secure the newly established international competitiveness, to bring inflation to below 5 percent by 1996, to attain sustainable growth of 5 percent primarily led by improved competitiveness and export performance, and quickly achieve primary and eventually, overall budget surpluses. These were to enable increased domestic savings, reduced current account deficits and to finance an increasing share of domestic investments.

As illustrated in appendices I and II, there is evidence that the sub-region recorded a positive growth as from 1994 at the macroeconomic level with GDP increasing averagely at 3.7 percent between 1994 and 2003. However, this falls below the expected 5 percent. At the same time, inflation has been contained at less than 5 percent during the same period. At the microeconomic level, however, the fruits of the growth have not trickled down to the common people, but rather, there has been a trickle up effect, through which most of the resources intended for the poor actually benefited the very rich. Poverty thus remains a major challenge in the sub-region.

Assessing the Level of Integration in the CEMAC Zone

In order to assess the level to which countries of the sub-region cooperate with each other, integration indices are used as proposed by the Economic Commission for Africa (ECA) (2002). In terms of trade among RECs members, only 10 percent of exports of countries belonging to RECs go to other REC members in Africa. Specifically, South African Development Community (SADC) countries trade more among themselves than any other REC in Africa, with 31 percent of exports and 24 percent of imports respectively originating or destined for member countries. Countries of the Economic Community of West African States (ECOWAS) rank second with only 17 percent of exports and imports originating or destined for other member countries. The CEMAC zone ranks tenth with an intra-trade index for exports and imports of less than 2 percent. The low level of intra-trade may be explained by the fact that a greater proportion of trade is informal. Details of trade indices for other RECs in Africa are contained in appendix III.

The United Nations Economic Community for Africa also came out with a composite index to measure the level of integration beyond trade. This was constructed on the basis of some integration indicators embodying trade among REC members, monetary; fiscal and financial integration, transport, communication; industry, energy; food and agriculture, and human development and labour markets. Each sectoral cluster comprises a subset of variables and the trend is calculated as a weighted average of the components of the subset. Results show that there is a discernible move towards greater integration, with a burst through 1996 and a slowdown thereafter, as can be seen from appendix IV. The average tendency towards integration in the whole region in 1994–99 was 4.7 percent, faster than the region's economic growth. Integration performance in the CEMAC zone during this period was moderate; increasing from 1994–97 and falling thereafter. The index shows that CEMAC countries performed better in 1997 than in 1999. The same trend was followed by SADC, Common Market for East and Southern Africa (COMESA) and ECOWAS. Union Economique et Monétaire l'Ouest Africaine (UEMOA), Economic Community of Central African States (ECCAS), Indian Ocean Commission (IOC), and the Mano River Union (MRU) recorded no particular pattern. On a yearly basis, however, CEMAC recorded considerable success despite the mediocre performance at the level of trade.

Constraints to Effective Development in the CEMAC Zone

Constraints on development are examined at two levels: constraints retarding economic progress, and those inhibiting effective integration. The impediments to economic progress in CEMAC are divided into three broad groups: historical and political oriented obstacles, economic policy obstacles, and institutional related constraints. Politically, the ruling elites constitute the source of corruption, mismanagement and greed in the sub-region. They have created their self-fulfilling prophecies by retarding the implementation of policies, by imposing bureaucratic hardships for investors, and generally creating negative impressions for potential investors. They use appeals to nationalism which often take perverse forms against local investors, as they are looked upon as unpatriotic. The absence of legitimised political institutions and processes for transferring power from one group of leaders to another has led to political instability, chronic unrest and uncertainty. The practice of democracy in the sub-region takes on modified forms: 'advanced democracy', 'gradual democracy', and recently, election rigging has become evident. In the CEMAC zone, the power of the pen is above the will of the people. All of these only help in putting off investors and creating conflict.

In terms of economic policy obstacles, poor physical infrastructure constitutes a drawback on economic development. There is no paved road that links member countries. Within countries, various governments do not pay enough attention to the maintenance of existing infrastructure. The CEMAC zone has the least developed road network in the whole of Africa. The various ports have the potential of being the best because of their central location but are generally not well maintained. Information technology is still regarded as a luxury in CEMAC countries. Labour codes are rigid and do not allow for the effective functioning of labour unions. Investment codes are inconsistent with industrial free zone legislation, reflecting the absence of well thought-out development programmes. Fiscal policies are not well designed and the result is fiscal fraud at all levels.

Institutionally, the judicial and legal systems are characterised by corrupt, inefficient practitioners, largely motivated by political and rent-seeking imperatives. Without the security of a court system, which is fair and competent; a legal documentation system, which is regularly up-dated and accessible, and a penal system, which fairly applies sanctions, there cannot be any confidence. Another major institutional constraint relates to a weak financial system. Despite this, the level of capital flight from the sub-region is frightening. This reduces capital for major investment projects. Government institutions act as major bureaucracies and slow down economic activities. Culture and religious norms also constitute an obstacle of an institutional nature.

Like with most RECs in Africa, CEMAC faces numerous functional problems in effectively achieving the objectives of the community. This shows that more often than not, governments fail to implement the treaties they sign, which in turn suggests that there is lack of political commitment in practice (in contrast to pronouncements). The loss of sovereignty leads to a lack of political commitment and this comes out as one of the leading obstacles to effective integration among the CEMAC countries. The supra-national bodies created do not have the powers as sanctioning authorities. The existing secretariat does not have the legal backing to force countries to fulfil their obligations.

One other major hindrance to integration is the implementation problems of harmonised policies. Major problems in this respect in CEMAC include lack of harmonised tariffs, customs procedures and tax policies as well as incentive packages for investments; problems related to donor support; lack of a common position on major macroeconomic policies like structural adjustment programmes; and disparities in laws relating to the operation of companies and relevant public offices.

Simultaneous membership of some countries of the zone in other regional groupings cause some problems. Three members of CEMAC are also members of the Communuaté Economique de Pays de Grand Lac (CEPGL), and ECCAS comprises CEMAC members and three others. This poses problems of multiple subscriptions. As Lyakurwa (1997) puts it, the usefulness of overlapping membership issue or more generally, the existence of subset groups within a larger group, has not enjoyed the consensus that other matters have received.

Compensation issues and variation in initial conditions constitute one other major problem associated with integration. This relates to the problem of the appropriate mechanism which ensures that gainers are compensating losers in the medium term and losses are minimised in the long run. Tax revenue loss is a case in point here. To aggravate this, countries of the sub-region exhibit differences in development levels and this implies that gains from integration are disproportionate. This explains why a country like Gabon always lags behind in many situations. The issues of complementarities are also directly related to compensation. This situation is compounded when tariff revenue is one of the most significant sources of government revenue for a country.

Poor private sector participation has also been observed in the CEMAC zone as a problem. As Aryeetey and Oduro (1997) and Aryeetery (2000) pointed out, the aspect of regional integration process in Africa has been singled out as one of the main factors for a weak private sector initiative. The participation of the private sector is hampered by a lack of government resources to ensure full participation. Even when these resources are secured, they are limited to the level of Chamber of Commerce officials. Moreover, lack of adequate knowledge to use existing information at the level of private sector associations is also noted as a major problem.

One major constraint to integration is low capacity to deliver on ambitious mandates. CEMAC has to cope with the ambitious mandates entrusted to it in its treaties and protocols, but it lacks the resources to do so. The gap between the allotments and payments is considerable and growing, even more so given estimates of its projected needs in the near future. The rate of collection against assessed contributions dropped from 100 percent in 1993 to just over 50 percent in 1998. Moreover, the contributions actually paid by member states barely cover operating expenses. This has led to an over-dependence on external assistance.

The NEPAD Initiative

Origin and Objectives

The New Partnership for Africa's Development (NEPAD) is a holistic and integrated sustainable development initiative for the economic and social revival of Africa. It is based on a constructive partnership between actors at various levels of development. The mandate of NEPAD had its genesis at the Organisation of African Union (OAU) Extraordinary Summit held in Sirte, Libya in September 1999. The Summit mandated President Mbeki of South Africa and President Bouteflika of Algeria to engage Africa's creditors on the total cancellation of its external debt. Following this, the South Summit of the Non-Aligned Movement and the G77, held in Havana, Cuba during April 2000, mandated President Mbeki and President Obasanjo of Nigeria to convey the concerns of the South to the G8 and the Bretton Woods Institutions. Realising the correlation between the two mandates, the OAU Summit held in Togo in July 2000 mandated the three Presidents to engage the developed North with a view to developing a constructive partnership for the regeneration of the continent during the G8 Summit in Japan in July 2000. During the 5th Extraordinary Summit of the OAU held in Sirte, Libya from 1 to 2 March 2001, President Obasanjo made a presentation on the Millennium Partnership for the African Recovery Programme (MAP), while President Wade presented the One People, One Goal, One Faith (OMEGA) Plan. The work of the four Presidents, (Mbeki, Obasanjo, Bouteflika and Wade), was endorsed. It was also decided that every effort should be made to integrate all the initiatives being pursued for the recovery and development of Africa, including the ECA's New Global Compact with Africa.

Thus, on 11 July 2001, NEPAD (or the New African Initiative [NAI] as it was temporarily known at the time), was presented to the OAU Summit of Heads of State and Government in Lusaka, Zambia. This was enthusiastically received and unanimously adopted. The globalisation and liberalisation of the world economy, and the increasing economic and political integration in other regions of the world during the 1990s, certainly stimulated African leaders to think this way. The NEPAD principle is thus based on the neo-liberal macroeconomic framework.

The primary objective of the initiative is to eradicate poverty in Africa and to place African countries both individually and collectively on a path of sustainable growth and development in order to halt the marginalisation of Africa in the global economy. At the core of the NEPAD process is its African ownership, which must be retained and strongly promoted, so as to meet the legitimate aspirations of the African people. While the principle of partnership with the rest of the world is equally vital to this process, such partnership must be based on mutual respect, dignity, shared responsibility and mutual accountability. The expected outcomes are:

- Economic growth and development and increased employment;
- Reduction in poverty and inequality;
- Diversification of productive activities;
- Enhanced international competitiveness and increased exports; and
- Increased African integration.

To achieve these objectives, NEPAD is structured into three components:

- The first component provides the preconditions for sustainable development, which are Peace, Security, Democracy and Political Governance Initiative; the Economic and Corporate Governance Initiative; and the subregional and regional approaches to development.
- The second component provides the sectoral priorities, which include bridging the infrastructure gap; the Human Resource Development Ini-

tiative; the Agriculture Initiative; the Environment Initiative; the Cultural Initiative and Science and Technology Platforms.
- The third component concerns the mobilisation of resources, referring to the Capital Flows and the Market Access Initiatives.

NEPAD has not been constructed in a vacuum. It is therefore linked to existing initiatives and programmes both in Africa and beyond. In providing the focal point and the overall strategic framework for engagement, NEPAD does not seek to replace or compete with these initiatives and programmes, but rather to consciously establish linkages and synergies between them. In this way, all activities focused on Africa can be pursued in an integrated and coordinated fashion. NEPAD is a mandated initiative of the African Union. The NEPAD Heads of State and Government Implementation Committee have to report annually to the Union Summit. The Chair of the Union as well as the Chair of the Commission of the Union are ex-officio members of the Implementation Committee. The Commission of the Union is expected to participate in Steering Committee meetings.

Outline of the NEPAD Initiative

Institutional Framework

This aspect relates to the political institutions that are needed to ensure a safe political environment conducive to sustainable development. Firstly, peace, democracy, security and political governance initiatives are concepts that are usually associated with stable political institutions such as excellent legislatures, judiciary or executive powers. These are preconditions for safe investments in a country, and for long African countries have been classified as high risk countries and have not been able to attract enough Direct Foreign Investments (DFI) that is necessary to help the continent emerge from underdevelopment. NEPAD seeks to address Africa's underdevelopment and marginalisation through a number of ways including promoting and protecting democracy and human rights in African countries as well as developing succinct standards of accountability, transparency and participation at national and sub-national levels (Baimu 2002).

Secondly, the political and economic integration of countries has been identified as an excellent way of overcoming underdevelopment. Institutions like the European Union, the Latin American Economic Union (MERCOSUR), Association of Southeast Asian Nations (ASEAN) have shown very good results in terms of promoting sustainable and widespread development in their respective regions. African countries have also attempted to organise themselves into economic and customs unions such as CEMAC, ECCAS, ECOWAS, SADC, COMESA, Arab Maghreb Union (AMU) and so on. NEPAD is requiring African countries to strengthen these institutions so that there will be a general improvement in the countries' situations as opposed to local improvements.

The Market Access Initiative of NEPAD provides formidable guidelines. Renewed political action by African countries to intensify and deepen the various integration initiatives on the continent is indispensable. To this end, consideration needs to be given to: (i) a discretionary preferential trade system for intra-African trade; and (ii) the alignment of domestic and regional trade and industrial policy objectives, thereby increasing the potential for intra-industry trade critical to the sustainability of regional economic arrangements. More so, economic and corporate governance initiatives are also on NEPAD's agenda.

Public Sector Framework

This dimension of sectoral analysis is centred on the role played by African governments in the struggle against poverty. First and foremost, bridging the infrastructure gap is predominant on NEPAD's agenda. In order to make effective use of a region's resources, there must be channels through which these resources can be processed, and there must exist appropriate systems to manage such resources. This implies that there is a need for sufficient and adapted infrastructure that will be used to increase value-added output in an economy. Most investors are afraid of coming to Africa because of the lack of a basic technical framework. NEPAD addresses this issue by emphasising the need for African countries to invest in technical infrastructure, transportation, energy platforms, Information and Communication Technology (ICT), water and sanitation.

Even more, human resource development is an important component of NEPAD's agenda. The Universal Declaration of Human Rights provides some basic human rights including the rights to life, education, feeding, shelter and health. It is the duty of governments to protect these rights; they also have to make effective use of their human resources by committing them to tasks that are clearly related to their abilities and potentialities. This equally brings the concept of discrimination in the picture. Governments are supposed to provide equal rights to all citizens of the state. NEPAD is particularly interested in this aspect of development as it places a high premium on bridging the education gap, reversing the brain drain, and ensuring health care for the African masses. Under this topic again, women and gender issues are of great importance, as African governments must make sure that women take part in the development process.

Also, the environmental initiative is a component par excellence of NEPAD's agenda. Though development requires the use of natural resources, sustainable development places more emphasis on the rational use of these resources. If there is no ecological environment, one vital input of the production process is lacking and as such, no sustainable growth can be achieved. NEPAD therefore has a good point in requiring governments to design legal platforms/frameworks oriented towards the protection of the environment.

A cultural initiative is not absent on NEPAD's agenda. Diversities in views have always been seen to be an excellent grounding for a multidimensional approach to problem solving. Africa is truly a cultural mosaic with a great multiplicity of diverse cultural backgrounds. NEPAD is advocating the consideration of all African cultures as well as the integration of such cultures into a Pan-African cultural basket that will serve to address development issues using a multicultural approach, and equally avoid the conspicuous marginalisation of some ethnic and tribal entities on the continent, which have plunged Africa into devastating massacres and all forms of extremism.

Private Sector Framework

From the liberal point of view, the private sector of an economy has a vibrant role to play in creating wealth. This school of thought proposes an equitable approach to development. NEPAD places a lot of emphasis on the use of private capital flows and the promotion of African exports under the market access initiative. In this component, NEPAD is directed towards ensuring that private sector resources are used to develop Africa and that the private sector deserves access to Africa's resources and markets. NEPAD is therefore promoting a sound approach concerning the financing of Africa's projects and the development of its economic activities.

Agricultural Sector Framework

It is true that African people whose economy relies heavily on agricultural products are presently suffering from the fact that western countries like the USA and European countries are highly subsidising their agricultural sectors. This acts as an impediment on the ability of the African agricultural sector to compete on the international market. Despite this situation, agriculture is still a vital aspect of Africa's economy. An overwhelming proportion of Africa's population characterised by high illiteracy rates rely on agriculture as their main income life-line. There is a crucial need in this case to restructure that sector of the economy so that it will really serve as a basis for Africa's development. This is much of the gospel NEPAD is preaching by devoting an entire sectoral priority to agriculture and by initiating plans designed to make African agricultural products available - and competitive of course - on the international markets.

Industrial Sector Framework

As pointed out by Klein (2003), a reduction of poverty passes through the creation of wealth by bringing growth processes to poor areas. This industrialisation of poor areas therefore entails the creation of jobs and the use of resources of such areas to create wealth by adding value to inputs. NEPAD, through the market access initiative, places a particular emphasis on the manufacturing sector of the economy and the diversification of production. By looking at the manufacturing part of the economy, NEPAD simply associates development and industrialisation. NEPAD seems therefore to be really oriented towards the industrialisation of Africa since most of the finances are raised through banking systems and established financial markets. NEPAD, through its capital and market access initiatives is trying to find ways of financing Africa's economy by mobilising private funds.

Human Resource Development Framework

In the view of Sanders and Meeus (2002), human resources are a critical part of a system and thus NEPAD places a particular emphasis on bridging the knowledge gap. The objectives in this vein include to work with donors and multilateral institutions to ensure that the International Development Goals (IDG) of achieving universal primary education by 2015 is realised; to work to improve curriculum development; quality improvements and access to ICT; to expand access to secondary education; and to promote networks of specialised research and higher education institutions. It also advocates that governments should increase education expenditures. NEPAD has also made the fight against the brain drain one of its priorities. Human resource losses have a negative effect on economies, especially those of Africa. NEPAD recognises this in Article 121 where it sets out the following 'to reverse the brain drain and turn it into brain gain for Africa, to build and retain within the continent critical human capacities for Africa's development and to develop strategies for utilising the scientific and technological know-how and skills of Africans in the diaspora for the development of Africa' (Sanders and Meeus 2002).

Science and Technology

NEPAD explicitly recognises that the region's economic recovery and transition to sustainable development will be achieved if science and technology are applied to solve pressing food production problems, communication limitations, environmental exigencies, diseases and energy insecurity. It has as its objective building a better comprehension of the status of science and technology in Africa, the mobilisation and improvement in the utilisation of the continent's capacities with respect to science and technology, promotion of innovative ways and means of financing science and innovation, integrating science and technology considerations into other programmes, and those of other sub-regional structures like the African Economic Community (AEC), and the building of a strong political constituency for science and technology in Africa's development.

Health Issues

NEPAD places a high premium on health. It recognises the interconnections between development and health. Articles 64 and 128 of NEPAD point to the fact that good health contributes to productivity changes and consequently to economic growth. Sound health policies are therefore a challenge for Africa to develop the capacity to sustain growth to levels required to achieve sustainable development. NEPAD in the health sector actions encourages African countries to pay more attention to health in their budgets and to phase in such increases in expenditures to be mutually determined (Sanders and Meeus 2002). NEPAD's objectives in the health sector include real gains in human development by controlling epidemies like HIV/AIDS, tuberculosis and malaria, thus increasing the population's capacities through improving the health and nutrition sectors.

Women and Gender

Recognising that women constitute a majority of the poor, and that they equally play key roles in agriculture and food security issues, their role in society must be strengthened. In promoting the role of women in all activities, NEPAD appeals to African leaders to take responsibility (among other things) for promoting the role of women in society and economic development through education and training, access to credit, and assuring women's participation in political and economic life (Wanyeki 2002).

Limitations of the NEPAD Initiative

Lack of Broad-Based Participation

As Mshana (2002) puts it, NEPAD is a 'Heads of States-Top-Bottom' project, almost exclusively owned by the New African Leadership Group. The penchant of this reigning African aristocracy to popularise it, has ended up reinforcing the perceptions that it is little more than a marketing exercise, targeted at the multilateral donor community and the western bureaucratic elites. The conceptions and subsequent merger of the two plans (OMEGA and MAP), into NEPAD were achieved without the participation of the ordinary African citizen, despite NEPAD's Declaration in Paragraph 5 that its success will be achieved only if it is owned by the African people united in their diversity (Kanyenze 2003).

The consultation with African civil society and think-tanks only started after NEPAD and its leaders had been presented at the Genoa G8 Summit of 2001 and the World Economic Forum in New York in 2002. The very fact that a supposed African initiative for poverty alleviation had to be unveiled at foreign forums rather than in front of the people it is alleged to serve, is a pointer to its lack of popular African commitment in the real sense.

Lack of Mandated Leadership

More fundamentally, questions are being raised regarding the mandate of NEPAD's leadership. A batch of African leaders is questioning the mandate of the implementing committee. President Moi of Kenya argued that none of the

East African leaders is in this Committee. Of late, one of the founding fathers, President Mbeki, expressed his fear regarding the leadership of NEPAD in his historic visit to Libya (Kanyenze 2003). This is a clear indication that NEPAD lacks focus and representation in its leadership. How then does it intend to holistically alleviate Africa's poverty sustainably with such a biased leadership structure?

Over-dependence on External Support

In the political sphere, NEPAD remains a quintessential African initiative that is dependent on western ideologies and aid. The almost inextricable link between NEPAD, the European Union (EU), the International Monetary Fund (IMF), the World Bank and the G8, contrasts with an almost entirely disconnected link from the very African people it is intended to safeguard. The concept of partnership, which constitutes the cornerstone of NEPAD, is more outward instead of inward oriented. It is based on the discredited neo-liberal approach, which promotes free market and trade. NEPAD enjoins African countries to implement far-reaching reforms and programmes without elaborating on what these really entail. The analytical part of NEPAD observed that the current phase of globalisation undermines African recovery and development, and yet the proposed solution is steeped in further integrating Africa into a faulty world economy, without addressing its inequalities and injustices (such as the absence of fair and just global rules, divergences in global market power, etc).

NEPAD also seeks to complement existing poverty reduction efforts by the IMF and World Bank and the enhanced debt relief programme initiated by the two institutions. It fails to interrogate these initiatives, which do have their own limitations, and are market-based. In fact, these are given precedence. In spite of its rhetoric about self-reliance, African-ownership and control, NEPAD depends largely on external funding (an estimated US$64 billion per year). Lessons from experience suggest caution in expecting benevolent inflows of 'unconditional' resources. Too much hope is placed in the basket of a 'new global partnership'.

Structural Impediments

NEPAD does not deal with the structural impediments to Africa's development. Although NEPAD points out these structural impediments, including an unfair and unjust world order that favours developed countries, and reliance on primary exports among others, it has no strategy of dealing with these hurdles, choosing to focus on integrating itself into the world. By failing to develop an alternative strategy based on a human development model, as opposed to its preferred growth (market) model, NEPAD fails to chart a new path for African recovery and development.

It lacks a labour market approach, and especially an employment strategy. NEPAD has not properly articulated a strategy to deal with unemployment and underemployment, yet unemployment is one of the main causes of poverty. More so, NEPAD has not strengthened the existing tripartite consultative framework and the institutions that could facilitate dialogue between employers and employees.

Lack of Political Cohesion

The political good governance initiative is not well developed - details are yet to be worked out. However, we know that deviant governments will be subjected to peer reviews, but this is only when they accept and become members of the African Peer Review Mechanism (APRM). Many African countries have not yet succeeded in adopting the basic democratic principles. Democracy is conceived in many forms with the power of the pen exceeding that of the people. The NEPAD initiative fails to specify the form of democracy it wants for Africa. In the absence of legitimate political institutions and processes for transferring power from one group of leaders to another, countries are subjected to chronic political unrest. The absence of a clear-cut distinction of the organs of government (executive, legislature and judiciary) poses a serious threat to democracy in the continent. The African judiciary is not independent and often receives directives from the Executive. The political atmosphere during elections in most countries is therefore often characterised by tensions and in most cases lead to conflicts. The organisation of elections is often accompanied by mass rigging, yet NEPAD is talking about good governance when it has not established a rigid, high profile, mechanism to ensure it.

In the nexus of human rights, NEPAD, although has made a magnificent attempt by including legal concerns on its sustainable poverty agenda, has not been cautious enough to avoid duplications of human rights structures and mechanisms. This melange could lead to confusion between structures in terms of legal functioning. An example par excellence of such legal overlap is between NEPAD and AU as clearly pictured in the Abuja, October 2001 meeting where it was decided that a sub-committee on peace and security focused on conflict management, prevention and resolution in Africa, be put in place. Given that the AU already has the Central Organ for Conflict Prevention Management and Resolution as one of its organs, the probability of the mandates of the two organs overlapping is very high (Baimu 2002).

Lack of a Comprehensive Human Development Programme

The NEPAD initiative places a lot of emphasis on bridging the education gap but fails to link it with the scourge of diseases like HIV/AIDS and the brain drain crises. Africa's health systems have been undermined to the extent that they are unable to provide even for the most basic health needs of its populations (Simms et al, 2001, Sanders et al, 2002). Old diseases such as malaria and tuberculosis have signed a new partnership with HIV/AIDS for Africa's underdevelopment. NEPAD does not pay cardinal attention to these issues. In its health sector objectives and actions, NEPAD encourages African countries to give higher priority to health in their budgets and to phase in such increases in expenditures to be mutually determined. It is difficult, if not impossible, to see how this would happen in the current weak economic climate on the continent (Sanders and Meeus 2002). Stephen Lewis, UN special envoy for HIV/AIDS, recently remarked of NEPAD, '... for all its talk of trade and investment, and governance and corruption and matters relating to financial architecture, there is only a pro-forma sense of the social sector, only modest reference to the human side of the ledger' (Lewis 2002).

In the domain of the brain drain, NEPAD's agenda conceived and articulated one of the continent most laming and perturbing factors—the brain drain—as one of its priorities (Article 121-122: Reversing the brain drain) in its Human Resource Development Initiative. A careful perusal reveals some queer traces of double standards. Paragraph 121 expresses its objectives in this sphere as:

- To reverse the brain drain and turn it to brain gain for Africa,
- To build and retain within the continent critical capacities for African development, and
- To develop strategies for utilising the scientific and technological know-how and skills of Africans in the Diaspora for the development of Africa.

To be frank, the first does not really look like an objective but a desired outcome. The issues in the second objective are ambiguous and deserve prudent explanation to decongest them and ensure clarification (Sanders and Meeus 2002). The grotesque paradox about the vagueness and speculative nature of NEPAD's brain drain clause is climaxed by the serious threats the brain drain represents in terms of sustainable human development in Africa. Estimates show that Africa spends 35 percent of Overseas Development Assistance (ODA) annually (approximately US$ 4 billion), on salaries of 100,000 foreign experts in all sectors (Pang et al, 2002). This is not an issue NEPAD can overlook.

Undermining Gender Issues

NEPAD has gone down the abyss of infamy in recent times especially amongst feminist critiques for its low-profiled placement of women within its organigram, its background and current installation of women's emancipation and gender amongst its components and above all its dismal rejection of the contemporary Gender and Development (GAD) notion for the less current Women in Development (WID). Without doubt, NEPAD's imaging of women is preposterous and deserves change. More so, NEPAD is formulated from a neo-liberal economic perspective and based on the modernist approach to development. By bypassing a mounting assemblage of current feminist critiques on the denigrating effects these economic policies' impact on African women in particular,

NEPAD has only revealed its ugly face that it has all this while hidden under a beautiful mask of women's concerns (Wanyeki 2002).

While there is some recognition of the need to address women's needs and existing gender gaps in the region's development through the implementation of NEPAD, the limited recognition of the systemic barriers and discrimination faced by African women (especially the biased land tenure system paramount in Africa), the misplaced emphasis on the need for self-development and self-improvement of women rather than on a need for African states to remove these systemic barriers and squarely address discrimination against women, puts in question the committedness of NEPAD to sustainably alleviate Africa's poverty situation, when a majority of the poor–women–are grossly neglected (Wanyeki 2002).

Conclusions and Recommendations

Conclusions

From the above discussion, a number of conclusions are discernible. Firstly, development efforts in Africa and particularly in the CEMAC zone have not been all roses. The socio-economic conditions have deteriorated significantly from the pre-1980 standard. The intensification of efforts at reinforcing cooperation between CEMAC countries has resulted in a negligible progress because of lack of real commitments backed by the means and political will. Paper rhetoric alone cannot overcome scarcity and institutional constraints.

Secondly, The CEMAC zone and generally sub-Saharan Africa continue to face the same developmental problems as in the past, with conflict, insecurity, poor governance, weak institutions, a mounting debt burden, and poor infrastructure topping the list.

Thirdly, the New Partnership for Africa's Development initiative confirms that African leaders are at the forefront of the struggle against underdevelopment on the continent. It is a well thought-out collection of ideas, which provide the basis of hope to the African people. Topping the agenda of NEPAD is peace and security followed by good governance, infrastructure, trade and investment, agricultural productivity and the expansion of information technology.

Fourthly, although NEPAD has been well received within the elite governing community, the initiative lacks foresight in many respects. The civil society groups have been extremely critical of its lack of political, economic and cultural creativity, and unless these are well targeted, the NEPAD initiative will remain a toothless bulldog.

Recommendations

In order to enhance economic recovery and sustainable development in Africa as a whole and in the CEMAC zone in particular, enormous efforts need to be deployed at country level, RECs level, the continental level, and at the international level. It is of paramount importance that NEPAD prioritises its programmes as this will facilitate follow up and control for effectiveness.

Topping the chart is strengthening good governance. NEPAD should come out with a time frame within which countries should show progress in their good governance programmes. There is equally the need to come out with a framework on the democratisation procedure for African countries. These are supposed to be monitored by the APRM and there should be provision for sanctioning deviant governments. This implies therefore that belonging to the APRM should be mandatory for all NEPAD countries. Human rights control mechanisms on the continent need to be harmonised. The independence of the African judiciary should be ensured and electoral systems must also be inclusive through various arrangements at the national or local levels. The leadership of NEPAD should be clear and patterned in an evolving manner to ensure the representation of all regions.

The NEPAD's security and peace initiative must be supplemented by efforts to help war-affected regions to develop economically. A 'Marshal Plan' for these countries is highly recommended. At the same time, support for conflict resolution should be intensified. Efforts by African countries and the United Nations to better regulate the activities of arms brokers and traffickers should be reinforced by the G8. There should be a concerted effort at eliminating the flow of illicit weapons to and within Africa. The western world, and particularly the G8, should support various efforts initiated by African governments and the civil societies to address issues relating to the linkage between armed conflict and the exploitation of natural resources.

In the domain of infrastructure development, the institution of regional support programmes for regional infrastructure can facilitate an overall infrastructure breakthrough on the continent. These should target particularly agriculture and communication.

The partnership principle embodied in the NEPAD initiative must be that of real collaboration. Thus, it must allow criticisms to flow from the South to the North. It must include the civil society groups in the development of the initiative. The promoters of NEPAD should listen to the many voices of criticism emanating from Africans engaged every day in the struggle for peace and security on the ground.

To strengthen the economic recovery process at the level of economic groupings as in the CEMAC zone, there should be provision for some consistency between national economic reform programmes and regional policy objectives. The duplication of membership of countries in many economic groupings and the proliferation of RECs in Africa contradicts reality. It is often suggested that the integration process would be more effective if there were fewer RECs and if member states were limited to membership in only one. This suggests that in the Central African sub-region and the Great Lakes, there should exist only one economic grouping. It is equally suggested that official correspondences in an economic grouping like CEMAC should be multilingual.

NEPAD should establish a consultative framework that would necessitate a social dialogue between the employers and the employees and also incorporate the issue of social and labour codes of conduct that must be respected in respective countries. There is need for national employment policies that should be balanced with community action.

In the domain of gender, NEPAD should establish a high profile and well-financed machinery for the advancement of African women. It should also establish a high-level feminist caucus or monitoring bench to ensure that all programmes validated for implementation are evaluated for Gender Sensitivity.

Strengthening health systems to meet health care needs of the population is necessary for effective economic recovery. More investment in health and health-related infrastructure is a prerequisite for achieving the above. Particular attention should be given to personnel in order to curb the crises of brain drain that characterises this sector.

The financing of NEPAD's activities should not only concentrate on G8 assistance and multilateral sources but also should include Multinational Corporations (MNCs) and subscriptions of member countries. The later should be a percentage of the GDPs.

To better coordinate the NEPAD activities in various countries, a Ministry of Regional Cooperation and NEPAD should be established in various African countries or special departments in charge of NEPAD activities be established in foreign ministries.

The elitist governing stratum in Africa, which constitutes less than 2 percent of the total population, should put on a 'human face' and follow their conscience as guiding principles for their actions.

Bibliography

African Development Bank, 2002, *Selected Statistics on African Countries*, Statistics Division, DRD, Phonix-Trykkeriet A/S, Arhus.

African Development Forum, 2000, 'Consensus Statement and the Way Ahead: Defining Priorities for Regional Integration', Addis Ababa.

Alemayehu, G. & H. Kibret, 2002, 'Regional Economic Integration in Africa: A Review of Problems and Prospects with the case of COMESA'.

Ake, C., 1981, *A Political Economy of Africa*, UK: Longman Publishers.

Ayeertey, E., 2000, 'Regional Integration in West Africa', Paper presented at the Policy Workshop organised by the OECD Development Center at the Graduate Institute of International Studies, Geneva.

Ayeertey, E. and A. Oduro, 1996, 'Regional Integration efforts in Africa: An Overview', in J.J. Teunissen (ed.), *Regionalism and the Global Economy: The Case of Africa*, The Hague.

Baimu, E., 2002, 'Human Rights Mechanisms and Structures Under NEPAD and The African Union: Emerging Trends Towards Proliferation and Duplication', Occasional paper N° 15; University of Pretoria.

CODESRIA, 2003, 'CODESRIA's 30th Anniversary Celebrations: Central African Sub-Regional Conference, Douala, 4-5 October 2003. Call for Abstracts'.

Department for International Development, 2002, 'New Partnership for African Development', *Issue* 19, 3rd quarterly.

DFID, 1998, 'Growing up together', *Issue* 1, 1st quarterly.

ECA, 2002, 'Annual Report on Integration in Africa. An overview', Addis Ababa.

Games, D., 2002, 'NEPAD: Boost for Business', *Business in Africa*, July/August.

IBRD, 2002, *Can Africa Claim the 21st Century?* Washington D.C., World Bank.

Kanyenze, G., 2003, 'Critique of The New Partnership for Africa's Development, (NEPAD)', *The Worker*, Twelfth Edition, Zimbabwe.

Klein, U.M., 2003, 'Ways Out of Poverty: Diffusing Best Practices and Creating Capabilities', Perspectives Policy for Poverty Reduction, World Bank Policy Research Working paper N° 2990; Washington D.C.: The World Bank.

Lewis, S., 2002, 'Africa Puts Fight Against AIDS at Forefront', *African Recovery*, Vol. 15, No 1-2.

Lyakurwa, W. et al., 1997, 'Regional Integration in Sub Saharan Africa: A Review of Experiences', in Ademola Oyejide, Ibrahim Elbadawi and Paul Collier (eds.), *Regional Integration and Trade Liberalisation in Sub Saharan Africa, Vol. I: Framework, Issues and Methodological Perspectives*, London: Macmillan.

Mshama, R. R., 2002, 'The New Partnership for Africa's Development (NEPAD): Its Success Depends on Participation of African People', *Echoes* No. 21.

Nathan et al., 2002, *Determinants of Poverty in Uganda*, Nairobi: AERC.

Ngwane, G. N., 2003, 'Africa's Development Problematique: The Case of NEPAD', *Insight Magazine*, May edition, Yaounde.

Nigerian Institute of Social and Economic Research, 2000, 'Reflections on Africa's Historic and Current Initiatives for Political and Economic Unity', Ibadan.

Pinstrup, A., P. and Pandya-Lorch, 2001, *The Unfinished Agenda: Perspectives of Overcoming Hunger, Poverty and Environmental Degradation*, IFPRI Publication, NW, USA.

Sanders, D. and Meeus, W., 2002, *A Critique on NEPAD's Health Sector Plan of Action*, Cape Town: Cape Town University Press.

Science and Technology for Africa's Development, 2002, 'Building the Foundation for Regional and International Collaboration: A Proposed medium Term Paper of NEPAD: 2003-2005', Yaounde, Cameroon.

South African Department of Foreign Affairs, 2002, *NEPAD Background: Introducing the New Partnership for Africa's Development.*

Wanyeki, L. M., 2003, *Women and Land in Africa Culture, Religion and Realising Women's Rights*, London: Zed Books.

www.allafrica.com

www.beac.int

www.hurilaws.org/nepad_art.htm

www.izf.net

www.uneca.org.

Appendix I: Real GDP Growth in CEMAC Countries: 1993–2003

Country	1990	1992	1993	1994	1995	1996	1997	1998	1999	2000	2001	2002	2003*
Cameroon	-5.4	-2.2	-9.5	-4.3	3.0	5.0	5.1	5.0	4.4	4.2	5.2	4.1	4.3
CAR	-0.7	-2.1	-2.5	5.0	2.0	-3.0	5.3	5.3	2.7	0.7	-0.4	0.6	-0.4
Chad	1.3	0.3	-2.9	4.0	4.0	3.0	4.3	4.6	0.2	-0.3	8.1	8.5	13.1
Congo	-0.1	2.7	-1.5	-4.6	2.0	5.0	8.3	3.7	-3.2	8.2	3.2	2.4	1.3
Equatorial Guinea	7.4	-13.7	7.3	6.8	38.0	31.0	71.2	17.7	23.2	14.2	65.6	20.9	10.1
Gabon	-2.1	-3.6	4.1	-16.1	4.0	3.0	5.7	3.5	-11.3	-1.9	1.9	0.1	1.0
CEMAC	-4.5	-4.6	-2.2	-2.0	4.5	4.7	6.3	4.6	2.3	3.3	5.8	4.0	4.0

* BEAC projections

. Sources: Extracted from BEAC, ADB and World Bank Documents, 2003.

Appendix II: Principal Economic Indicators 1993–2003 (% Growth)

Year	1993	1994	1995	1996	1997	1998	1999	2000	2001	2002	2003
GDP	-8.1	-3.0	4.2	4.4	5.4	4.6	-0.3	3.3	5.8	4.0	4.0
Oil Sector	0.3	0.8	0.4	0.7	1.3	0.5	-0.9	-0.4	1.3	0.7	0.6
Non Oil Sector	-0.4	0.3	3.8	3.7	4.0	4.1	0.5	3.7	4.5	3.3	3.4
Demographic growth	2.4	2.6	2.5	2.5	2.5	2.5	2.5	2.5	2.5	2.5	2.5
Inflation	-0.4	34.9	9.9	4.4	5.9	2.4	0.5	1.2	4.3	3.0	2.6
Government Revenue	-13.8	37.1	31.1	14.5	24.7	-7.0	7.0	38.8	8.0	0.3	-0.4
Government Expenditure	-3.7	19.6	6.1	5.5	26.7	12.2	-14.9	9.8	20.4	2.1	-2.3
Credits to the Economy	-6.7	0.9	8.1	-2.3	17.3	14.0	4.4	11.8	7.4	6.0	7.3
Monetary Stock (M_2)	-6.6	32.2	2.6	1.1	14.9	-0.7	6.3	25.6	6.3	15.2	9.5
External Protection Rate	14.8	36.4	36.9	50.9	60.0	39.1	46.9	70.7	63.4	66.6	75.3
Speed of Circulation (GDP/M_2)	9.0	7.8	8.3	7.5	7.1	7.0	7.2	7.0	6.9	6.3	5.3
Exports (fob)	7.5	73.6	12.6	22.5	13.5	-19.7	24.5	53.9	-4.1	0.6	-6.3
Imports (cif)	7.9	75.0	13.4	9.1	24.6	7.5	-4.5	12.4	39.5	-6.1	4.1
Exchange Rate	-0.4	-14.3	9.1	12.4	-5.6	-17.4	20.2	47.3	-3.7	1.0	-7.0
Gross Domestic Demand	-0.3	0.2	5.6	6.7	7.4	6.6	-0.3	8.1	17.6	-2.3	10.7
Total Consumption	0.0	-3.3	2.6	6.5	-0.2	5.2	2.0	4.2	7.7	2.5	5.9
Public Consumption	-0.2	0.6	-0.9	-0.5	1.3	1.3	-1.1	1.0	1.4	0.5	0.3
Private Consumption	0.2	4.0	3.5	7.0	-1.4	3.9	3.1	2.3	6.3	2.0	5.6
Gross Investments	0.3	3.5	3.0	0.2	7.6	1.3	-2.4	3.8	9.9	-4.8	4.8
Public Investments	-1.0	-0.1	-0.4	0.0	2.8	0.5	-1.8	1.0	1.0	-0.2	0.1
Private Investments	-0.6	4.4	2.3	0.7	5.0	0.7	-0.5	2.6	8.9	-4.1	4.8

Source: Extracted from BEAC and World Bank Documents, 2003.

Appendix III: Exports to other REC members

	Individual intra-REC exports as share of total intra-REC exports		Share of intra-REC exports in total Africa exports		Individual intra-REC exports as a share of its total exports	
	Percent	Rank	Percent	Rank	Percent	Rank
CEMAC	1.1	10	0.1	10	1.9	11
CENSAD	12.8	3	1.3	4	3.6	
CEPGL	0.1	12	0.0	13	0.5	12
COMESA	9.3	4	1.0	5	6.0	6
EAC	4.7	7	0.5	7	18.1	1
ECCAS	1.3	9	0.1	9	1.9	10
ECOWAS	19.9	2	2.12	3	10.2	5
IGAD	4.4	8	0.5	8	13.5	2
IOC	0.7	11	0.1	11	4.0	7
MRU	0.0	13	0.0	12	0.3	13
SADC	31.3	1	3.3	2	12.8	3
UEMOA	5.9	6	0.6	6	11.2	4
UMA	8.6	5	8.6	1	3.1	9

Source: Extracted from ECA Documents, 2002.

Appendix IV: Composite Integration Index by REC

REC	1994	1995	1996	1997	1998	1999
CEMAC	100.0	127.5	133.8	134.1	132.5	122.0
CEPGL	100.0	91.0	89.9	95.1	91.0	87.3
COMESA	100.0	110.1	123.0	125.2	127.2	118.3
EAC	100.0	114.7	120.3	118.5	120.5	119.2
ECCAS	100.0	124.6	128.1	132.0	126.8	121.7
ECOWAS	100.0	117.3	132.2	131.0	137.7	134.2
IGAD	100.0	112.4	116.4	119.5	120.8	119.2
IOC	100.0	116.2	126.2	118.3	123.8	109.6
MRU	100.0	90.2	96.4	119.3	109.3	117.1
SADC	100.0	113.7	124.8	127.2	133.2	132.9
UEMOA	100.0	117.4	130.5	132.3	134.7	136.2
UMA	100.0	112.3	125.0	124.8	119.2	121.7

Source: Extracted from ECA Documents, 2002.

6

Checking Rebels or Chasing Fortunes: Foreign States' Elites and the DR Congo Conflict (1997–2002)

Oladiran W. Bello

Introduction

The Democratic Republic of Congo (DRC) conflict involves a complex set of actors, both state and non-state, from within and outside the Congolese state, all motivated by a diverse, and often conflicting, set of interests and agendas.[1] One important aspect of this internationalised civil conflict, which has attracted considerable attention in the global media, academic and official circles, is the role of foreign interventionists. Yet, as evident in the deluge of sensational and often conflicting analyses of the Great Lakes crisis,[2] it would appear that a satisfactory perspective for grasping and explaining the issues involved, and the foreign belligerents' motives, is yet to emerge.

While some observers have pointed to widespread economic agendas as a central raison d'être in the war, all the belligerents have denied such allegations, explaining their participation either in terms of legal agreements/commitments owed to the Kinshasa government or in pursuit of their own legitimate security interests abroad. An examination of both the strident official pronouncements of some of these governments and the tone of debates within international bodies reveals that the great stress placed on the security concerns of Congo's neighbours is somewhat justified.[3] Yet, one important dimension of the conflict that must necessarily feature in any coherent explanation is the politics of resource control among intervening states' military and political elites. This dimension has remained firmly outside the focus of mainstream debate, or at best has been treated as part of the criminality of war, rather than subjected to systematic analysis.

Admittedly, the considerable ferment in official and intellectual circles not only reveals a groundswell of contradictory understandings and interpretations of the Congolese impasse, but it also underscores the urgent need for fresh approaches for an understanding of the apparent 'privatisation of the state'.[4]

This paper argues that although the initial impetus for intervention was provided by the threat of transborder incursions by insurgents based in the DRC, the ultimate explanation for the prolonged stay of the Rwandan Patriotic Army (RPA) and Uganda People's Defence Forces (UPDF) in the Congo will have to be sought in the realm of opportunistic exploitation, to wit, resource expropriation both for war financing and the elites' own material aggrandisement. We, therefore, investigate first the complex security questions confronting the Ugandan and Rwandan leaderships at the initial stages of the conflict. We then probe the interplay of factors that led to the emergence of 'resource scramble' as a key dynamic in the conflict. The final section shows how resource control politics has manifested itself, and concludes with an analysis of the 'Kisangani debacle', in which two historical allies, though confronting similar security threats, fell out with each other and clashed in a frenzy of resource plunder that produced one of the most intense and destructive battles of the war.

Rwanda and Uganda: The Complex Security Situation

The roles of Rwanda and Uganda have elicited the greatest interest among analysts of the Congo conflict.[5] Yet, accounts of their basis for intervening in the DRC have been anything but consensual. For the victorious RPA government that took power after the trauma of the 1994 Rwandan genocide in which more than half a million Tutsis and moderate Hutus were slaughtered, the most pressing task was to disarm Hutu *genocidaires* who had fled to Eastern Congo, dismantle the refugee camps under their control, and permanently tackle whatever security threats they posed to the new administration.

Aside from internal restructuring,[6] the government moved to douse the security threats posed by elements of the Hutu *Interhamwe* and ex-FAR (Forces Armées Rwandaises) forces that perpetrated the genocide. This was the initial basis for Rwanda's involvement in Congolese affairs right from the ascension of the victorious RPA to power. From the perspective of the Kigali regime, comprehensively removing the *genocidaire* threat involved at least two things: disarming the armed insurgents within the vast refugee camps of eastern Zaïre (as Mobutu's Congo was then called) and resolving once and for all the question of citizenship for Congo's Tutsi population. To that end, Kigali spear-headed, first covertly and later overtly, the offensive that toppled President Mobutu (who as part of his support for the defeated FAR had in 1995 provided troops to assist the Hutu-led government of Juvenal Habyarimana in resisting the RPA's onslaughts on Kigali).

It should be noted that Rwanda's objective in the war that deposed Mobutu and brought Kabila to power, as for Uganda and Angola, was the removal of both the insurgency threats from across the Congolese frontiers, and the hostile Kinshasa regime which it believed was actively involved in undermining Rwanda's security interests.

However, the security dividend which Rwanda expected from its support for Kabila did not materialise. First, the security situation along Rwanda's border with the eastern Congo did not stabilise considerably as the Interhamwe/ex-FARs continued to launch attacks into Rwanda. By early 1998, top Rwandan officials were even expressing doubts about the wisdom of installing the 'incompetent' Kabila in Kinshasa.[7] A second issue whose importance was probably exacerbated by the Rwandans' experience of genocide was the fate of the *Banyamulenge*, the Congolese Tutsi minorities who, despite being long domiciled in the Kivus of Eastern Congo, had been denied citizenship. It should be noted that while the Tutsi Banyamulenge started the Rwanda/Uganda-led rebellion which brought Kabila to power, Kigali in particular had become disillusioned with the new government's failure to swiftly address the question of their citizenship.

Kabila was also reluctant to give in to pressure from his allies to deploy more troops to porous border areas or allow their own forces to tackle Interhamwe and Uganda's Allied Democratic Forces (ADF) insurgents operating from bases in the Congo. Besides the internal sensitivities to perceived Tutsi domination of his government, he also became increasingly concerned about the danger of continuing to entrust his security networks to the Rwandans and Ugandans. In the run-up to the August 1998 military offensive by Rwanda and Uganda, the Kinshasa government therefore deliberately promoted fears of Tutsi irredentism. Earlier in that month, broadcasts urging violence against Congo's Tutsis were being aired on Congolese state radio. In words strikingly similar to those preceding the 1994 Rwandan genocide, the persuasive broadcasts exhorted:

> People must bring a machete, a spear, an arrow, a hoe, spades, rakes, nails, truncheons, electric irons, barbed wire, stones and the like, in order, dear listeners, to kill the Rwandan Tutsis... wherever you see a Rwandan Tutsi, regard them as your enemy. Be ferocious. You will detect the enemies and massacre them without mercy.[8]

Phillip Reyntjens has spoken of a 'bi-polar ethnic set-up' in the Great Lakes region in which different groups like the 'Bantu' oppose themselves against 'Hima', 'Hamites' or 'Nilotics', just as the Hutu are opposed to Tutsi in Rwanda and Burundi'.[9] This fragile inter-ethnic mix in the region was exploited by Kabila apparently as part of his strategy for countering the rising influence of Rwandan and Ugandan forces in his country, and with it the power of Congo's Tutsis. The approach, ultimately, was counter-productive as it bolstered whatever initial justification Kigali and Kampala had for deploying forces and materials to support the breakaway RCD rebels.

Two other developments also highlight the widening gulf between the erstwhile allies. In July 1998 Rwanda made a volte-face by acknowledging its role in the ADFL advance on Kinshasa. Apparently intended to embarrass Kabila, the Congolese government's domestic popularity plummeted to a new low among many Congolese who resented the fact of their own government being a lackey of their eastern neighbours. On the international scene, frictions with the UN human rights panel investigating rights abuse allegedly committed during the 'liberation' war also lost the government political goodwill as it came under the opprobrium of international opinion. Kabila's frustration at this time was well summed up by Reyntjens:

> [Kabila's government] realised it was doing Kigali's dirty work, as most killings of Rwandan Hutu refugees had been the RPA's responsibility. This was Kabila's dilemma: either he pointed an accusing finger at his Rwandan allies (at the risk of antagonising them and, at the same time, admitting they had fought his war) or he assumed full responsibility (and admitted to being guilty of war crimes against humanity and possibly genocide).[10]

In late July, Kabila reacted to rumours that his estranged allies might be plotting to topple him by dismissing his Rwandan Chief of Staff, James Kabarebe. This move did not assuage the feelings of his external backers who already saw his several cabinet reshuffles as a systematic attempt to undermine their influence in Congolese affairs, while their security concerns remained unaddressed. It is interesting to note that allegations of war plundering also seeped into the official tirade being traded at this time - something that had already come into public debate in the wake of high-profile mining contracts, concluded by Kabila as Alliance des Forces Démocratiques pour la Libération du Congo Zaïre (AFDL-Alliance of Democratic Forces for the Liberation of Congo-Zaïre) marched towards Kinshasa amidst widespread looting among retreating Zaïrean forces. For example, Victor Mpoyo, a Congolese minister, accused a Ugandan official of smuggling Congolese diamonds, gold and forest products. As will be argued later, at this time the Rwanda-Uganda alliance seemed to have steered clear of 'war profiteering' activities. Hence, claims that they were after Congolese resources as the original motive of intervention is weakened by this evidence. Only in the context of domestic dissatisfaction with years of resources mismanagement and, perhaps, the reactive intervention of Kabila's foreign allies, do economic considerations first emerge as a plausible motive for intervention.

For Uganda, the Allied Democratic Forces (ADF) making incursions into Western Uganda from bases in Eastern Congo have been a long standing menace which the army of Uganda has been hard pressed to dislodge. Already stretched thin by the Lord's Resistance Army's (LRA's) incursion from southern Sudan, Kampala had a strong interest in going after and destroying the ADF in the Congo. It also had a stake in the fortune of the Rwandan government, as key members of the RPA were part of President Museveni's National Resistance Movement (NRM) successful guerrilla campaign in the 1980s. Indeed, Uganda not only served as a launching pad for the RPA's successful campaign to take power in Rwanda, Ugandan intelligence, war materials and logistics were instrumental in its success.[11] Museveni therefore had some self-interest in helping to keep the RPA in power to forestall any substantial Tutsi refugee flow into Uganda should his allies lose power.

When on 26 July 1998 Kabila ordered all foreign troops to leave the Congo, he in effect set the stage for a joint effort by these two historically linked armies to try dislodging him from power. With the characteristic swiftness with which troops were deployed 15 months earlier, the remainder of the ADFL still loyal to Kabila came under rebel attacks jointly co-ordinated by Rwandan, Ugandan and Burundian forces.

Although the security reasons offered by these two allies to justify intervention appear compelling, many have questioned the long term wisdom of the military option because of its potentially long term damaging effect on the Rwandan and Ugandan regimes. Not only does it raise the spectacle of a Hutu revanchism (because of the alliance that will naturally coalesce between desperate Ugandan and Rwandan insurgents and their host government in Kinshasa), even more damning is the prospect of a settlement along the lines preferred by the Kabila regime, which is the total withdrawal of all interventionist forces in the Congo. Yusuf Bangura succinctly summed up this situation:

> In the long term, Rwanda and Uganda face heightened tension and insecurity in eastern Congo, whether the government of Congo wins the war or not... If the east falls to the government hands, then Rwanda and Uganda will have a large, outspoken, unfriendly and potentially rich neighbour (a wounded lion) to the west of their countries... If on the other hand the east remains a contested zone, it is unlikely that Congo will accept the buffer that Uganda and Rwanda will ultimately want to create on Congolese territory.[12]

The security dilemma in which this leaves Kagame and Museveni, when factored into the economics of foreign intervention, certainly provides the most compelling perspective for understanding the continuing military stalemate in the Congo.

The Economics of Foreign Involvement

While it remains to be seen whether all foreign forces deployed in the Congo were sent there for the defence of concrete national security interests (Zimbabwe, with one of the most robust presences in the war, rather surprisingly, does not use the excuse of a direct security threat which other key participants have been able to deploy to make their case), there can be no doubt that the arrival of military and political leaders on the scene was soon followed by the establishment of war profiteering networks covering deals in forest and agricultural products (coffee, timber and ivory), illegal taxation, and illicit mining of gold, diamonds, cassiterites, and coltan. The latter, in particular, is a high-demand white malleable metallic element used in strategic high-tech and aerospace industries for producing mobile phones, computers, playstations, electronic capacitors and rectifiers, surgery and dental tools, turbine blades and anything that needs passive capacitors to maintain the electric charge of a computer microchip.[13]

The Economist described very graphically the evolution of events which led to the current regional crises in the Great Lakes:

> In the 1990s Congo became a proxy battleground for civil wars in Angola, Rwanda and Burundi. The governments of these countries sent their armies into Congo partly to pursue their own rebels. Once inside the country, both armies and rebels found mines, hardwood forests, coffee plantations and much else that they could exploit. None of the foreign armies or rebel groups will be poorer when they leave Congo than when they came in.[14]

It should be noted that while none of Rwanda, Uganda and Angola's political heads have been directly implicated in allegations of extensive plundering perpetrated in the DRC, close family relatives, top-ranking officers and political associates have been revealed to be involved in what the UN panel of experts referred to as the 'illegal exploitation' of resources. Allegations that first came out about foreigners involved in illegal economic activities in the DRC war pointed either at top Ugandan political figures, military elites, civil servants or close family members of the political leadership. Evidence from the Safiyatou Ba-N'Daw-led UN Panel of experts investigating illegal exploitation of minerals and other products in the DRC (henceforth Ba-N'Daw Report)[15] suggested in April 2001 that many foreigners, including two top Ugandan military functionaries who had at various times been relieved from their posts, are involved in many of the illegal deals going on in the Ugandan-occupied north-east of the DRC. The first, Major General Salim Saleh, is President Yoweri Museveni's younger brother and is said to control a chain of companies with his wife, including the Victoria Group and Air Alexander. These companies have been listed as involved in illegal businesses in the DRC. It was the same Saleh who was pardoned by President Museveni for making an 'honest mistake' when he admitted to secretly buying Uganda's largest bank.[16] The other, Major James Kazini, commander of the UPDF, was also said to have discovered business opportunities early in the DRC war, and accordingly organised men and troops to facilitate the ventures. The Ba-N'Daw Report described him as Saleh's 'executing arm and right hand'. He later confirmed these reports when he admitted flouting President Museveni's order banning business dealings by public servants serving in the war in the Congo.[17]

As on the Ugandan side, some private business people were also mentioned either as fronts or collaborators with Rwandan officials who did business in the Congo. Aziza Kulsum Gulamali, who was said to deal in gold, coltan and cassiterite in Rwandan-controlled Bukavu, seems to have established such a thriving business partnership with Rwandan forces that her past antecedent as financier and arms supplier to the Burundian Hutu Forces pour la défense de la démocratie (FDD) rebels mattered very little to the RPA. As the Ba-N'Daw Report notes:

> She was recently appointed by RCD-Goma as General Manager of SOMIGL, a conglomerate of four partners, which obtained the monopoly for the commercialisation and export of coltan. This monopoly has strengthened her position as a major player in the trade in coltan in the region. RCD-Goma, in an attempt to explain this partnership, said that she is a very useful person and would bring $1 million to RCD monthly. Mrs. Gulamali is famous for forging customs declarations, especially for the products she exports. Confronted recently with a false customs declaration where coltan was declared as cassiterite, she replied, 'in this business everybody does that'. (Ba-N'Daw Report, paragraph 19).

Madam Gulamali's claim on the widespread nature of sharp business practices in rebel-held territories indeed matched reports making the rounds as early as January 1999 of large quantities of resources, particularly timber, being smuggled out of the eastern Congo. Andruale Kapanga, Congolese ambassador to the UN, alleged that Rwanda and Uganda 'were plundering Congo of its minerals and other resources'. He claimed Congolese 'know the timber that is going to Uganda'.[18] By May, Uganda's Revenue Authority (URA) nabbed two consignments of timber worth about $30,000. As Joseph Olanyo notes of this seizure:

> It is not clear how the forest permit for Uganda was issued five days after the goods, which are on transit from the DRC, landed at Entebbe. Although the timber originated from Kisangani where the Congo forest officials should have issued the authority, an Ugandan document was instead used on entry at Entebbe. Another irregularity is that the goods were not manifested on entry into Uganda. There was also no declaration on entry to Customs by the captain of the aircraft. It had no Congo Customs Transit or Export documents, neither did the Congo forest officials give export (sic) clearance and permit.[19]

Indeed, there is clear evidence indicating that smuggling networks were widespread in Rwandan- and Ugandan-occupied territories. The complex alliances formed between business interests and political/military elites from the side of

Congolese rebels, particularly the Rassemblement Congolais pour la Démocratie (RCD) factions, and their foreign backers have been behind the shady dealings in minerals, timbers and other resources in areas outside the de facto control of government. Apparently, the Ba-N'Daw Report's mention of widespread illegal structures of exploitation is a reference to the highly organised channels through which such resources find their way from the Congo to both Rwanda and Uganda for onward export to the destination markets. It notes that regardless of the looter, the pattern was the same. Rwandan, Ugandan and/or RCD soldiers, commanded by an officer, visited farms, storage facilities, factories, and banks and demanded that the managers open the coffers and doors. The soldiers were then ordered to remove the relevant products and load them into vehicles (Ba-N'Daw Report, paragraph 32).

Hence, between September 1998 and August 1999, the Panel claimed, the occupied parts of DRC were drained of existing stocks of minerals, agricultural and forest products. Once the stockpiles were exhausted, the exploitation shifted into the 'active extraction' stage. Direct extraction was carried out either by individual soldiers for their own benefit, organised by commanders of the occupation forces, or by foreign nationals for the army or commanders' benefit. Occupying forces also brought labour from their own countries, such as Rwandan prisoners brought to the Congo to dig coltan.[20] In its analysis of intervening states' official production and export figures, the Panel found inconsistencies in Ugandan exports noting how 'diamond exports from Uganda [started] only in the last few years, coincided surprisingly with [her] occupation of eastern Congo'. To this allegation, the Ugandan central bank has suggested that some exports might be 'leaking' over the borders with Congo.

On Rwanda, the Report notes that the authorities themselves acknowledge that their country 'has no production of diamond, cobalt, zinc, manganese and uranium'. Yet, figures from the World Trade Organisation, the Diamond High Council and Belgian statistics revealed that Rwanda has been exporting diamonds. Like Uganda, the timing of these increases in mineral production is also noted to have coincided with the deployment of troops in the Congo. Analyses of the two countries' military budgets reveal similar discrepancies. For instance, while two percent of Ugandan GDP officially goes to defence (estimated to be about $110 million for the fiscal year 2000), about $126 million was spent on the military in 1999 (representing an overspending of $16 million) (Ba-N'Daw Report, paragraph 117). Ugandan officials have argued that it could well be that the economy enjoyed a boost from Congolese products being exported through Ugandan ports.[21] They observed that recent improvements in the GDP (which, presumptively, the re-export economy has brought) permitted 'an increase in absolute terms of the military budget while keeping the military budget at the agreed 2 percent of GDP' (Ba-N'Daw, paragraph 142). One implication of this argument is that the UPDF war effort has at least partly been financed (directly or indirectly) by illegal mining and commercial activities in the DRC war. The same appeared to be true of the Rwandan army, whose calculated war expenses far outstripped its official defence budget of $63 million, and is estimated to have made up to at least $250 million over a period of 18 months by simply selling the coltan that intermediaries buy from small dealers at $10 per kilo. Rwandan President Kagame himself, as the UN Panel noted, has agreed in this regard that the conflict is a 'self financing war'.

Yet, the big risks associated with the lucrative timber and diamond trade across the Congo-Uganda border implies that only well-protected investors can survive in such a harsh business climate. Reports of business ventures established by Rwandan and Ugandan military officers, state officials and close family members should therefore hardly come as a surprise. Yet, judging by the tone of domestic debate in both states – Ugandans' fears for example that commencement of the DRC war 'has seen a serious threat to Uganda's so-called economic miracle'[22] – it would appear that military and political elites, together with their cronies in the private sectors, have been the primary beneficiaries of whatever economic gains accrued to intervening states in the DRC, not their publics. While it is indeed difficult to verify such reports as the one on 'six companies operating in Eastern Congo in which President Museveni's wife, his brother, Vice-President [now President] Kagame and James Kabari [Kabarebe] are alleged to have shares',[23] it should nevertheless be reiterated that evidence exists to suggest that political and military leaders did soil their hands in the DRC war.

As argued earlier, it is clear that the looting from eastern Congo is not *strictu sensu* the official policy of the entire Ugandan government in the DRC war. The example of the URA confiscation above illustrates this, and it was even reported to have complained to the Ugandan defence ministry at an early stage about revenue loss from unchecked, and untaxed, products entering or leaving the DRC through the Entebbe military airport. To be sure, while Rwanda and Uganda manifestly lacked the internal resources to sustain their elaborate military campaigns, support for war operations from illegally exploited resources does not make profiteering elites executioners of their states' 'official policy' any more than a corrupt manager acts in the name of his company's shareholders. War entrepreneurs have an interest in sustaining their 'venture', and this is even easier when 'keeping in business' will not provoke questions by their own taxpayers at home. Profiteering elites in this sense are not much different from warlords who loot to sustain war and also enrich themselves.

Resource Control Struggles and the Kisangani Debacle

Fighting broke out between Rwanda's RPA and the Ugandan People's Defence Force in August 1999, and again from May to July 2000. Violent confrontation between the two allies had swiftly followed the emergence of splinter factions within the RCD, with the Wamba dia Wamba-led RCD-K backed by Uganda and the Jean-Pierre Ondekane faction supported by Rwanda. The initial fighting on 7 August 1999, culminated in the 14 August take-over of Bangoka airport by Uganda's third battalion, with hundreds of soldiers killed on both sides. President Museveni in an open letter published in the official government tabloid claimed 'there was no battle for Kisangani, but there were armed clashes in Kisangani' because in 'a military sense' 'a [soldier] would not place too much premium on controlling buildings in town unless he has finished capturing all the airports, ground of tactical importance overlooking the river and the roads'.[24] He therefore attributed the fighting to 'wrong actors' who 'most probably had political, economic, criminal or confused aims in their minds'.[25] The President, citing struggle for control of the banks as one possible reason, promised that a joint investigation by the two governments would expose those behind 'this criminal circus'. As if to lend credence to that part of Museveni's explanation that suspected 'confused aims' in the war, by mid-August, broadcasts from Radio Liberté at UPDF's headquarters in Congo, were speaking of the Rwanda-backed faction of the RCD as 'defeated fascist forces supported by a small neighbouring country'.[26] In Rwandan official circles, criticisms were levelled against the Ugandan President who gave free rein to extremists in the military, while Ugandans also expressed resentment at Rwanda's 'vain and inappropriate' regional ambitions.

Jean Baptiste Kayigamba, apparently in a concealed reference to the subterranean moves and carefully orchestrated schemes on both sides to attain supremacy in Kisangani, observed that if there is anybody to be surprised by the Kisangani fighting 'it should be both the Ugandan and Rwandese publics; not the two authorities in both countries'.[27] In his subsequent investigations in Kisangani into the real cause of fighting, he established that the 'August 7 attack was also meant to create political and military space for Wamba dia Wamba and turn him into a faction with a seat in Kisangani'.[28] It is indeed difficult to think of any objective security reason that could lead to such a spectacular fall-out between the two Great Lakes allies other than the quest to exert supremacy over this Congolese town, described by the BBC as a 'strategic city for the Congolese diamond trade'.[29]

It is therefore not surprising that despite the establishment of a joint command to manage 'breakdown in communications among commanders' and 'unresolved issues of divergence of objectives and priorities',[30] tensions again boiled over between the two rival forces on 5 May 2000. In the 'six-day war' in June, over 650 people were left dead and hundreds more became homeless.[31] So profound was the animosity between the two sides that during and after the hostilities, religious buildings were not spared, health centres and hospitals were full of wounded civilians and dozens of corpses had to be removed from the streets by social workers. It was not until July, after the Rwandans had pushed back the Ugandans, that the UN Observer Mission, MONUC, was allowed to take control of the situation.

The ease with which forces change sides when interests diverge provides a useful perspective from which to view the numerous wars/insurgencies in the region, and motivations for the never-ending resource scramble in the DRC. For instance, it was only logical that Kabila should find allies amongst his former adversaries - including the ex-FAR and *Interhamwe* - once he fell out with their own enemies. This paved the way for one of the most spectacular shifts in alliances in the conflict, perhaps rivalled only by Angola's decampment from the anti-government coalition that saw Mobutu out of office in 1997. It is at this point that the objective calculus of the military balance matches the realism of economic looting.

The fact of alliance fluidity among actors in the Great Lakes, and the widespread resource scramble seen in the Congo, two seemingly independent sets of events, could arguably be traced to the same generic sources: the desperate need to fend off at all cost serious security threats emanating from neighbouring states, and exploiting opportunities for war finances provided by Congo's weak state structures but immense resource endowments. In the network of transborder alliances spawned in the region – the curious alignment between Rwanda's Tutsis and Museveni's NRM/A before their respective rise to power; Angola's dramatic decamping from its Rwandan-Ugandan allies in 1998 – the presence of hard calculations of interests is an unmistakable thread underpinning the relations of actors.

Rwanda and Uganda's calculations of power must therefore be seen as understanding the fundamental requirement that their security interests are best safeguarded when backed with the necessary material resources. Their armies' part in the economic plunder of Congo, like those of other participants, is therefore from the outset an inexorable policy course. What this means is that Rwanda's regime felt so threatened by the activities of *Interhamwe* and ex-FAR rebels in the Congo that regime survival became an overriding and urgent concern over and above the need to rein in 'erring' military and political functionaries in the DRC war. This will invariably be a viable course for a leadership confronted with the demands of repelling a regime-threatening insurgency on very limited internal resources. To be sure, while the economic outlook of Rwanda and Uganda was anything but buoyant at the start of hostilities, it was always apparent that the scale of their commitments in the Congo war would provoke questions on the sources of their finance.

This is the sense in which economic plundering is a necessary logical outcome of military intervention by resource-poor countries such as Rwanda and Uganda in a richly endowed weak state like the DRC. The effect of weakly institutionalised political processes, foreign policy decisions inclusive, was clearly visible in the manners in which troops launched operations into the DRC. The political leadership in all intervening states took the decisions to commit troops abroad without recourse to parliamentary approval, even in countries like Uganda and Zimbabwe where there is at least some degree of parliamentary oversight over executive action. In Uganda's case, the parliament for a long time opposed the Congo operations because 'not only was there no approval from the house, but [the operations were] also too costly'.[32] In such situations where troop deployment was not subject to constitutional control, military commanders answerable only to the political head have considerable leeway in deciding how to conduct operations. This is more so in the cases of Rwandan and Ugandan leaderships whose history of revolutionary struggles conduces to a near total fusion between the core executive and the military functions of government. The implication of all these factors is to underscore the danger of viewing all foreign interventions as capable of being interpreted through a conventional foreign policy lens. It does make the most sense to disaggregate and move below the level of the state architecture in order to explain the politics of resource control among Africa's interventionist elites.

Elites, Privatised States and Disguised Expectations of Personal Benefits

It would seem that one of the striking observations that comes out of a careful examination of interventionist governments' official pronouncements is the way the leaders tried to distance themselves from alleged economic crimes by foreign forces in the Congo. Since the release of the UN Panel report, and other independent inquiries, which indicted senior state officials, close family members and private individuals with links to political heads in Rwanda and Uganda, the official line has consistently been to label such actions as 'misconduct' on the part of 'bad eggs' in the government and military. In both Kigali and Kampala, investigative panels such as the Ugandan Porter's Commission have even been established to probe 'serious acts of misconduct'. This provokes questions on the link between the activities of individual functionaries and the policies of states that they represent.

Does plundering in the DRC represent the official policy of governments involved in the war? Or is it another classical manifestation of the African public ethic where personal interests take precedence over the general will? Providing answers to these questions will necessarily involve an examination of the internal working of governments in Africa which, in the overwhelming number of examples, are poorly institutionalised.

As Charles Onyango-Obbo poignantly notes of the popular perception of the Ugandan ruling elite:

> when I mentioned that yes I am a Ugandan... I would be asked about the 'timber we hear you people are looting from Congo', I found that funny because in Uganda... people talk about some crooked officers and businessmen who are making a fortune in the Congo.[33]

He further notes that '[b]ecause the ruling movement was not unanimous about our intervention in the Congo, and indeed a lot of opposition to it, the campaign could not be carried out as a formal activity of the government'.[34] It could be argued that the lethargic response of the Ugandan government in dealing with reports of corrupt dealings by its officers in the DRC is tied to the grave worry and alarm with which Kampala regards the rebel threat on its borders with the Congo. Perhaps because of the huge cost involved in simultaneously confronting the LRA in the North and ADF to its south-east, Museveni's government has shown itself willing to allow the officers' ranks to 'supplement' with whatever war-generated resources could reduce the burden on Uganda's own internal resources, and crucially as part of that 'conspiracy of silence', allow the military and political elite a free hand in the daily routines of the occupation. This, arguably, is the background against which the reckless resource control politics in the conflict is being played out by political and military elites. Onyango-Obbo is again apt when he argued that, as a consequence of the informalisation of state processes, 'decisions as to which officers and soldiers to deploy in the Congo are not taken as openly as with operations against the Lord's Resistance Army rebels in the north'.[35] Thus, he notes, 'a lot of officers, who were on suspension or were semi-retired pop up with command positions in the Congo'.[36]

An examination of the Ugandan official response to similar allegations in 1966 that the then Colonel Idi Amin, head of the Ugandan forces deployed to aid Zaïrean rebels fighting the government, was involved in gold and ivory smuggling from Zaïre, does not differ very much from the present. Daudi Ochieng, an Ugandan MP, charged that 'three ministers received and shared sh2.5m ($400,000 then) while Amin had been given a gratuity of sh34,000', and duly presented as proof a photograph (!) of Amin's bank account.[37] The then Minister of Internal Affairs, Felix Onama, claimed 'Amin's relatives from the Congo had crossed the border into Uganda and handed their cash to [him]'.[38] When Ochieng petitioned further and asked that findings from government's investigation of the matter be made public, Premier Milton Obote responded thus: 'May I suggest that in future you divorce politics from security matters. Your writing and statement have all given the impression that you find it difficult to separate the two'.[39]

The point to be drawn from this may not be so much that the Prime Minister indulged an officer who eventually plotted his overthrow, as that weakly institutionalised governments lack strict procedures for dealing with allegations of 'gross misconduct' such as economic pillage by their state functionaries abroad. Onyango-Obbo argues that:

> Foreign wars have a peculiar corrupting influence on armies partly, it seems, because they lack a moral frame of reference. In a home war, things are easier. You protect members of your party, tribe religion and kill the rest. Not so in a war abroad; it calls for a lofty philosophical purpose (e.g.

> defending human rights, or preventing the advance of fundamentalism) which African armies have neither the intellectual depth nor experience back home to cope with. It is not long before the armies turn into plundering forces, and the few idealists in the military who opposed it get marginalised or silenced - or get swept by cynicism and simply join the looting.[40]

The conduct of foreign elites in the DRC war should therefore be seen not just as the preferred course among those who direct the affairs of state, but more fundamentally, as the consequence of state weakness, and in a sense, a democratic deficit, which creates room for elites' expectation and pursuit of personal interests in the name of, and at the expense of, the state. On this, Onyango-Obbo commented on the perceived internal rot that the Congo venture has caused within Museveni's ruling National Resistance Movement:

> It seems that some leaders concluded from the experience of opposition to the Congo war within the Movement, that the Movement itself was a problem. The response, apart from disrupting the coherence of the security establishment, seems to have been to undermine the limited 'democracy' within the Movement... the feeling of alienation and frustration among Movementists [party faithfuls] has grown sharply over the last year. It is likely that the president is feeling the heat. It is clear that a feeling of insecurity pervades the minds of his close hatchet men.[41]

Hence, even as late as July 2001 when the UN mission began its renewed mandate to oversee the withdrawal of all outside forces, Rwanda stuck obstinately to its position that troops would certainly not withdraw until, in accordance with the Lusaka peace accord, the 'negative forces' were disarmed.[42] Uganda also stuck to the same line, in spite of the opinion polls conducted in Kampala in September 1999 which indicated that 'a majority of Ugandans [about 81 percent] are opposed to the UPDF presence in the Democratic Republic of Congo'.[43] In the Ugandan Parliament, law-makers wondered why the 'high military expenditure' involved in the Congo operations did not stop ADF attacks on western Uganda while 'there have been persistent allegations of the involvement of senior UPDF officials in illicit trade in Congo'.[44] Owing to the persistent domestic and international pressure, Rwanda and Uganda only reluctantly committed themselves to withdrawing troops from the DRC, while their continuing support for Congolese proxies has witnessed continuing violence in the east of the country even as political negotiations for a national government continued in Kinshasa between government and rebel groups. With what looks like the implementation of at least parts of the Lusaka agreement and progress in the Inter-Congolese Dialogue now taking place, mind-boggling reports in the global media of continuing resource plunder only underscore the extent of the problem posed by the resource control element in contemporary African conflicts.

What does the role of Uganda and Rwanda in all these tell us about the 'workings' of governmental processes in Africa? At a minimum, it indicates that the conventional notion of the state as the entity which aggregates the public good over and above individualist interests is not very relevant to many African states, be they military dictatorships, 'neo one-party states' or even the fragile 'democracies' of the type that are now taking root in a number of countries. On this, Abdul Raheem Tajudeen was very apt when he observed that:

> There is nothing unique about diversity of interests; however, when personal interests clash with the protection of the public ones, those entrusted with the protection of the public good must act. From Harare through Luanda to Kigali and Kampala, there is more than ample evidence or strong perception that the war had become business and the business is now war.[45]

In the final analysis, Rwanda and Uganda, it would appear, cannot be indifferent to the choice of leadership in Kinshasa. Unlike non-border states such as Zimbabwe and Namibia, security threats emanating from within Congo clearly provide a basis for their involvement in the DRC. Yet, an attempt to be so closely involved as they have sought with their military intervention will always generate a backlash, or resentment at the very least, from both the Congolese government and people. It also creates rooms for rebels opposing them to continue to seek alignment with elements within the Congolese state in a strategic partnership aimed at a common adversary. This security dilemma, when factored into gains that Rwandan and Ugandan soldiers and the political class make from illegal profiteering activities, provides the most compelling perspective for understanding the continuing military stalemate in Eastern Congo. To be sure, despite the unassailable security explanations on which the case for their initial intervention was built, the subsequent refusal to pull back troops from inside the Congolese hinterland (despite assumption of full control over the security situation along their respective borders), as well as behind-the-scene meddling in the continuing fighting in the east exposed the one plausible explanation for the protracted foreign occupation of the DR Congo: the on-going plunder of its vast economic resources. This enduring resource motive runs through the various strands of our preceding analysis, and was well supported by evidence from very diverse sources.

Notes

1. The DRC government and its allies (Zimbabwe, Angola, Namibia, Sudan and Chad) engaged three major rebel factions (RCD-G, RCD-K and Mouvement de

Libération Congolais (MLC) supported by either Rwanda or Uganda. Local armed militias like the Mai-Mai and foreign rebel groups like Rwanda's Hutu Interhamwe/ Ex-FAR and Uganda's ADF are allied to the DRC government while Congolese Tutsi militias (Banyamulenge) join the insurgency. There are also other foreign insurgent groups like Angola's Uniao Nacional para a Independencia Total de Angola (UNITA) operating from bases in the Congo.

2. Some of the claims include the emergence in the region of 'a war zone from Luanda to Asmara', a 'greater ethnic conflict in Central Africa', the rise of the first 'authentic African powers', the beginning of 'the First African World War' and 'the second scramble for Africa', etc. See Filip Reyntjens, 'The Second Congo War: More than a Remake', *African Affairs*, No 98, (1999), 241-50; William G. Thom, 'Congo-Zaire's 1996-97 Civil War in the Context of Evolving Patterns of Military Conflict in Africa in the Era of Independence', *The Journal of Conflict Studies*, Vol. 19, No. 2, 1999, pp 93-123; Ibid, p.120; David Shearer, 'Africa's Great War', *Survival*, Vol. 41, No. 2, 1999, pp. 89-106; and *The Times*, 22 April 1997, p.18, respectively.
3. Representative here is the Report of the Security Council Mission to the Great Lakes Region, 15-16 May 2001. Its greater sensitivity to intervening states' security claims, in contrast to the Ba-N'Daw-led Expert Panel's focus on resource exploitation, made it more acceptable to Rwanda, Uganda and Burundi.
4. My use of this term is inspired by Jean-François Bayart, Stephen Ellis and Beatrice Hibou, *The Criminalisation of the State in Africa*, (Oxford: The International African Institute in association with J. Currey, 1999).
5. Burundi, chasing its own Hutu insurgents in the DRC, is also involved in the fighting. The activities of the major intervenors, namely Rwanda and Uganda, is however the main focus of this chapter.
6. Paul Magnarella, *Justice in Africa: Rwanda's Genocide, Its Courts and the UN Criminal Tribunal*, (Aldershot: Ashgate, 2000) presents an historical overview of internal developments in post-genocide Rwanda.
7. See Michael McGreal, 'Why Threatened Rwanda turned on Kabila', *Electronic Mail & Guardian* (Johannesburg), 20 August 1998.
8. Quoted in Michael McGreal, op.cit.
9. Filip Reyntjens, op.cit, 244.
10. Ibid., pp. 245-6.
11. As late as 2001, debates were still on in the Ugandan public about 'Uganda's arms said to have been taken by Tutsis when they invaded Rwanda in 1990'. See *The New Vision* (Kampala), 31 May 2001, p.19.
12. Yusuf Bangura, 'Museveni, Kagame Blew Up Golden Chance in Congo', *The Monitor*, (Kampala), 1 September, 1998, p.20.
13. See *New African*, No 397, June 2001, p.30; and *The New Vision*, 5 August 1999, p.17.
14. 'Congo and its Neighbours', *The Economist*, 21 June 2001.
15. Report of the Panel of Experts on the Illegal Exploitation of Natural Resources and Other Forms of Wealth of the Democratic Republic of the Congo (April and November 2001).

16. 'Uganda: Profiles of Corruption', *The New Vision*, 29 December 1998.
17. My personal discussion of the Porter Commission's Report with the Ugandan Ambassador to the UN, H.E Prof. Semakula Kiwanuka, Uganda House, New York, 23 May, 2002.
18. *The Crusader*, (Kampala) 9 January 1999, p.1.
19. *The New Vision* (Kampala), 27 May 1999, p.17.
20. Personal discussions with the journalist Juliana Ruhfus, co-participant at an SOAS conference in which she shared insights on her fieldwork in eastern DRC, SOAS, London, 17 November 2001.
21. As the Ugandan Ambassador to the UN told me, allegations of looting from Congo ignore the long existence of a transborder network of economic exchange between Ugandan and Congolese traders.
22. See *The New Vision*, (Kampala), 12 September, 1999.
23. Report of the Tanzanian *Daily Mail*, 14 January 1999, cited in Reyntjens, op.cit, p.249.
24. 'There Was No Battle for Kisangani Town', *The New Vision*, 24 August 1999, p.6.
25. Ibid.
26. *Sunday Monitor* 29 August, 1999, p.28.
27. Ibid.
28. Ibid.
29. BBC Online Reports updated 5 May 2000.
30. These were the words in which the Ugandan Ambassador to the UN described the causes of the Kisangani clashes. Personal interview at the Uganda House, New York, 23 May, 2002.
31. BBC Online Reports updated Friday, 21 July, 2000.
32. See 'Why Ugandans Want Out of the Congo', *Sunday Vision* (Kampala), 12 September 1999.
33. *The Monitor* (Kampala), 24 November, 1999, p.10.
34. Ibid.
35. Ibid.
36. Ibid.
37. *The New Vision*, 26 August 1999, p. 21.
38. Ibid
39. Ibid
40. *The Monitor* (Kampala) 24 November 1999, p. 10.
41. Ibid.
42. *Africa Confidential*, Volume 42, Number 14, 13 July 2001.
43. *Sunday Vision*, (Kampala) 12 September 1999.
44. Ibid.
45. 'Enough for Our Need, Not Enough for Our Greed', *The New Vision*, 26 October 1998.

7

The Youth and Environmental Education in Cameroon: A Study of Secondary School-based Environmental Clubs

Andrew Wujung Vukenkeng

Introduction

Environmental education whose aim is raising awareness and nurturing friendly environmental attitudes amongst the population, cannot be complete without an examination of non-formal environmental education through bodies such as clubs and non-governmental organisations. The proliferation of school-based environmental clubs in Cameroon, as a forum for creating practical awareness on environmental issues, is likely to have a considerable impact on the youth. The contention of this study whose aim is to examine the role of school environmental education, is that if the youth are made aware and can understand the serious consequences of human activities regarding the environment, they will be able to appreciate the need to avoid such activities, or adopt new ones which will minimise those consequences and become better advocates for environmental protection.

The observations which animate this study centre on the circumstances of the creation of these clubs. Concretely, which activities do these initiatives carry out? By their nature, do they respond to the on-going environmental crisis? Is their emergence necessitated by this crisis? We first of all attempt to situate environmental education in the global context of environmental policy in Cameroon. To this end, we throw some light on the objectives and tools of this policy. Thereafter, we examine the goals and strategies of environmental education in the country. We end with an examination of environmental clubs in the North West and South West Provinces.

The Place of Environmental Education in Environmental Policy in Cameroon

Environmental protection and conservation are already a long tradition in the developed world. Developing countries recently gained inspiration from the experience of the West and opened departments to take care of their environment, which may be relatively undamaged. Environmental departments such as the Ministry of Environment and Forest (MINEF) are charged with the elaboration and implementation of environmental policy. This Ministry set up co-ordinated actions to achieve the desired environmental sustainability returns, and has had the following specific objectives:

i) To supervise and evaluate the ecological impact of development activities on the environment,
ii) To elaborate, control and apply the norms of the management of natural resources,
iii) To educate, inform and sensitise the public on environmental problems,
iv) To assemble, organise, disseminate all relevant information on the environment and ensure the application of cooperation treaties/conventions on the protection of the environment,
v) To provide inventory and planning in the area of forest exploitation, and
vi) To implement specific policy on wild life and protected areas.

To achieve these objectives MINEF has been organised along the following-lines to achieve the following objectives. The Department of Environment is charged with environmental studies, extension and control at the Central, provincial and divisional levels. The service of Forestry is charged with inventory, planning and statistics, administration and control of activities of exploiters. The service of wildlife and protected areas is called upon to implement policy on wildlife and protected areas. The service of administration and finance is in charge of all administrative and financial problems of the ministry. Finally, the technical operations unit takes care of special units such as wildlife reserves, National parks, leisure parks, Botanic gardens and zoos.

In the above organogram, only the service of the environment uses mainly education as a tool to achieve environmental sustainability returns. The other departments rely on legislation, effluent taxes and subsidies, treaties/conventions, monetary policy, and direct government spending to achieve their objectives.

From the foregoing environmental education can be seen to comprise one of the tools of environmental policy in Cameroon. What remains now is to get to know the goals and strategies of this particular tool of environmental policy.

Manases Ngome considers the modern concept of environmental education to be an improvement on and a derivative from fairly established elementary social practices which make people aware of the serious consequences of their activities for the environment. Here, the main problem is how to bring about such an awareness and understanding and at the same time persuade people to adopt and learn new ways of doing things with long-term environmental benefits. In fact, according to Fonkeng and Tamajong (1995: 4), 'responsible educational planning which reflects environmental/biospheric awareness would give more meaning to schooling and is likely to generate a more sustainable development'.

It is in response to the above observation that the national action plan for the environment spelt out the following objectives:

i) Environmental policy: to increase the level of awareness and knowledge of environmental problems and threats;
ii) To bring about a better understanding of the causes of environment problems;
iii) To disseminate the necessary knowledge, skills, and technology that will help reduce environmental degradation and encourage conservation; and
iv) To persuade people to adopt environmentally friendly activities.

A concerted multifaceted effort from a plethora of common initiative groups, non-governmental organisations and government is made to translate these objectives into action. However, this effort is compromised by the fact that it is difficult to deal with all environmental problems at the same time, since they differ in their nature, causes, extent and urgency. Time and other economic resources also impose a limit on the efforts of these environmental actors.

Meanwhile, environmental educators are open to three strategies or methods of education – formal, non-formal and informal education. The choice of any one method would depend on practical considerations rather than the inherent merit of any one type. However, these methods are complementary.

The goal of formal environmental education is eventually to condition the population to adopt environmentally responsible attitudes and behaviour by integrating the facts, principles, definitions and value concepts of the environment into the institutionalised educational system of Cameroon. This could be achieved either by introducing a new subject called Environmental Education or introducing environmental concepts as well as modifying existing concepts in subjects such as geography and nature study at the primary level, and civics, ecology, biology, and geology at a more advanced level.

As concerns non-formal environmental education, it aims at transferring knowledge and skills through organised activities so as to alter opinions, attitudes or behaviour. This type of education which is problem-orientated and targets institutions such as clubs, NGOs, groups and specific social categories such as farmers, women, teachers etc, can be effected by creating opportunities for the target groups to be exposed to material of pedagogic value through the mass media, special printed material (e.g. posters), exhibitions, demonstrations and shows. For this type of education to be effective, it needs to:

- be precisely targeted;
- be persistently delivered;
- use a variety of delivery systems;
- be appropriate and relevant to the problems and needs of the target group;
- be based on reliable data; and
- avoid situations of conflict.

Informally, some sections of the population in the country acquire environmentally useful information because of their proximity to conservation projects or accidental exposure to newspaper articles and television programmes.

From the foregoing, we have identified environmental education as a tool of environmental policy in Cameroon and situated it in its proper framework. More specifically, we have reviewed the objectives and needs of non-formal environmental education which is our focus in this communication. To what extent and with which difficulties do school environmental clubs meet the objectivities of environmental education policy in Cameroon is the logical and central question in this investigation.

Methodology

A sample of 22 secondary school environmental clubs was studied. Seventeen of these clubs were run by the Cameroon Baptist Convention (CBC) and Presbyterian Church in Cameroon (PCC) schools in the North West and South West Provinces of the country. Two Catholic mission school clubs, two public school clubs and one lay private school club were also studied. The under-representation of environmental clubs run by Catholic mission schools, public schools and lay private schools in the sample is explained by the quasi-absence of these environmental initiatives in these schools. On the other hand, the large proportion of Baptist and Presbyterian school clubs in the sample are co-ordinated and encouraged by the CBC-PCC-DED-EZE-in service-training programme.

To obtain the required information, a structured questionnaire was designed, pre-tested and administered to school environmental clubs. The questionnaire was designed such that it comprised of both closed-ended and open-ended questions so as to allow club coordinators/members to better express themselves. Here, information was sought on the motivations, successes and difficulties of the clubs. Reports on CBC and PCC club activities presented by their co-ordinators during their August annual seminars organised by the CBC-PCC-DED-EZE-in service Training programme were also examined. Intensive interviews with the CBC–PCC school club co-ordinators were also conducted during their August annual seminar of 2001. Data were analysed using simple descriptive statistics.

Proliferation of School Environmental Clubs

Creation and Composition of Clubs

The study showed that school environmental clubs have existed as far back as 1983 in the study region, but have failed to take their activities seriously and to sensitise the public regarding them. However, the recently created clubs which constitute 54 percent of the sample have joined the few old clubs to renew their interest in environmental education. These environmental club initiatives which group both teachers and students together, are known by different appellations. According to Nsobe (1996) these clubs exist under labels such as 'Friends of nature, lovers of nature, Earth club' etc. Our survey showed that in addition to the above appellations, some of these clubs bear names such as Environmental Education club, Voice of the Environment, Better Environmental Partnership or simply Environmental club.

Tracing the origin of these clubs, it was found that the idea to create and run these clubs came from teachers, from an external source such as a non-governmental organisation, or jointly from students and teachers. No club indicated that the idea to create the group came solely from the students. Some 58 percent, 23 percent and 19 percent of the clubs traced their origin/creation to teachers, an external source, and jointly to students and teachers, respectively.

Student enrolment into the clubs ranged from 15 to 138 students. The modal range of club membership was 40–60 and average membership per club stood at 46. The mean number of boys and girls in these clubs was 19.3 and 27.1 respectively. The distribution of club membership by class of study revealed the modal class to be upper six followed by Form III. This finding suggests the inadequate motivation/interest of junior students to join these environmental initiative groups. According to age distribution, members were shared equally between the age groups 10–15 and 16–20.

Objectives and Activities of School Environmental Clubs

With the emergence of school environmental clubs, we wanted to know if they effectively provided solutions to their environmental problems, pursued specific objectives, and functioned well. Are they talk shops or field clubs? Investigating with these questions in mind we found that the activities of these environmental initiatives rotate around environmental education and protection. Generally, these clubs aimed at introducing the school community to environmentally useful information and activities. More specifically, these clubs aimed at initiating activities that bring about environmental sensitivity and commitment in different ways.

First, three-quarters of the clubs organised study trips and excursions to protected areas and critical environmental sites such as Kilum mountain Forest project/Lake Oku, Mbinkar Mountain Forest, Tubah watershed, Bakingili and Lake Barombi.

Second, the clubs conveyed environmental messages through lectures, stories, drama/sketches, songs, poems, and discussions/debates on feast days or special events such as the hunting season, Earth Day, Food Day, World Population Day, Wetlands Day, the World Environment Day. The clubs were equally involved in environmental hobbies such as flower, herb, fruit and tree gardening, keeping of pets and bees. In fact, about half of these clubs were involved in the beautification of their campuses, and this proved to be a practical demonstration of the beauty of nature and provided valuable learning opportunities for their members and the entire school community.

Clubs of the CBC and PCC schools participated in an environmental drawing/painting competition organised by the CBC - PCC - DED - EZE In-service Training programme. Students who distinguished themselves in this competition were sponsored for a six day excursion to the Korup National Park in Mundemba.

Apart from carrying out environmental activities within the school setting, some of these clubs encouraged their members to practise similar activities at home. Here, through the exhibition of environmental activities to neighbouring local communities, the clubs were able to promote awareness on community-oriented activities which more appropriately would ensure environmental sustainability. The extension of club activities to local communities is a practice to be emulated by other environmental cluster groups, for this approach leads to many multiplier environmental friendly activities and returns.

Finally, coordinators of environmental clubs especially those of the CBC – PCC schools participated in environmental workshops and seminars organised by the CBC-PCC-EZE-DED In-service Training programme in partnership with the Bamenda Highlands Forest project. Precise information and knowledge on the rational exploitation of natural resources acquired during these seminars was later on passed on to club members through their co-ordinators. In this way club members were equipped to be better advocates of environmental protection and conservation.

Management of School Environmental Clubs

Organisation and Co-ordination of Environmental clubs

Though school environmental initiatives involved both students and teachers, their organisation and coordination was incumbent more on teachers who served as a link between members of the club on the one hand, and the school administration and external organisations on the other. Besides the teacher co-ordinator, all but one of the clubs had a pure student executive bureau. The teachers' role in these clubs was mostly one of co-ordination. The actual running of the clubs was in the hands of the students. However, at the tertiary level of education students can single-handedly run these clubs. At the primary school level, the organisation and coordination of these clubs would entirely be in the hands of the teachers, since most of pupils are still too young to assume leadership roles. Whatever the level at which these clubs are organised there would be the need to define clear rules binding members. In fact these rules should define the terrain over which members manoeuvre.

Financing of School Environmental Clubs

The proper organisation and coordination of a school environmental club would depend on its resources, especially financial resources. The clubs studied had a very wide range of activities such as study trips, excursions, gardening, building of embankments to check erosion, sending of environmental messages etc. These activities required a lot of funds which they could not easily raise. Some 45.5 percent of the clubs indicated that they financed most of their activities solely with members' contributions; 14.5 percent, 19 percent, 9 percent and 9 percent of the clubs used funds from members' contributions, income raised from their activities, administration, members contribution, external funds, school administration and members contributions, and solely from external sources, respectively. In the case of a few clubs funds were raised during special fund raising activities such as exhibition and presentation of sketches and drama. Some of these activities while generating income through the market system drew the sympathy of environmental friendly members of the public who generously supported the clubs.

An in-depth interview of co-ordinators of some environment clubs revealed that the financial situation of these initiatives was a mixed one. The co-ordinator of the environment club of Joseph Merrick Baptist College (JMBC) Ndu, shouldered almost single-handedly the burden of financing the club's activities. However, few staff members of the club occasionally offered some assistance. According to the club coordinator of the Presbyterian Secondary School, Bafut, the story was a little bit different. During the early life of the club, its activities were financed solely with contributions from members but in the long run, the club received the financial support of the London-based Living Earth organisation for the presentation of a project on the management of waste items in the school. To the co-ordinator of the Nature Club of Government Bilingual High School Kumbo, club activities were considerably constrained by inadequate funding to the extent that talk shops were preferred to expensive field trips.

Hence we find that these clubs like other organisations need finance to run their activities which are largely new to members and very demanding both in time and money. Unfortunately these funds are not easy to obtain. It is recommended that while these clubs intensify their self-financing strategies, they should also emulate the example of the environment club of P.S.S Bafut and others by coming up with environmental friendly projects which can be financed by governmental and non-governmental organisations.

Motivations: Successes and Difficulties

As we saw earlier the idea of creating environmental initiatives in school settings largely came from teachers and external sources, mostly non-governmental organisations. This shows the limited interest students had in these initiatives. Minang (1997) holds that to some of the students, field trips, interschool visitations and ego fulfilment constitutes the primary motive of belonging to these clubs. However, the emergence of these clubs was a response to persistent appeals from governmental and non-governmental organisations to join in the global concern with environmental degradation.

Schools in the past had launched club initiatives in domains such as music, art, debating and drama, but not in environmental education. When environmental clubs became fashionable, they embraced the management or control of waste items in the immediate school environment. In fact most of the clubs developed an appropriate waste management strategy whereby waste materials are sorted into plastics and paper, metallic and iron objects, and organic matter. The plastics and paper are incinerated using controlled fire. The metallic and iron objects are either dumped into a pit or sold to local manufacturers of pots and spoons. The organic matter is allowed to decompose and subsequently used as manure in the school garden. Next, these clubs were found to be involved in environmental hobbies such as herb, flower, fruit and crop gardening, bee keeping etc. Through exhibitions and theatrical shows, singing, poetry, short stories and debates, the clubs improved students' creativity as well as providing other valuable learning opportunities. Finally, and not the least, a good number of clubs extended their activities to excursions. These field trips were mostly sponsored by external bodies to provide study and leisure opportunities to the students. During these excursions the student benefited from the triple strategy of learning i.e. learning by hearing, seeing and doing. In this way students' understanding of vague environmental concepts which they heard in their geography lessons or from other media was heightened.

These clubs did not make their way without difficulties. They confronted a number of problems: lack of finance, administrative bottlenecks, time constraints, inadequate interest from students and inadequate environmental literature.

All the clubs studied indicated that they had experienced some difficulties financing some of their activities - especially activities such as field trips which required substantial amounts of funds. Only two clubs received some financial assistance from the school administration and only two donor organisations had ever provided financial assistance to these clubs. As a result, the activities of some of the clubs were low-keyed with emphasis placed on talk-shops rather than fieldwork.

Meanwhile some school administrators are not very cooperative with coordinators of school environmental initiatives. Apart from withholding financial support from these clubs on the pretext of scarcity of funds, they complicated things for club coordinators each time a project was funded by an external body. To one club co-ordinator, his club was completely sidelined from the execution of a club project to fence a herb and crop garden which was funded by the CBC -PCC-DED-EZE In-service Training programme. This attitude killed the enthusiasm of the club and almost brought its activities to a standstill. Another club co-ordinator declared that he encountered administrative bottlenecks when he organised a field study for members of the club. Funds for the project in question were disbursed directly to the club co-ordinator and this did not please the Dean of Studies who in retaliation refused to give permission to two other staff members of the club who had to act as facilitators on the trip. Some school administrators were found to delay messages they had received addressed through them to environmental clubs. Some of these messages never reached the clubs.

Moreover, regular school programmes were found to occupy the students for most of the time. This constrained them from having regular meetings. In addition visits of important personalities and some special organised activities occasionally grounded club activities. The fact that the majority of the clubs met only fortnightly for about two hours could not enable them to accomplish their full agenda of activities for a given academic year.

Another worry was the inadequate interest from students, especially junior students in these initiatives. It seemed apparent that environmental issues were new to them and more so demanded a lot of their time and effort which they preferred to use for academic pursuits.

Finally, some of the clubs actually confessed to have been using mostly the trial and error method in whatever activity in which they were involved. In fact they did not have enough information or professional literature on environmental issues. This made it difficult for the clubs to define appropriate environmental messages in theatrical shows or to design clear activities, exercises, or games for the students. This problem is really acute given that the secondary school teaching core in service had little or no training in environmental education and teaching and learning materials are limited both quantitatively and qualitatively.

Conclusion

The analysis of the experience of school environmental clubs in Cameroon reveals their growing importance as focal points for environmental education for the youths, conditioning them to adopt environmental responsible attitudes and behaviour. Motivated by the need to join in the global fight against environmental degradation, these clubs carried out a wide range of activities amidst difficulties. The essential question posed by this study is the place accorded them by the country's educational policy. Lessons learnt from these initiatives should be taken seriously and not be ignored when examining environmental education policy.

From a policy perspective, an important conclusion is that greater attention should be given to these school initiatives as a forum for creating practical awareness on environmental issues amongst the youth. To this end, the National Action Plan for the Environment would be incomplete without the chapter on environmental education policy dwelling on school clubs. This policy will be expected to establish, co-ordinate, supervise and guide the activities of these school environmental initiatives. Such a policy should equally address the problems of inadequate finance, teaching and learning materials, in-service training of the teaching core especially club co-ordinators, as well as encourage the growth and development of environmental education departments in the teacher training colleges and higher institutions of learning in the country.

References

Chikelem, D., 2001, The Methodology for Civic and Environmental Education (A Cross-curricula Approach for Teachers of Primary, Secondary and Post-secondary Schools).

Fonkeng, E.G. and Tamajong, E., 1996, 'Integrating the environment in Educational planning: some proposals', in OSCISCA Working Paper No. 26 of January 1996, Yaoundé.

Living Earth, 1998, *The Foundation Unit: Beyond Talk*, London: Living Earth.

Living Earth, 1998, *Environmental Education in Action*, London: Living Earth.

Minang, P.A., 1997, 'Environmental Education in Cameroon: Can it Elicit Environmentally correct Behaviour?', *Cameroon Post* Newspaper, 9 February, 1997, p. 5.

Motaze, A., 1989, 'Perception de l'environnement au Cameroun', Department Seminar, CRESS, Yaoundé.

Ngome, M., n.d., 'Environmental Education in Cameroon: Problems and Prospects', unpublished Mimeograph.

Nsobe, E.M., 1996, 'Running A School Environmental Club', *Cameroon Post* Newspaper, 28 July , p. 5.

Obasi, M. N., 1996, 'Towards an Environmental Management Policy in Cameroon', *Cameroon Post* Newspaper, 20 August 1996, p. 5.

Vukenkeng, A.W., 1997, 'Financing A School Environmental Club', *Cameroon Post* Newspaper, 28 July 1997, p. 5.

Vukenkeng, A.W., 1997, 'Beyond School Environmental Clubs', *Cameroon Post* Newspaper, 28 July 1997, p. 5.

Vukenkeng, A.W., 1997, 'Greening Bamenda: The Responsibility of the youth', Cameroon *Post* Newspaper, July 1997, p. 5.

Vukenkeng, A.W., 1997, 'Domestic Animals become Environmental Enemies in Kumbo, Nso', *Cameroon Post* Newspaper, 8 April 1997, p. 5.

Vukenkeng, A.W., 1997, 'Man Everywhere but no water in Kumbo', Cameroon *Post* Newspaper, 28-30 April 1997, p. 5.

Vukenkeng, A.W., 1998, 'Environmental sustainability: A pre-requisite for sustainable Economic growth', in proceedings of North West Economic s Teachers Association (NOWETA) seminar of 6-7 February 1998 at P.C.H.S Mankon, Bamenda, Cameroon.

Vukenkeng, A.W., 1998, 'German family introduces an alternative to the Eucalyptus tree in Kishong', *Cameroon Post* Newspaper, April 1998, p. 9.

Vukenkeng, A.W., 1998, 'Generate income from refuse', *La voix du paysan* Newspaper, No. 33, April 1998.

Vukenkeng, A.W., 2002, 'Introductory concepts in Environmental Economics for Secondary Schools', in *Economic Focus*: A publication of NOWETA Bui chapter, Cameroon.

Vukenkeng, A.W., 2002, 'Environmental Protection as A Policy objective in Cameroon', in *Economic Focus*: A publication of NOWETA Bui chapter, Cameroon.

Vukenkeng, A.W., 2002, 'The Experience of the Triple Strategy of learning during the Excursion to the Korup National Park', in the Environmental Education journal of the CBC - PCC - EED -EZE, In-service Training Programme.

8

From Village to National and Global Art: Whose Art?*

Walter Nkwi

Introduction

Histories of art inevitably reflect the minds and feelings of authors, who are almost as diverse as the artists about whom they write and create. Works of art in general are more than aesthetically pleasing objects, more than feats of manual skill and ingenuity. They deepen our insight into others and ourselves; they sharpen our awareness of our own and other moods of thought and religious creeds; they enlarge our comprehension of alternative and often alien ways of life. They help us to understand and explore our own nature (Honour and Fleming 1995). Some works of art, especially of Africa, reflect the soul of the people; it is their 'god' and the fortunes as well as the misfortunes of the society are attributed to the 'raggedness/happiness' of a work of art. Different meanings therefore, and different definitions, have been given to works of art by various authors. What cuts across all these meanings is the universal consumption of the works of art.

For a while the study of African art was carried out on iconographical level, but today that same study could be read as an historical phenomenon (William 1966: 59–74). More often than not the works studied had moral and religious undertones (Davidson and Buah 1965:159). The statues of African art are or were often carved to honour ancestors, kings and gods. Art served a function in society and if it was divorced from its function, it lost a part of its meaning. In being thus linked to religion, African art was not different in content from the art of all other peoples who lived in an age of faith (see Williams 1966:63; Harris 1987:37; Ki-Zerbo 1978:22–23; Thomas 1995:3–10; Nettle 1987:46–79; Fichner-Rathus 1992; 1; Mary Ann-Frese et al. 1993:200).

The European incursion on the African continent led to looting of African works of art, which included the theft of *Afo-a-kom* in 1966, from the Kom *fondom* of the North West Province of Cameroon. The *Afo-a-kom* literally means the '*Kom* thing' and measures 64 inches high. Its face is smeared with copper. It holds a sceptre of power and stands behind a throne. It also has an embroidered crown made of the same material. The exhibition of the phallus not only stresses sex but also seems to point to lineage and tribal continuity, as well as fertility, which the Kom people hold in high esteem. Its three toes signify the Kom motto which is 'child, food and prosperity'.

The kom *fondom* is one of the largest in the North West province of Cameroon - popularly known in colonial historiography as the Bamenda grassfields (Chilver and Kaberry 1967 and 1968; Nkwi 1976; Fanso 1989; DeVries 1991). Like most West African Kingdoms (*fondoms*) in the nineteenth century (Forde and Kaberry 1967:1-260), Kom expanded from its Laikom nucleus to incorporate ten 'vassal states' – Baiso, Mejang, Mejung, Mbengkas, Achain, Ake, Ajung, Mbesinaku, Mbueni and Baicham (The Author 1976). In order to hold these incorporated states intact, Fon Yuh (1865–1912) carved the *Afo-a-kom* - an almost life-size figure which he bestowed with sacred qualities. This was because the incorporation of these 'satellite states' was his handiwork. By so doing he succeeded in making the Kom and these vassalages look up to the *Afo-a-kom* as their very existence, their symbol of unity, their very heart and soul. It also legitimised Fon Yuh. In the local context he was an imperialist who aimed at building an empire. When the Germans attempted to subjugate the Kom in 1905 he ferociously retaliated and humiliated them (Kiawi 2001).

In 1966 *Afo-a-kom* was stolen from its storage sanctuary and was 'mysteriously' spirited away by thieves using a highly organised system of logistics 'that included Land Rovers, trucks and air planes' (*Times Magazine* 5 November 1973). The Kom wept at the loss of their 'God' and the consequences of its absence were telling in the *fondom*. The news in 1973 that it had been found in the United States of America and was to be conveyed home to Kom was greeted with much euphoria and vivacity. This paper revisits this commonly told story but focuses on the relationship between art and such ideologies as unity, nation building and regional identity. The paper draws inspiration from the theft of the *Afo-a-kom* to conclude that African works of art could be used to achieve nationhood. However, before we embark on achieving this goal, it is crucially relevant to revisit some of the existing literature on the *Afo-a-kom*.

Afo-a-kom in Literature

Tamara (1984) handles *Afo-a-kom* within the context of the art of Cameroon. He makes an inventory of some of the works of art found in the Kom *fondom*. Tamara (1973) focuses the royal art of the Bamenda Tikar in general. Here, the *Afo-a-kom* and its companions are shown. In these two works the theft of the

Afo-a-kom is passively treated. Brasch and Schneider (1974) describe the complexities involved in trying to retrieve the *Afo-a-kom* from the diaspora. They also explore the role of the western press in the return of the statue.

Burnham (1974) describes how the *Afo-a-kom* was stolen, how it wandered and how it came back to the Kom people (its original home). According to him, the *Afo-a-kom* is the 'sacred Idol' of Kom. Ellis (1974) gives an eyewitness account of the homecoming of the *Afo-a-kom* in the *National Geographic*. Like Burham, he sees *Afo-a-kom* as 'sacred'. Ferretti (1975) dwells lengthily on the Kom ancestral land and the exile, rescue and return of *Afo-a-kom*. He concludes his book with Cameroon Art and a postscript in which he provides a descriptive analysis. His work, quite journalistic in nature, was a source of great inspiration to me. Shanklin (1976) chronicles the 'odyssey of the *Afo-a-kom*' in which she gives the American and Kom versions of the story about the idol. She treats the *Afo-a-kom* alongside other idols in the Kom palace and disagrees with Ferretti's journalistic version about Kom, Cameroon and the statue itself, a point with which I strongly disagree. The Author (1975) handles *Afo-a-kom* as 'the return of a stolen god'. As the title suggests, he specifically treats the return of the *Afo-a-kom*. He has one principal informant, Bobe Jonny Ngong, whose eyewitness account leads him to the conclusions that he makes in the work. The Author (1976) mentions *Afo-a-kom* in a footnote and in relation to a carving school which was opened by Fon Yuh, the creator of *Afo-a-kom*. In his other work with Warnier (1982), they also mention the *Afo-a-kom* as a symbol of great achievement of Fon Yuh. Greenfield (1996) shows how sometimes cultural property is returned after requests have been made through diplomatic channels. She cites the example of the *Afo-a-kom* which was returned after a formal request was made by the Cameroon government.

From these works, the authors have handled the *Afo-a-kom* saga from journalistic and informative perspectives. As far as linking the *Afo-a-kom* to the themes of unity and regional identity is concerned, very little has been done. Neither has the scientific dynamics surrounding the theft of the *Afo-a-kom* nor the *Afo-a-kom* after 30 years has been given adequate attention. As a result, this paper will attempt to open these yet unopened pages. It will critically examine how the pivot of the Kom 'nation' - *Afo-a-kom* - was stolen from its village shrine and became national and global art. To whom then did it belong? Implicitly, the paper also attempts to show how African works of art could be used to forge nationhood; an enigmatic dilemma to most African leaders and political theorists who still hold that nationhood can be decreed. By so doing the enquiry will add meaning to the *Afo-a-kom*. The objective here is not to debunk the conclusions drawn by the various sociologists, anthropologists and journalists cited above in its entirety. Rather, it attempts to explore the theft of *Afo-a-kom* with particular attention given to the relationship between art and themes such as unity, nation building and regional identity.

The crisis of identity, belonging and citizenship in the last decade of twentieth century Cameroon needs further elucidation. The year 1990 saw the invention of new forms of ethnicity in Cameroon in the form of 'autochthony' and 'allogenes' where some citizens were branded as 'sons of the soil' while others were branded as 'strangers'. Cameroon is made up of ten provinces and more than 250 ethnic groups. In the South West Province, an umbrella political elite association that was formed in the 1990s with the complicity of the ruling party excluded 'non-natives' of the province. Consequently, descendants of migrants whose birthplace was not the South West Province found themselves in the cold. The Southwest province was not an exception. In the other nine provinces of Cameroon the issue of citizenship, strangers and belonging was equally questioned. This was instigated by the indigenous political elite who felt that the influence of strangers/migrants in their municipalities would derail their victory in elections. It had happened in the 1992 Municipal elections and on the eve of the 1996 elections, the constitution was revised. This constitution explicitly and tacitly mentioned in the preamble and in article 57,3 – the state's 'obligation to protect minorities and preserve the rights of indigenous populations', moreover, it requires that chairpersons of each regional council 'shall be an indigene of the Region' while its '…. Bureau shall reflect the sociological components of the region.'

The 1972 constitution had apparently been a sharp contrast to the 1996 constitution. Its preamble stated that:

> The people of Cameroon, proud of its cultural and linguistic diversity… profoundly are of the imperative need to achieve complete unit, solemnly declares that it constitutes one and the same nation, committed to the same destiny, and affirms its unshakeable determination to construct the Cameroonian fatherland on the basis of the ideal of fraternity, justice and progress… Everyone has the right to settle in any place and to move about freely… No one shall be harassed because his origin.

This shows the level of unity in Cameroon in 1972. By November 1973 the *Afo-a-kom* was identified more on the basis of 'symbol of unity'. The 1996 constitution replaced this emphasis on the rights of every national citizen by an emphatic respect for the rights of 'minorities' and 'indigenes' (Geschiere 2001:98). These latter terms have a specific background worth revisiting here. These words are borrowed from the discourse of the World Bank which since the 1980s has increasingly stressed the need to protect 'disappearing cultures'. According to the World Bank parlance 'minorities' and 'indigenes' refer, for instance, to 'pygmies', hunters and gatherers or even to pastoralists. In Cameroon these words were given a sharp twist in content and meaning by political elites. This was in order to win elections at all cost and remain in power.

This paper appears at a time when this crisis of identity, belonging and citizenship has engrossed the attention of historians, sociologists, anthropologists, political scientists, religious leaders and 'jacks-of-all-trades' in Cameroon and beyond (See Mamdani 1996; Nyamnjoh and Nkwi 1997; Jua 1997; Konings and Nyamnjoh 1997, 2000, 2003). It is therefore hoped that it will tickle constitutional theorists about the vanity of decreeing identity, belonging and citizenship more especially because *Afo-a-kom* once acted as a symbol of identity not only to the Kom, but also to Cameroon and America. In so doing, perhaps constitutionalists may draw inspiration from it and correct the obnoxious 1996 constitution in Cameroon which nakedly branded some citizens as autochthons and others as allogenes. They might draw the lesson or they might neglect it, but the choice of the latter will be at their own peril.

The paper is structured as follows. After the general introduction, there is a literature review which is in turn followed by a description of the methodology of data collection. It then looks at the definition and purpose of African art before highlighting the various myths that surround *Afo-a-kom*. The next section focuses the *Afo-a-kom* in the 'diaspora' and its impact on the *fondom*. The peregrination of *Afo-a-kom* from America back home constitutes the subject of the following section. The last section centres on the *Afo-a-kom*: a thing of the Kom; a thing of Cameroon or a thing of America: Whose art?; *Afo-a-kom* after thirty years.

Methodology of Data Collection

The data that served as input to this paper came from two sources: primary and secondary. Primary data were collected from a sample of local actors who were at least 30 years old and were selected through a systematic random sampling technique in the Kom *fondom* where the impact of the *Afo-a-kom* was most felt. Two techniques were used here: observation and interview. We observed that the story of the *Afo-a-kom* was received by every Kom indigene irrespective of the age group with a lot of emotion and that there was some sense of pride among the Kom people when they talked about the theft and return of their invaluable god. It was fascinating how united the people were because of a work of art which most of the people had never even seen and whose creator had died long ago. We equally realised that non-Kom indigenes especially of the Grassland area talked boastfully of the *Afo-a-kom* to assert the greatness of the Grassland culture. Non-grasslander Cameroonians often made reference to it to assert the greatness of the Cameroonian culture and heritage. Then it dawned on us that a single work of art could actually give a group of people a sense of belonging. To collect more data, to prove our hypothesis, we carried out a number of interviews in which we asked open-ended questions that would help us determine the place of works of art in a society which is riddled with divisive tendencies. Secondary data were collected from books and articles in libraries and archives.

Definition and Purpose of African Art

According to Hugh Honour and John Fleming (1995), most works of African art were created for a purpose, whether religious, social, political or exceptionally, to express the artist's inner vision. Fichner-Rathus (1992: 3-24) suggests the following purposes of African art: to create beauty; to provide decoration; to reveal the truth; to immortalise; to express religious values; to express fantasy; to record and commemorate experience; to reflect the social and cultural context; to protest injustice and raise consciousness; to elevate the commonplace. In the context of this paper *Afo-a-kom* exemplified the raising of consciousness while at the same time it played a religious role in the Kom *fondom.*

Works of art such as the Altar of the Hand, Benin, illustrate the skill with which the Benin manipulated bronze, as well as the importance of symbolism to their art. The many figures, which have been cast in relief around the circumference of this small work, are meant to venerate the king and glorify his divine office. The king is the central figure in both the relief and in the freestanding figures on top of the altar. He holds the staffs of his office in his hands and his head is larger than those of his attendants. (Fichner-Rathus (1992: 472-478). The centrality of this configuration points to the fact that Benin art symbolised unity and sacredness. The population looked up to this art for guidance.

In the seventeenth Century Osei Tutu and his friend Okomfo Anokye worked together using a 'golden stool' to forge the heterogeneous Akan groups into a cohesive strong union. Basil Davidson (1977: 242-243) vividly captures the situation in the following words:

> Okomfo Anokye declared that he had a mission from Nyame, supreme god of the Akan. Nyame, he declared, had ordered him to make the Asante into a great people. To spread this message the new Asante ruler, Osei Tutu who was working closely with Anokye called a vast assembly of people. At this gathering Okomfo Anokye brought down from the sky a wooden stool that was partly covered in gold causing this stool to come to rest on Osei Tutu's knees. Having done this, Okomfo Anokye announced that the golden stool contained the soul or spirit of the whole Asante people. He told the chiefs and people that their power and health, bravery and welfare, were all symbolized in this stool and the chiefs and people accepted this. (Also see Ayittey 1992:49; Fage 1969:169; Webster and Boahen 1980:85; Ajayi and Crowder 1976:25).

The above quotation is an eloquent and classic illustration of how Osei Tutu and Anokye used a work of art (the Golden Stool) to convince people that it was their soul. 'All these states recognized the Golden stool created by Osei Tutu as the symbol of their soul and unity, the king of Kumasi state or division (Oman) as their paramount king or Asantehene, and all of them recognized the great oath... ' (Webster and Boahen 1980:85). By so doing the incongruous Asante empire was united. When the chiefs and the peoples gave their recognition, Osei Tutu then began to make laws for the Asante groups, who were thus welded into a union and among the first of his laws was one of common citizenship which forbade anyone to speak about any of the old separate histories of the now united groups (Davidson 1977:243).

By the same token, Fon Yuh (1865–1912) of the Kom *fondom* of the North West Province of Cameroon carved the *Afo-a-kom.* It is not known exactly when he did so but speculation suggests that it was after he had incorporated assorted 'peoples' into the *fondom.* The main purpose of *Afo-a-kom* was to hold these vassal states in a union. The *Afo-a-kom, ab initio* acted as a symbol of unity, the god and soul of the Kom. If African works of art played a religious role as well as a unifying one, as the story of the Golden Stool illustrates, the *Afo-a-kom* was no exception. To fully appreciate this role it will be necessary to look at the various myths concerning the statue before considering its meaning.

The Myths Surrounding *Afo-a-kom*

The various myths and/or versions surrounding the *Afo-a-kom* were gathered during fieldwork in the year 2002 and the first half of 2003. These versions were as follows.

Version One

Afo-a-kom was carved by Fon Yu (1865-1912), the most powerful ruler of Kom. The Fon was supposed to see it once in his lifetime. If he saw it twice he was going to embrace death. Fon Nsom Ngwe saw it twice and had to die.[1]

Version Two

When *Afo-a-kom* was stolen in 1966, Fon Alo'o Ndiforgu died shortly thereafter. Its theft heralded hunger, increasing deaths, and impotency and infertility became the order of the day in kom.[2]

Version Three

The short reign of James Yibain (1989-1994) was because the theft, and the suffering of *Afo-a-kom* in the United States was attributed to him.[3]

Version Four

During the annual traditional dances, which took place every January, sacrifices were offered in honour of *Afo-a-kom* with the belief that it would cleanse the *fondom* of many ills. This explains why during the absence of the statue, there was no annual dance for seven years.[4]

Version Five

The Fon never slept during the absence of *Afo-a-kom* and this was attributed to the theft of 'the heart of kom'. There were times during this period that the predecessor of the Fon, Fon Ngam, used to mysteriously appear to the Fon, Fon Nsom Ngwe, playing his guitar (*ilung*) asking the whereabouts of the Afo-a-kom.[5]

Version Six

During this period (1966–1973) many traditional council sessions in Laikom (capital of Kom) failed or ended prematurely either through infighting or quarrelling because of the absence of the Afo-a-kom.[6]

Version Seven

Hunting was unsuccessful, with not much game being obtained, especially in the royal hunt often known as *Ibyem-I-kwifoyn*.[7]

Version Eight

The *Afo-a-kom* was our 'god'. Many good things happened to us. But during its absence with continuous tribulations in the *fondom* the kom were led to invite somebody from Bambui to carve *Afo-a-kom*. Of course things did not work as well.[8]

A Critique of the Interviews

The discourses provided by the local actors/observers concerning the *Afo-a-kom* saga cannot be taken uncritically. First of all we shall assume that these myths were true and thus accept them. Yet a scientific diagnosis of the myths reveals that the Kom were perhaps infatuated with their wooden statue. For instance, it is quite debatable that birthrates were reduced and high death rates were recorded. A visit to the archives of the four main maternity homes in the *fondom* shows that between 1966 and 1973 there was an increase in birthrates by at least 10 percent. I was born in 1967, (one year after the theft of the *Afo-a-kom*) and my two younger brothers were also born before 1973. This is just a tip of an iceberg to show that birthrate never reduced within this period. A similar visit to the archives of the health centres in the *fondom* revealed that those who died within this period were aged and therefore were likely to die. From this we can conclude that any increase in the overall percent of the death rates within this period was negligible.

Furthermore, to say that the fon was not to see the *Afo-a-kom* twice, still provokes further debate. *Afo-a-kom* was carved by Fon Yuh and for him to have decreed that a fon could not see it twice in his life time as a fon is quite doubtful. Yet many observers felt that Fon Nsom Ngwe saw it twice-when he was installed and in 1973 when it returned from America, thus leading to his death in 1974. It is quite difficult if not impossible to prove that he died because he had seen the statue twice. Yet he had seen it. As at 1974, the fon was well above 70 years and considering the fact that African life expectancy age limit is about 60 years and considering the fact that he travelled from Laikom to Yaounde by land at his age, it could therefore be concluded that the fon died because he was aged and stressed rather than the fact that he had seen the *Afo-a-kom* twice.

Further debates and controversies are provoked when impotence/fertility as well as the death of fon Alo'o Ndiforgu are mentioned. Scientifically, impotence is a situation in which somebody is unable to have full sex or an orgasm, while infertility is the act of being unable to reproduce. These scientific connotations make the centrality of the *Afo-a-kom* with regards to impotence and infertility incomprehensible. The death of fon Ndiforgu could be attributed to two issues. First, he was quite old. As he was born c. 1880 and ruled from (1954–1966) it could be logically concluded that at a ripe age of 86 he must have gladly met his death. Second, he was the fon who witnessed the *Anlu* women revolution of 1958-61 in which all the 'state institutions' were abused and the fon was constantly called by name thereby breaking a *fondom*'s taboo.

The absence of annual dances in the *fondom* could be attributed to a shift in the belief systems and a change in attitudes of most of the Kom towards traditional institutions. The change in attitude will be fully examined elsewhere in this paper. What should be noted here is the fact that 'westernisation' rather than the absence of the *Afo-a-kom* could have caused the absence of annual dances. After all, many informants told me that after the return of the *Afo-a-kom*, annual dances never took place again. The appearance of a dead fon playing a guitar is more of the minority Kom view who still believe in life after death than the absence of the *Afo-a-kom* in the *fondom*. By the way, no one ever testified that he ever saw him. Every one heard so.

The issue of hunger is more psychic than real. Universally, natural forces such as drought and floods cause hunger. It could also be caused by the attitude of people towards farming. This means that laziness could have caused hunger. The situation in the Kom *fondom* between 1966 and 1973 never revealed the contrary. There was drought which lasted less than one year. For the most part the Kom had developed a lazy attitude towards farming since to a very large extent, they believed and trusted so much in the *Afo-a-kom*. Even the poor catch in game could have been attributed to the tactlessness of the hunters and their dogs. Instead, the Kom saw this as the absence of the *Afo-a-kom* in the *fondom*. The bottom line fact about all these discourses shows how infatuated the Kom had been with their god. It also shows how ritualistic *Afo-a-kom* had become to the Kom. To further elucidate how infatuated the Kom were, *Afo-a-kom* was stolen not by a foreigner but a Kom. What surrounded this theft is what the next part of this paper will turn to.

Scientific Dynamics Surrounding the Theft of *Afo-a-kom*

The issue at stake here is why the *Afo-a-kom* was stolen despite its presumption ascendant role in the *fondom*, and assuming that James Yibain stole it. That it was even stolen by a Kom reveals the minority view that the *Afo-a-kom* was not a god. The nineteenth century saw European penetration into the Bamenda grasslands (Moisel 1913:150, Hunt 1925: para.18-21; Hawkesworth 1924: para.9-10; Chilver 1966. The Germans were taking the lead (Rudin 1938). They were in search of labour for their plantations. A by-product of this main objective was the introduction of a new form of exchange, money. With the introduction of money almost everybody wanted to become a *nabob* (a very rich person). When the Germans were expelled from the territory in 1916 the British continued. The theft of the *Afo-a-kom* therefore was for pecuniary motives directly or indirectly.

The Europeans also came as researchers and missionaries to the Kom fondom. The missionary effect on the Kom *fondom* was quite subversive given the fact that its creed as well as preaching saw a shift from indigenous cultural practices towards 'a western oriented one' (see DeVries 1998; 38-68). The cultural allegiance, which some Kom people had for the *Afo-a-kom* dwindled and *ipso facto,* did not command the respect that it had before colonialism. They saw it simply as a 'piece of wood' rather than the 'god' or 'soul' of the fondom. This permitted its theft. But *Afo-a-kom* could only have been sold if there was a demand for it. Here the role of European researchers becomes pivotal.

The researchers had possibly seen the *Afo-a-kom* during some of the annual dances in January and taken pictures of the statue. More to this, the fon used to give out to them some tokens of works of art. In return the researchers would give some money or fancy goods to the fon. This courtesy aroused the appetite of the retainers or palace guards. When the Europeans demanded the *Afo-a-kom* in place of a ransom Yibain tipped Yuh Ndi who was nearest to the sanctuary. In the night of 1966 they stepped into the shrine and the *Afo-a-kom* was folded in a mat and head loaded to Fundong (the administrative headquarters of Kom situated 6 km from Laikom) where a standby Land Rover whisked it away into the diaspora. The fascinating pictures were sent back to Europe and its sight alongside some Cameroonian works of art attracted dealers. This subsequently led to the theft of the *Afo-a-kom*. The demand of the *Afo-a-kom* by European/American art dealers and the supply by the Kom interacted, thereby leading to its theft.

It is a paradox that 'our god' was stolen by some of us. What comes out from all these, is the fact that the *Afo-a-kom* was an embodiment of Kom itself. It was the 'God' of Kom *fondom*. This was corroborated by Paul Gebauer (1975:26), who lived and worked with Kom people as a missionary and an anthropologist. He had this to say:

> The heartbeat of dynamic religion throbs in Cameroon art. Kom was and the *Afo-a-kom* was no exception... It is in the Sculpture that we meet the

> greatest variety of expression and find so much that is of first quality. It is important to note the dynamic function of the object is primary, its form secondary.

From these words the importance of the *Afo-a-kom* was hardly in doubt. But there is more to be added regarding the *Afo-a-kom*. 'To the people of Kom it was what the Declaration of Independence is to Americans, what the Magna Carta is to Englishmen, what a saintly relic is to Christians, what the Wall of Jerusalem is to Jews. It is at once religious, political, historical and social; it is the tangible symbol of the Kom nation – its one constant through decades of German and British invasion and subjugation; it is the rock that the changes forced upon this nation by Catholic and Baptist missionaries could not dislodge' (Ferretti 1975:6).

In the context of all these shifts there was an honest and sincere sense of loss in the Kom nation, the village identification had crumbled. The heart and the blood vessels of the *fondom* had been removed when the *Afo-a-kom* was pilfered from its storage in 1966.

Afo-a-kom in the Diaspora, 1966–1973

The years 1966 to 1973 were those of frustration and disillusionment in the Kom *fondom* following the theft of *Afo-a-kom*. Persons suspected of contributing to the theft of the statue were interrogated, intimidated and beaten up by the police. They included Samuel Tufoin, Ngam Njam, Yuh Ndi and James Yibain.[10] All of them had a close relationship with the palace. There were, as well, much bad feelings between the suspects, accused and accusers; victims and victimizers. While in the field, informants attested to the fact that total darkness descended on the *fondom* and people were at a loss, and every mishap was attributed to the absence of *Afo-a-kom*: the *fon* was never sleeping; there was poor harvest, there were many more deaths, the royal hunting was not as fruitful as before.[11]

Two important issues emerge from the above discussion. The first one concerns the mishaps of the *fondom*, which were entirely attributed to the loss of the *Afo-a-kom*. This is an indication that works of African art in general and *Afo-a-kom* in particular created consciousness, identity and nationhood among the Kom people. They always felt rightly or wrongly that the *Afo-a-kom* protected them as their 'god' but now that it had been stolen, anything bad in the kingdom was seen and interpreted in terms of its absence.

The second issue deals with the police investigation, the intimidation and the beatings of suspects. Ahidjo's government saw the *Afo-a-kom* not from the perspective of a Kom cultural artefact but from that of Cameroon as a nation, and took upon itself the responsibility to safeguard this cultural heritage. *Afo-a-kom* had been gradually passing into an emblem of national art. Nevertheless, it was central that one could first identify *Afo-a-kom* as a Kom possession rather than a national treasure.

With the prevailing general unrest, it was believed that no amount of sacrifices could sanctify the *fondom* in the absence of *Afo-a-kom*. Likewise it was believed that the offering of sacrifices without the *Afo-a-kom* would be useless.[12] Despite the fact that many informants saw this mishap through the prism of *Afo-a-kom*'s absence, Shanklin (1976:70) holds the contrary. According to her there were instead high birth and low death rates, a point that provokes further research..

The apotheosis of disillusion with regards to the absence of *Afo-a-kom* was reached in October 1968. The Kom believed they could never regain their stolen 'god'.

Consequently, they went to Bambui – a border *fondom* with Kom and hired a carver, Robert Toh. His job was to carve a substitute.[13] After carving it; it was rejected for several reasons. It lacked the symbol covering of beads as the original. Second, it had not been honoured with sacrifices. The Kom further claimed that no living artist in Kom was talented enough to make such a carving and that the original one was needed in the *fondom*.

When the *Afo-a-kom* went into the diaspora, in America, Aaron Furman took it to his gallery. It was later installed in the museum of African art in the United States. While here it drew wide attention and became an object of exhibition as one of the most important pieces of African art. One must ask here whether it was a Kom thing, a Cameroonian or an American thing? It is logical to say that the *Afo-a-kom* had assumed a global dimension. This can be further illustrated by the fact that in April 1973, it was the central piece of exhibition in a Dartmouth College of Art exhibition (Ferretti 1975:45). The pivotal issue that surrounded this exhibition was identity. Francis Nkuo, a member of the Kom elite contacted the Cameroonian Embassy, identified the *Afo-a-kom* and thus informed and thereby initiated its discovery for those in Cameroon who had always cherished it (*Washington Post* 1973:5).

The general cry in Kom and the world was that the *Afo-a-kom* should be brought back. Sympathisers in the United States questioned the morality of American ownership of it. According to the director of galleries at Dartmouth College, Churchill Lathrop, 'If I personally owned it my conscience would be bothering me a great deal. But there is a little different situation here... isn't the real villain the man who smuggled it out' (*Time Magazine*, October 1973).

Apart from the concerned Americans there was a deeper feeling elsewhere regarding why *Afo-a-kom* should be returned. The year 1973 was the climax of two related issues, which kept the American government on her toes. The first was the Watergate Scandal that brought the government of Richard Nixon to near collapse. The second was the protracted Vietnam War, which equally jeopardised the American government. The fact that the press (in both Cameroon and America) was taking a keen interest in the *Afo-a-kom* caused enough of a stir to lead the Americans to return *Afo-a-kom* to its base. What was more important was the fact that under the auspices of the United Nations agency UNESCO, in the early 1970s, the concept of the restitution of cultural property began to crystalise. This revolved around two basic issues; the removal of such property as a result of the previous colonisation of a newly independent state, and the issue of the continued elicit worldwide traffic in art treasures (Greenfield 1996: 185).

Following the UNESCO convention to return cultural works of art Belgium sent back at least forty objects to Zaire; in 1973, the Brooklyn museum returned a stela fragment stolen from the Piedras Negras to Guatemala in 1974. The National museum of New Zealand, Wellington, by informal arrangement returned a mask to Papua New Guinea Museum, Port Moresby (Greenfield 1996:261-262). What is important is that these cultural works were returned through intergovernmental or institutional negotiation and domestic legal suits. But the return of *Afo-a-kom* was an exception. It was finally returned after a request had been made through diplomatic channels (Greenfield 1996:273)

The 'Long March' of *Afo-a-kom* from New York to Laikom via Yaounde and Bamenda

The journey of the *Afo-a-kom* to Kom involved some key personalities whose roles were pivotal. These figures included Craig Kinzelman and Evan Schneider, and various personalities in the Cameroon Embassy in the U.S. Craig Kinzelman, an American Peace Corps Volunteer who worked in the Bamenda grasslands started the crusade for the return of the *Afo-a-kom* by contacting the American Ambassador and some leading Cameroonian government officials. Through his efforts there was widespread pressure to return the statue (*Time Magazine* November 1973: 1).

Gilbert and Evans Schneider, who considered Kom to be their second home because they had lived in Kom for a very long time, also played a tremendous role in seeing to it that the *Afo-a-kom* was returned. Gilbert Schneider on the one hand provided photos of the *Afo-a-kom*, the kom people and the royal compound. All these were used by the *Times* as follow-ups surrounding the status of the *Afo-a-kom*. When he attended an African art conference of the Hampton Institute in New York in 1968 he was shocked to learn about the presence of *Afo-a-kom* in America. He said:

> I could hardly believe it... I knew of course how fantastically powerful a piece it was, a functioning piece... Although I was amazed to see it there because I knew what it meant to the Kom and the *Fon*, it hurts me too. To have such a piece removed is quite unusual. I felt especially something that meant so much to a people. (Ferretti 1975:70).

These words of Schneider underline the importance and fame of the *Afo-a-kom*. According to him it was impossible to accept that the *Afo-a-kom* was out of Kom.

He had worked with the Kom and knew the fame and importance of the *Afo-a-kom* to them. Oral tradition holds that his brother, Evans Schneider, was the first in Kom to know the whereabouts of the *Afo-a-kom.* Working with Kinzelman they impressed on the international community the unrest in the kom *fondom* as a result of its absence (*Times* 1973:6).

If the *Afo-a-kom* finally returned, the efforts of Thaddeus Nkuo, Johnson Ndimsi and Ambassador Francois Xavier Tschoungui, all of Cameroon Embassy in Washington ought to be applauded. Nkuo, above all, a son of Kom, had worked to ensure its return. He declared that the *Afo-a-kom* was something which money could not buy. Back in Kom there were great preparations for the return of their god. According to most informants life would go back to normal if the *Afo-a-kom* returned home. The euphoria and conviviality of its return invigorated the fon and his council, *kwifon*, who decided at a meeting held at Laikom, the capital of Kom, on the 28 of November 1973 that money would be offered to have the *Afo-a-kom* returned. 'If the money is not enough, we will give him anything he asks for' (*Times* October 1973:4). One wonders how much the people of Kom would have raised to have the *Afo-a-kom* flown to Cameroon. Of course, the statement simply illustrated the importance of the *Afo-a-kom* to the Kom *fondom.*

On 10 December 1973, *Afo-a-kom* left New York for Cameroon. On the eve of its departure a buffet party was held at the Cameroon Embassy and the Cameroon Ambassador to America, Francois Xavier Tschoungui played host, and addressed the *Afo-a-kom* in the following words:

> As for you, eternal tranquility,
> Return hence to your ancestral land.
> Return hence to look after the dead and living.
> You symbol of love and unity, be forgetful of Upheaval and blasphemy.
> Your sojourn here has been nothing
> But a nightmare which will soon vanish.
> Forever forget your uncomfortable appearance
> In this sophisticated technology whose
> Achievements turn to overlook human
> Consideration. Return. (Ferretti 1975:3; *Washington Post*, November 1973:2).

The Ambassador viewed the *Afo-a-kom* as eternal in its functions, thereby acknowledging it as a 'god' who was the custodian of the living and the dead. The words 'unity and diversity' had some added importance, which cannot be taken uncritically. From the onset the *Afo-a-kom* was carved to maintain the unity of a heterogeneous *fondom.* Kom was and is made up of Mbueni, Baiso, Mbengkas etc. that are not Kom speaking but considered to be part of the *fondom.* This means that the *Afo-a-kom*'s cardinal purpose was to maintain the unity of the *fondom* and thus remain as a Kom thing. On the other hand, the Ambassador's speech could be viewed as a 'government slogan' (Shanklin 1975:63). Cameroon is made up of approximately 250 ethnic groups. After 1961 President Amadou Ahidjo's main objective was to forge national unity in a diverse cultural milieu. He 'achieved' this objective on 20 May 1972 through a referendum (see Ngoh 1996). What comes out from all these, is the way that Tschoungui use the *Afo-a-kom* as a symbol of 'Love' and 'unity'. He did not see the *Afo-a-kom* as belonging to the Kom but rather as belonging to Cameroon as a nation. This is more plausible because he was representing Cameroon and not Kom. Implicitly the *Afo-a-kom* was carved to maintain unity in a diversified Kom *fondom*. What is even surprising is that he did not pronounce the word 'Kom' in all his speech. The *Afo-a-kom* was therefore a Cameroonian thing. Identity and consciousness was near complete.

The *Afo-a-kom* arrived in Yaounde on 10 December 1973 and was displayed in the National Tourist office. While in Yaounde a controversy arose as to where it should be kept - Yaounde or Laikom. According to the Minister of Information and Culture, Vroumsi Tchinaye, *Afo-a-kom* was to remain in Yaounde because it belonged to Cameroon. Gussman and Robbins who had travelled from America with specific instructions to install the statue at Laikom were confused. The *fon* of Kom, Nsom Ngwe, however, brought them out of their psychic quagmire by telling the Minister that he would bring all the Kom people to live in Yaounde.[14] The *Fon*'s statement ended all controversy and on 11 December the Cameroonian Airforce Cariban plane flew to Bali, Bamenda, transporting the *Afo-a-kom*. From thence it was transported by road to Fundong and finally to Laikom.

While at Fundong, the Minister of Information and Culture told the people that '*Afo-a-kom* must now serve as a symbol of national unity... this statue though it originated here in Kom, no longer belongs only to the Kom tribe... it is now the property of Cameroonians'. This sudden interest expressed by the Cameroonian administration gave the Kom people both Kom speaking and non-Kom speaking some sense of pride and engendered some renewed sense of belonging, as everyone wanted to be identified with the origin of the statue. He also emphasised the government's respect for tribal tradition within the context of Cameroon national unity (see *Weekly Bulletin* No. 33/73, 1973). The Minister's 'unity' was not limited only to the Kom *fondom*. He had wanted the statue to stay in Yaounde and it can be deduced that the *Afo-a-kom* had taken on the trappings of a national emblem symbolising national unity. The issue of unity in this paper need further clarification. Unity with focus to the *Afo-a-kom* has two meanings: first, the *Afo-a-kom* was used by fon Yuh to hold the heterogeneous Kom *fondom* together. Second, the *Afo-a-kom* was used by the Cameroon authorities in 1973 to the effect that it symbolised national unity. In this sense National unity was re-emphasising what had been achieved in 1972 through the referendum in which 99.9 percent of the population voted for a unitary state. One of the effects of the 1972 referendum was the supplanting of the federal structures which were instituted in 1961 thereby giving birth to the united Republic of Cameroon. The United Republic of Cameroon broke down the federal Republic into seven provinces. In 1984 either by accident, design or political expediency, the name was shortened to Republic of Cameroon by a Presidential decree.

The immediate effect of this Decree was the birth of regional identity. The erstwhile West Cameroonians who are English speaking saw this as a way of marginalising them. This was because Republic of Cameroon reminded them of the former Republic of Cameroon that existed before Reunification in 1961. As a matter of fact since 1984, national integration has been jeopardised by ethno-regional jingoism, fanned and sustained by the state. The notion of national unity is ridiculed and people in the 1990s are overtly encouraged to demonstrate stronger loyalties to their ethno-regional or sub-national groups than to the Cameroon nation. Priority is given to belonging to a group first and the nation second and this state of affairs engenders the crisis of citizenship as full acceptability in one's fatherland suffers from a delimitation of a geo-ethnic order. It is only when the Cameroon national team is winning in a competition that all ethnic loyalties are submerged. The *Afo-a-kom* had emerged in 1973 and almost neutralised ethnic boundaries as insinuated in the speeches of Tsoungui and Tchinaye. To crown it all, it can be concluded that the *Afo-a-Kom* aroused nationalism in the sense that the cream of Cameroon's political elite expressed their wish that the *Afo-a-kom* return to Cameroon.

Again informants in the field testify to the fact that when *Afo-a-kom* was transported from Bali to Kom, school children, men and women, boys and girls came out in great numbers and lined up along the road.[15] Everybody appeared resplendent and there was great excitement and the firing of den guns filled the air. This was a simple proof that the *Afo-a-kom* had transcended tribal boundaries at least momentarily. It was not only the Kom who came out to receive their 'god' but people from Bali, Mankon, Babanki and Bambui including the minister's entourage from Yaounde. The *Afo-a-kom* had thus become a national art treasure.

The Place of *Afo-a-Kom* after Thirty Years

The whereabouts of the *Afo-a-kom* among the Kom today is not known. Most of the people in the field had doubts if the statue was in the *fondom* or not. While some accepted that it was in the palace and had never gone out since 1973, others denied and argued that since they heard that it went out for the second time in 1977 they do not know whether it has ever returned to the *fondom*. Yet others still claimed that the statue was in the village and could be given out, provided money was involved. Few people explained that after its return, the fon decided that the statue should remain in its sanctuary for sometime before it could come out. It was only to be seen by the *kwifon*, the second in command to the fon, who each day prepared different sets of purification rites designed to rid the *Afo-a-kom* of all the profane influences to which it was subjected during its seven years absence. Even after the purification rites, it was alleged that the annual dance had never been organised and *ipso facto* the statue had never been brought out.

The above opinions are quite interesting given the fact that this is a god whom the people attributed almost all the fortunes/misfortunes of the *fondom* to it. From these views, the fact that the position of the *Afo-a-kom* in Kom has changed cannot be denied. Change is a gradual and inevitable process. The change of attitude towards the *Afo-a-kom* never came as a bang but as a whimper. It was not abrupt but rather slow and at different times. From when it was carved till 1966, it commanded unalloyed respect. Between 1966 and 1973 the Kom mourned its absence and finally from 1973-2003 its importance and affection to the Kom had dwindled, waned and petered out.

Some people maintained that the statue had lost its value long before it was stolen. Others felt that it was after its theft or recovery that people lost confidence in it. Yet others saw Christianity as a major factor that necessitated the change. According to this school of thought, Christianity came up with ideas such as the belief in one God who made heaven and earth and who is the provider of life. Christianity also provided explanations to mysterious happenings, which people, with their traditional ideas, had never understood. These teachings catalysed by the absence of the *Afo-a-kom* in the *fondom* forced a majority of the people to change their belief in it.

Still, there were other people in Kom who have not changed and have even vowed never to betray their only god. It could be said here, that since change is gradual, these few may one day change or one day the community shall come to depend on the *Afo-a-kom* again.

Western education could also be advanced as one of the factors that necessitated the change of attitude towards the *Afo-a-kom*. This fact cannot be refuted because with the introduction of western education, many ignorant minds caused many parents to send their children to school to obtain the 'white man's way' of doing things. This gradually cystallised into the western educated elite who diverted from the aspects of their culture that failed to give them enough satisfaction. By doing so, the importance which they previously attached to the *Afo-a-kom* was substituted by the Almighty God, whom they believe was more supreme than their wooden statue.

The role of fon Yibain (1989-94) is equally important as far as the change of attitude towards the *Afo-a-kom* is concerned. Some informants described him as money minded fon who did not take pride in the *fondom*'s treasure and as a result caused the Kom to change their attitude towards their own god. As an heir apparent, he stole the *Afo-a*-kom and sold it to the Americans. When he came to the throne in 1989 he sold most of the carvings which accompanied the *Afo-a-kom* during the annual dances. These 'Kom things' as they were called, assisted the

Afo-a-kom in performing miracles as the Kom claimed. They were usually stored in the same hut and always came out together. But when Yibain came to power, he decided to make money by selling these things. This made the Kom to describe the *Afo-a-kom* as a 'bird without its wings.' Since its wings were clipped, it was certain that its powers had been reduced. The only alternative for the people was to look for another god who still had its powers and there was no other god which was more powerful than the white man's God.

From the above illustration it is logical to conclude that the *Afo-a-kom* after thirty years of arrival in the *fondom* from the diaspora has lost its intrinsic meaning to the Kom . It is nothing more than a piece of wood albeit the minority view, which still hold that the *Afo-a-kom* has not lost its importance. To the people of the North West province, and Cameroon in general, the *Afo-a-kom* has been reduced to a touristic figure.

Conclusion

This paper has highlighted the contrast between a Constitutional decree regarding identity, belonging and citizenship, and the reality of the grass roots response to the theft and return of a famous traditional icon, the *Afo-a-kom*. The issue aroused national unity and consciousness and Cameroonians of all walks of life and ethnic background momentarily identified with the *Afo-a-kom*. It had thus promoted national unity. The paper has succinctly examined how the pivot of the Kom 'nation' (*Afo-a-kom*) was stolen from its village shrine and as a result transformed it into a national and global artefact. The question 'To whom then did it belong?' is answered with the revelation that many Cameroonians momentarily united around it. Drawing inspiration from this, the paper attempted to show how African works of art could be used to forge nationhood, an enigmatic dilemma to most African leaders and political theorists who still argue strongly in favour of the fact that nationhood could be achieved by decree. In other words, it has explored the rapport between art and themes such as unity, nation building and regional identity, at a time when citizenship, identity and belonging constitute a vexing issue in the politics of nation building in Cameroon.

Nation-building as employed in this paper does not involve the transfer of commitments and loyalties from narrow or parochial levels of ethnic groups to larger political units. That one is Kom, Beti, Bulu, Bakweri or Hausa is a matter of identity; one cannot transfer it. It involves the widening rather than transfer of horizons of identity of parochial units to include larger units such as the state. Paradoxically, in the 1990s following the whirlwind of political pluralism, Cameroon political authorities in an attempt to cling to power started questioning her own citizens by branding some as 'strangers' and others as 'sons of the soil'. This was on the backdrop of the World Bank's view of protecting the minority groups like the pygmies. In Cameroon it was given a sharp twist and the minority was interpreted to mean the indigenes of any locality.

It is on these bases that this paper has argued that instead of decreeing identity, belonging and citizenship as it was done by the 1996 constitution in Cameroon, the *Afo-a-kom* saga outlined in this paper could serve as a practical alternative of achieving this identity. Both in the Diaspora and at home, the *Afo-a-kom* stood as an object of identity and displayed remarkable dynamism to the socio-political situation in Cameroon. In a way, it aroused national unity and consciousness and many Cameroonians of different strands of opinion and ethnic backgrounds momentarily identified with the *Afo-a-kom*. It had thus stood out as a temporary symbol of national unity. Unfortunately, thirty years after its return from the United States, the importance and euphoria once generated in the people by the *Afo-a-kom* has gradually dwindled until it has become a mere piece of wood for touristic purposes. The virtues of consolidating national unity that once were found in this work of art have equally died with this slain esteem for the statue. There is therefore a dire need for strategies to be instituted at various levels especially on the part of the government to reawaken the value of artistic works in indigenous populations if national unity must be achieved in Cameroon in particular and Africa in general.

In so doing within the realm of the democratic experience in Cameroon since 1990, the paper contends that nationhood is not attained by decree, but by the deeply felt sentiments of the people themselves transcending the colonial hangover.

As a final remark, the *Afo-a-kom*, had moved from an inherently Kom symbol to a national and international artistic treasure. Under these circumstances, it functioned both as a particular symbol of Kom unity but had also become a universal possession, as it is the case with all great works of art.

Notes

* I am grateful to Messrs Henry Kam Kah and Ayunwi Neba for proof reading the first draft of this paper, and Professor Preben Kaarlshom for the comments which he made when the paper was first presented during the cultural studies workshop, 2–7 February 2004 in Bangalore, India.

1. Interview with Bobe Bartholomew Nkwain, 10 February 2002, Njinikom. He witnessed the reign of Fon Ngam till his death in 1974 and maintains that even before his death many people had spread rumours that he was going to die because he had seen *Afo-a-kom* twice.
2. Interview with Bobe Ambrose Beng, Njinikom, 14 March 2002. This version was further supported by Nawain Anna Ayumchua. Interview 20 March 2002, Njinikom. These respondents all lived through the era of the theft of *Afo-a-kom* (1966–73) and one could gather that normal life in the palace had come to a standstill.
3. Interview with Henry Yuh Ndi; Fundong, 8 June 2002. He spoke with bitterness because he attributed the theft of *Afo-a-kom* to James Yibain and himself. James

Yibain had used him to collect the *Afo-a-kom* from the storage sanctuary but failed to honour his promise to give him some money.

4. This version was strongly supported by Omer Mbang, Bartholomew Chia Kiyam and Francis Nkwain. Interviewed on separate occasions and individually on 10, 11 and 12 of June 2002, Njinikom. All of them were Kom elites who were living in the diaspora, and always attended the annual festival. They all stated that for seven years they had not come home for the annual dance.
5. This school was championed by Joseph Nyongou Kuh and Ephraim Lawyer Ajoff. Interview at Fundong 13 and 15 August 2002. Although they strongly believed that Fon Ngam mysteriously appeared before the *fon* asking about the *Afo-a-kom*, one wonders whether that could be true. It might have just portrayed the Kom mind regarding life after death.
6. Interview with Bobe Ambrose Beng, Njinikom 15 September 2002. He was the president of Njinikom traditional council when *Afo-a-kom* was stolen. He could vividly cite the circumstances when he went to Laikom for a meeting and everything ended up 'in smoke'.
7. *Ibyem-I-kwifoyn* was a royal hunt in which all the quarters in Kom were involved in the month of April each year. According to Aaron Ngam, interviewed at Fundong, 13 March 2003, there was a low catch from this hunt because of the absence of *Afo-a-kom*. Peter Nkwi corroborated this version (interview at Wombong, Njinikom, 4 April 2003). He was a hunter during this period, and held that the catch was always low, an indication that something wrong was happening in the *fondom*. This, according to him, was the absence of 'our god' *Afo-a-kom*.
8. This was group interview held at Fundong and Belo on separate occasions. Respondents consisted mostly of octogenarian women who lamented bitterly about 'their god' which was carried away from the *fondom*. Interview 14 May and 30 May at Fundong and Belo respectively.
9. Interview with Aaron Ngam, Fundong 14 March 2002. He was 75 years old at this time and had lived during the era of Fon Yuh I. According to him Fon Yuh transferred some of his supernatural powers to the statue. This version contradicts an earlier version given to The Author in 1975, by Johnny Ngong. He gave this version when he was 90.
10. These people were knights and nephews of the ruling dynasty of Kom. When James Yibain became the *fon* of Kom 23 years afterwards in 1989, the first rewards to Henry Yuh Ndi as a result of the theft came in 1990. Yuh testified to me that Yibain gave him 7,000frs. He also said that Yibain on his deathbed in 1994 told him that he should continue to wait for more rewards as a result of the *Afo-a-kom* affair. He further said that his death would hasten the coming of those rewards. Interview with Henry Yuh Ndi 17,18,19 and 20 March 2002 at Fundong, Kom.
11. Interview with Bobe Mumukom Augustine, 25 March 2002. He was 30 years when *Afo-a-kom* was stolen in 1966. His view was further supported by Yindo Mbah, Quarter head of Njinikom. Interview 30 May 2002.

12. Interview with Ngam Njam, 16 March 2002 at Laikom. He was present when Robert Toh was invited to carve another *Afo-a-kom*. He testified that many Kom notables showed dissatisfaction about the carver.
13. Ibid, interview 4 April 2002.
14. Interview with Francis Ngam Chia Fundong, 6 March 2003; He is a notable prince of Kom palace and besides that he accompanied the fon to Yaounde to receive the *Afo-a-kom* in December 2003.
15. I was personally involved when I was in class one, St Anthony's Primary School, Njinikom. There were no classes on this day. It was the first time I saw a caravan of Land Rovers - something in the neighbourhood of 50 - and guns were fired almost endlessly into the air when these Land Rovers passed on to Fundong; carrying the fondom's 'god'.

References

Ayandele, E.A.; Afigbo, A.E.; Gavin, R. J. and Omer- Cooper, J.D. ,1971, *The Growth of African Civilization: The Making of Modern Africa Vol. 2: The Late Nineteenth Century to the Present Day*, London: Longman.

Ayittey, G. B., 1993, *Africa Betrayed*, New York: St. Martin's Press.

Ben-Amos, P., 1980, *The Art of Benin*, London: Thames and Hudson.

Blier, S. P., 1982, *Gesture in African Art*, New York: Kahan Gallery.

Brasch, W. M. and Schneider, G.D., 'The Press Meets the *Afo-a-kom*', *African Art* 8, 1:50-53:84-86.

Burnham, S., 'The True Adventure of the Sacred Idol of Kom', *Esquire* (May) 81, 5: 177-21.

Chauvet, J-M., 1966, *Dawn of Art: The Chauvet Cave*, New York: Abrams.

Chilver, E. M. and Kaberry, P.M., 1967, 'The Kingdom of Kom', in *West African Kingdoms in the Nineteenth Century*, edited with an introduction by Daryll Forde and P.M. Kaberry, Oxford: OUP.

Chilver, E.M. and Kaberry, P.M., 1968, *Traditional Bamenda: Pre-Colonial History and Ethnography of the Bamenda grassfields*, Buea: Government Printing Press.

Davidson, B., 1965, *A History of West Africa, 1000-1800*, London: Longman.

Davidson, B. with F.K. Buah, 1977, *The Growth of African Civilization*, London: Longman.

Ellis, W. S., 1974, '*Afo-a-kom*: A Sacred Symbol Comes Home', *National Geographic*, July: 140-148.

Fanso, V. G., 1989, *Cameroon History for Secondary Schools and Colleges: Vol.1 Pre-Historic Times to Colonial Times*, London: Macmillan.

Fagg, W., 1967, *The Art of Western African: Sculpture and Tribal Masks*, New York and Toronto: New American Library.

Fagg, W., 1965, *Tribes and Forms in African Art*, London: Methuen.

Fagg, W., 1966, *African Tribal Sculptures*, 2 Vols. London: Methuen.

Fonlon, B., 1967, 'Idea of Culture: Culture as Fruit and Harvest', Abbia N° 16, March: 5-25.

Fichner-Ruthus, L., 1992, *Understanding Art*, New Jersey: Prentice-Hall.

Ferretti, F., 1975, *Afo-a-kom: Sacred Heart of Cameroon*, New York: The Third Press.

Greenfield, J., 1996, *The Return of Cultural Treasures*, Cambridge: Cambridge University Press.

Harris, J. E., 1987, *Africans and their History*, New York: New American Library.

Honour, H. and Fleming J., 1995, *The Visual Arts: A History*, New York: Abrams.

Jua, N., 1997, 'Spatial Politics, Political Stability in Cameroon', Keynote Address to a Workshop on Cameroon: Biography of a Nation, at Amherst College, Amherst, MA.

Ki- Zerbo, J., 1978, *Histoire de L'Afrique Noire: D'Hier à Demain*, Paris: Hatier.

Konings, P. and Nyamnjoh, F., 1997, 'The Anglophone Problem in Cameroon', *The Journal of Modern African Studies*, 35, 2, 207-209.

Konings, P., and Nyamnjoh, F., 2000, 'Construction and Deconstruction: Anglophones or Autochtones?' in P.N. Nkwi (ed.) *The Anthropology of Africa: Challenges for the 21st Century*, Yaounde: ICASSRT.

Laude, J., 1966, *Les arts de l'Afrique noire*, Paris: Livre de poche.

Leuzinger, E., 1960, *Africa: The Art of Negro Peoples*, New York: McGraw-Hill.

Mamdani, M., 1996, *Citizen and Subject: Contemporary Africa and the Legacy of late Colonialism*, Cape Town: David Philip.

Nettle, B., 1987, 'Africa Art', in *The New Book of Knowledge*, Connecticut:Grolier Incorporated.

Ngoh, V. J., 1996, *History of Cameroon since 1800*, Limbe: Presbook.

Nkwi, P. N., 1975 'The Return of a God', *Abbia* 29- 30: 121-128.

Nkwi, P. N., 1976, *Traditional Government and Social Change: A Study of the Political Institutions among the Kom of Cameroon Grassfields*, Fribourg: Fribourg University Press.

Northern, T., 1984, *The Art of Cameroon, Washington* DC: Smithsonian Institution.

Northern, T., 1973, *Royal Art of Cameroon: The Art of the Bamenda Tikar*, Hanover, Center Art Galleries.

Nyamnjoh, F.B., and Nkwi, P.N., 1997, *Regional Balance and National Integration in Cameroon: Lessons Learned and the Uncertain Future*. Yaounde: Asc/ICASSRT.

Williams, D., 1966, 'An Outline History of Tropical Art', in Joseph Anene and Godfrey Brown (eds) *Africa in the Nineteenth and Twentieth Centuries*, Ibadan: Ibadan University Press.

Section II

The Weird Wind of Democratisation and Governance

9

Traumas, Memories and 'Modern' Politics in Central Africa

E. S. D. Fomin

Introduction

Modern political development in Africa since the 1950s is largely concerned with the changing fortunes of a plethora of ethnic entities that make up the present states in the continent, which European colonialists created.[1] One of the strategies that these colonialists used in creating and keeping these colonies was to play one ethnic entity against another.[2] And all the strategies, risks and crimes associated with the enterprise of colonisation were for the supreme interest of the colonialists. The antagonism, hatred and resultant conflicts that have characterised and bedevilled the development in these postcolonial states in Africa can to a great extent be traced and blamed on their colonial foundations.

The civil wars and conflicts that have torn some of these states apart and left lasting traumatic memories among the citizens of these colonial patchworks, usually have their roots in ethnic, tribal and regional hatreds of a long-standing nature. These ethnically based conflicts are often rehearsed and resuscitated through mourning idioms in dirges, lullabies, folktales and other cultural manifestations such as dances, art and naming.

Memories and fears of the recurrence of traumatic events such massacres in inter-ethnic feuds have influenced the politics of modern African states tremendously, especially in the change of rulership from one ethnic or tribal group to another.[3] The glaring cases in recent history in Africa include those of Rwanda, Burundi, Somalia, Cameroon, Central African Republic, Chad, Congo, Nigeria and Sudan. These conflicts and others factors have retarded development in Africa in general and Central Africa in particular during this post-colonial era.

The conceptualisation or re-conceptualisation of African development politics has not yet adequately addressed this phenomenon of memory and mourning as a factor inimical to the emergence of democratically strong states in Africa. In Ghana, some years ago, some Africanist scholars believed that the problem of revisiting traumatic events, especially those related to the slave trade could be solved by what they called collective amnesia.[4] In fact, the role played by memory and mourning in the body politic of many emerging nations in Africa is becoming increasingly and commonly manifested in the voting patterns and in the appointments to top government positions. This study will focus on the Republic of Cameroon to show the way this trend has evolved, manifested itself, and retarded political development in the country since it became independence in 1960. The essay will discuss the background to the development of this phenomenon in Cameroon, the post-colonial manifestations of the phenomenon in the body politic of the country, and the effects it has had on its political development.

Background: Geo-Historical Basis

Cameroon is medium-sized state with a population of some fifteen million persons and a land area of 624,240 km^2.[5] It is located in the heart of Africa, sharing boundaries with the Republic of Nigeria to the West, the Republic of Chad to the North East, Lake Chad to the North, Central African Republic to the South East, Republic of Gabon and Equatorial Guinea to the South-East and the Atlantic Ocean to the South-West. From the Atlantic Ocean, at the Gulf of Guinea it spans many climatic and vegetation regions of which equatorial, tropical, Sudan and Sahel regions are the main ones.

Administratively, Cameroon is divided into ten provinces. Each province is made up of many ethnic entities. The melting of these over two hundred ethnic entities[6] into a nation has been complicated and compounded by memories of traumatic experiences that date back to the colonial period 1884–1960/61, memories which have been perpetuated in the post-colonial era.

A common policy of the three colonial powers that ruled Cameroon was the perpetration of ethnic conflicts among certain ethnic groups for their administrative exigencies. During the brief but memorable German colonial rule in Cameroon (Kamerun 1884–1916) they created antagonism amongst many ethnic entities by subjugating and subordinating unfriendly ones to their collaborators, thus engendering bitter memories and mourning that have continued to govern the relations among such groups to the detriment of nation building in this patchwork called Cameroon.

There are many examples of ethnic entities whose relations are governed by memories of traumatic events dating back to German colonial rule in Cameroon. Lebang and Lewoh, Ndungatet and Lewoh - all neighbouring states in Lebialem Division of the Southwest Province of Cameroon - have remained hostile to each other because Lewoh is accused of having collaborated with the German colonialists who exiled the Asonganyi and Tongwa, kings of Lebang and Ndungatet respectively.[7] Not only do they remember with grief and anger the exile of these rulers who were considered sacred, but also the traumatic and terrifying scenes of seeing the Azi Palace of Lebang and some of its most secret and sacred objects burnt down by the German invading forces.[8]

The popular idiom that describes the relations between these neighbours is to refer to Lewoh as traitors and this is found today in the writing of some Lebang elite[9] and folk songs of the traditional people. However, these neighbours belong today to the same administrative unit and cooperate as such, but these traumatic memories are evoked from time to time to transform trivial conflicts into majors ones.[10]

Further to the North-East of Lebialem in the Grassfields of Cameroon, one finds other interesting examples of traumatic and memorable events that German colonists created and left behind for the indigenous peoples. The Nso and their kith and kin, the Bamum, often have hostile relations because the Germans used the latter to defeat and humiliate the former. The other Bamileke people of the grassfields treat the Bamum with disdain because they welcomed the German colonialists who are believed to have desecrated their kingship and other traditional values of the area.[11] It is difficult if not impossible for a Bamum to enjoy popular support among Bamileke. Their neighbours believe that the Bamum royal emblem, which is a snake with two heads, signifies the slyness and treachery of the Bamum people.

The Germans were not the only European colonialists who provoked traumatic conflicts among ethnic groups in Cameroon. The British and the French, who ousted the Germans in Cameroon, created their own problems for the people. Both appeared to have perpetuated the German practice of punishing unfriendly ethnic groups in favour of friendly ones. They punished former friends of the Germans and restored their deposed enemies to their thrones, thus Asongayi of Lebang was reinstated against Ajongakuh who had succeeded him when he was exiled,[12] a real cause of terrible traumatic memories for Ajongakuh and his supporters.

In the Bamenda Grassfields, for example, the British colonial administrators quickly liberated Meta villages that had previously been under the suzerainty of Bali – to the chagrin of the Bali lords. They continued to live within the precinct of the Bali fondom. The memories of the traumatic experiences under the Bali have continued to promote hostilities between Bali and these one-time subjects of the Bali empire up to recent years.[13]

The French colonialists also sowed seeds of conflicts that created lasting ethnic mourning and hatred among states in the Bamileke region. French officials went to great length to manipulate the local succession process in order to ensure the selection and installation of those whom the administration considered would be submissive chiefs.[14] Such manipulations created terrible conflicts, which have had disastrous and traumatic consequences. There are many examples of such cases of manipulation. In 1926 the paramount ruler of Banjoun died. His rightful successor was Bopda but the French colonial administrator, intervened to impose Kamga.[15] The people of Banjoun, including members of the royal family, were split into two opposing camps that engaged in acts of hatred and sabotage with lasting traumatic memories.

Colonial administrative activities—there were many more than those mentioned here— strained relations and created traumatic memories between groups and ethnic entities in Cameroon, and they have continued to influence the body politic in this country in the post-independence period. Many ethnic entities continue today to recall such traumatic events in deciding whether to give or withhold their support when someone from a particular ethnic group seeks a public elective office.

Post-Colonial Manifestations

Cameroon became independent over forty years ago but the country has not made progress commensurate with its rich human and natural resources.[16] The contention of this paper is therefore that Cameroonian development efforts, as in the case of many post-colonial nations in Africa, have been bedevilled, among other ills, by the antagonism, hatred and hostilities emanating from memories of traumatic events that have governed the relations among the numerous ethnic entities that make up this country. The main post-independence issues have had to do with the acquisition and maintenance of power by Amadou Ahidjo, first president of the Federal Republic of Cameroon 1960–1982 and his successor Paul Biya, since 1982.

The reign of President Ahidjo started in the midst of events that divided regions and cultural groups and resulted in conflicts that left deep traumatic memories in many citizens. He first became Prime Minister of French Cameroon in 1968 after the French neo-colonialists had liquidated his main opponent Ruben Um Nyobé and Felix-Roland Moumie, leaders of Union des Populations du Cameroun (UPC) party, because of its radical anti-colonial attitude.[17] President Ahidjo was therefore set up as a French stooge and he worked closely with the French to repress anti-neo-colonialists.[18] The destruction of the UPC as a political party and the murder of many of its leaders left traumatic memories in the Southern and Western regions that have continued to affect Cameroon's development politics negatively.

In fact the UPC remained outlawed throughout the one-quarter century reign of Ahidjo. But most of its members remained antagonistic to him and his regime as a matter of policy.[19] The party colour, red, and its emblem, the crab, seem to have been designed by their leaders to keep this history of bloodshed and resistance alive. It was because their members and leaders kept these traumatic memories alive through solidarity among them and hatred against Ahidjo's regime that it did not disintegrate under him.

Ahidjo worked hard to establish a unitary party system in the country. Of course, the UPC was not an element in the unitary party group. A few individual members of the UPC like Mayi-Matip Theodore joined Ahidjo's parliament after the remnants of the senior leaders of the party who were still in the country and who surrendered on their own were killed in 1971. The Catholic bishop of Nkongsamba diocese who was purportedly implicated in their trial was exiled and died in exile.[20] The reign of Ahidjo also saw the institutionalisation of very repressive measures termed emergency laws which were used to cow persons with radical political views.[21]

Albert Mukong in his book, *A Prisoner Without A Crime*, 1990, recounts how he and other Cameroonians suffered many years of imprisonment, often in some of the worst prisons in the country, usually without formal trial.[22] The memories of this reign of terror, brutalities and tortures affected development in Cameroon negatively. Ahidjo himself became a prisoner of fear and went from one totalitarian act to another.

In 1966, he created a Unitary Party, the Union Nationale Camerounaise (UNC), which deprived Cameroon of the exercise of genuine plural party democracy. In the climate of the times, it was possible for him to abolish Federalism in Cameroon in 1972 with ease, to the chagrin of many Federally-minded Cameroonians, especially the Anglophones. He instituted the 20 May Day Celebrations to mark this abolition of Federalism. And to his opponents this celebration is the occasion of mourning the loss of democracy and freedom.[23] The political imbroglio in Cameroon today called the Southern Cameroon Question or the Anglophone problem is rooted in the traumatic memories of this high-handed fraud.[24]

The manipulation of political life in Cameroon by this neo-colonialists agent made him many enemies who have bitter memories about life under his rule, and who resent those who were associated with him.[25] Ahidjo's high-handedness that caused bitter memories among Cameroonians was not limited to political figures. There are the experiences of whole villages that Ahidjo´s armed men burnt down to ashes because their inhabitants agitated against one of his unpopular acts. Ahidjo himself was forced to live in exile when he resigned in 1982 as the head of state of the United Republic of Cameroon. In fact the way he ended left also bitter memories in his supporters and seemed to justify the adage that 'those who live by the sword shall perish by the sword'. Thus Paul Biya, his constitutional successor, took over against the background of the need for a leader who could bring about national reconciliation.

But Ahidjo and his clique were not happy with the rapid loss of control to Biya and decided to stage a come-back in coup d'état on April 6, 1984. The coup failed disastrously and led to the start of another reign characterised by fear, antagonism and traumatic memories. Thus despite the lofty philosophy[26] expressed by President Biya in his book, *Communal Liberalism*, his reign since 1984 has been characterised by traumatic experiences which have drawn the country into deeper underdevelopment. Perhaps one of the most traumatic things remembered about the reign of President Paul Biya is that the remains of late President Ahidjo, who died in exile, are still outside the country. His relations and political supporters are very bitter about this situation, and politicians opposed to Biya have exploited it to campaign against him and his ruling party.[27]

Paul Biya, a Christian from the Southern part of the country, more precisely from the minority Beti ethnic group, succeeded Ahidjo who originated in the Moslem North in October 1982, amidst great relief and high expectations from the Southerners. In the euphoria of the succession, Biya and his supporters christened his reign the 'New Deal' which was to be characterised by rigor and morality.[28] The New Deal was to rid the society of bribery and corruption, nepotism and tribalism and the laissez-faire attitude among public servants. But so little did this promise materialise that Ahidjo's men took up arms to over to overthrow President Biya in the military coup already referred to.[29] It was abortive but many people were killed in a counter offensive. The killings that resulted from this abortive coup d'état have had traumatic effects on Cameroonians.

Another event during the rule of Biya that created mourning of national dimensions was the birth of the SDF opposition party in May 1990. Hitherto, Cameroon had remained the one-party state that Ahidjo had bequeathed. Despite his rhetoric, Biya was not yet quite ready for multiparty democracy by 1990. But John Fru Ndi and his huge support for the SDF turned out to launch a new political party in Bamenda, the headquarters of the North West Province. Six youths were killed by government troops in the aftermath of the occasion, which had been banned, but the supporters and their leaders carried it out in defiance of the ban.[30]

In 1992, the SDF was again pitted against the CPDM, in the first multiparty presidential elections in Cameroon since Ahidjo introduced the unitary party politics in 1966. In those elections, John Fru Ndi, the SDF Chairman, was the main contender against the incumbent Biya, the CPDM candidate. Fru Ndi is said to have won but Paul Biya purportedly used the Supreme Court to reverse the results to his advantage. Much protest ensued, especially in Bamenda, the home town of John Fru Ndi and the headquarters of his party. Many houses were burnt down, one party leader, Tita Fomukong, was killed and the situation was tense and volatile. Paul Biya using his powers as head of state imposed a state of emergency on Bamenda, a dusk-to-dawn curfew was decreed, and Fru Ndi was placed under house arrest. This has remained a major source of bitterness among Fru Ndi's supporters. They often remember the trauma of this episode and refer to it as the 'Stolen Victory'.[31]

The SDF has exploited these two events to create intense and lasting traumatic memories in their supporters. The spot where the jubilant youths were killed on the fateful day of the launching of the party was quickly renamed Liberty Square instead of City-Chemist Round About. Supporters of the party have composed many songs in honour of their martyrs, and the anniversaries of the events are occasions of great fanaticism by SDF Party men.[32]

In the 1992 Presidential elections, Paul Biya chose the Lion as the symbol for his ballot papers. His opponents referred to him mockingly as the lion man. Little did they know that he was indeed going to become a lion as regards Cameroon's budding democratic practice. He seized victory for himself in that election and has since ignored criticisms from within and without concerning the conduct of elections. For example in the 1996 and 2002 legislative elections his party scored comfortable majorities due to what his critics believe was ruthless high-handed manipulation using administrative officials.[33]

The opposition parties, especially the SDF, have been unable to check this ruthlessness through the courts.[34] They have resorted to the rhetoric of hatred against Paul Biya and the CPDM. Many opposition party candidates and their supporters remember and mourn with bitterness what they consider to have been the blatant cheating that cost them their seats in the last two elections. In the last celebrations of the 20 May Day, SDF supporters marched in black T-shirts as a sign of mourning of the death of democracy again in Cameroon. This is as they claim, because of the lack of fairness in elections and the manipulation of results by divisional and sub-divisional officers who are used by government to run elections.[35]

The Consequences for Cameroon's Development

Cameroon, like most African nations, remains underdeveloped since independence in 1960 despite her huge natural and human resources. The perpetuation of underdevelopment in the midst of these riches is largely blamed on the type of development politics that has been practised. And a very important contributor to this underdevelopment syndrome is the extent to which memory and mourning of traumatic experiences of the politics of the country have affected development. The way Cameroonian politicians as well as traditional rulers have exploited these traumatic experiences in their governance seems to have been inimical to the political, economic and social development.

The Anglophone problem, or what some people called the Southern Cameroons problem, which is a major political imbroglio in Cameroon today, has been built on the memories of the neglect of this component of the country by her Francophone rulers.[36] The attempts by these rulers to reduce the Anglophone component to a political non-entity has produced Anglophone nationalism which threatens the unity of Cameroon today. Anglophone nationalists are very determined to regain the statehood of the Southern Cameroons.[37]

Anglophone nationalism is the product of memories of the former state of West Cameroon, which the Francophone leaders have obliterated to the great distress of Anglophones in the country.[38]

The Anglophones in Cameroon have continued to evoke traumatic memories and mourning to advance the struggles for their statehood through the organisation of meetings, demonstrations and by their writings.[39] There are many leaders in this struggle, which is carried out under an organisation called the Southern Cameroons National Council (SCNC). Many of these figures and other activists are in jail.[40] The most recent occasion of mourning that the Cameroon government thought the SCNC men would exploit to foment trouble was the burial of one of the SCNC leaders, Dr. Martin Luma, in Tiko South West Province of Cameroon on Saturday 17 May 2003. Indeed the atmosphere was tense as armed military men invaded the premises of the deceased and later arrested some SCNC activists outside the compound.[41]

The SCNC remains a hot potato in the palm of President Biya. The strategy to evoke traumatic memories has ramified to involve the occupation of Cameroon embassies by SCNC activities abroad.[42] In the preface to his 'Catechism of the Southern Cameroons Question', Ambassador Henry Fussong, himself one of the national leaders of SCNC states, 'After 40 years, the Southern Cameroonians are now very angry. Four decades after attainment of self-determination in 1961, have brought nothing but economic misery and deprivation, socio-cultural betrayal and political exclusion. We have become the object of fragrant violation, inalienable rights and basic freedoms, brutal repression, intolerance, insensitivity and in transience, utter bad faith, ridicule and contempt'.[43]

Another event that is often remembered with bitterness is the SDF so-called 'Stolen Victory'. As discussed earlier, John Fru Ndi's followers have never forgiven President Biya and his CPDM supporters for robbing them of victory in the 1992 Presidential elections. And as the SDF has a large following in the country, the political situation in Cameroon remains volatile. The CPDM leadership has since spent more time and resources in preserving itself than developing the country. Appointments to top government positions, government contracts and development priorities go to tribesmen of the people in government, regardless of competence.[44]

As far as this situation is concerned, it is unfortunate that the more the affected persons raise their voices the more the government in power indulges in the practice of loading particular areas and persons with government amenities as a way of maintaining their loyalty. Again it is believed that because of the same considerations many persons in high government positions defraud the country with impunity. This explains why the country today is considered as one of most corrupt countries in the world. In 1998 and 1999 Transparency International ranked Cameroon the most corrupt country. Many Cameroonians see this corruption syndrome as a new culture which is blamed on traumatic memories by the opposition and fear by members of the ruling party.

The supporters of President Ahidjo and those of his successor Paul Biya still remember and exploit traumatic experiences of the conflict between them in their relationship. President Biya has remained in power since 1982. He seems unprepared to give up power because his supporters, mainly from the Southern part of the country from where he originates, are said to be afraid of revenge if power goes to the North. Similarly the northerners are also said to be determined to regain power because according to them the North has been badly neglected during Biya's tenure of power.[45]

The Northern politicians, especially those not in Biya's government, and most of them former men of Ahidjo, are ganging up to form a coalition that will fight the next presidential elections in 2004. If they succeed, they might just continue to perpetuate the type of tribal and regional politics that has plagued this country since independence. Today, Cameroon is divided more along tribal and ethnic lines than it was many years ago.[46] The practice of promoting ethnic bigotry built on memories of traumatic relations among the ethnic entities of this country was given the support it needed in the preamble of the 1996 constitution. Thus Cameroon is further apart as a united and strong nation today than decades ago.[47]

The tribal and ethnic phenomena that have affected the development of Cameroon negatively are not limited to the conflict between Northerners and Southerners of Ahidjo and Biya respectively. There are development projects that have been affected because of ethnic and tribal antagonisms resulting from memories of traumatic events that affected people in one part of this country or the other. For example the main road linking Bamenda in the Northwest and Mamfe in the Southwest Province, which is part of the trans-African Highway from Cameroon to Nigeria, was supposed to be diverted through Mbengwi in Momo Division when S.T. Muna was still the speaker of the Cameroon National Assembly. Muna was from Momo Division. This diversion was to deprive the Bali, who are ethnically antagonistic to the Meta of Momo. This is clearly illustrated by fact that the road was rediverted through Bali when S.T. Muna retired from politics. Unfortunately the road had not been constructed before his retirement.[48] It can be recalled that this road from Bamenda to Mamfe, Kumba and (Victoria) Limbe was the main highway of the Southern Cameroons before reunification with the Francophone component of Cameroon. But it had been so neglected that it had become virtually impassable before Muna retired. Thus few Anglophones could forgive him for allowing the neglect of the road by his collaborators, the Francophone rulers.[49]

There are also a number of ethnic conflicts which are constantly remembered and used to block development initiatives. Ndungatet people in Lebialem division are known to have refused to benefit from a pipe-borne water project because it would also be of advantage to their neighbours in Lewoh, with whom they have had hostile exchanges in the past over land. Even among the northerners of Cameroon who were seemed politically united by Ahidjo, there have been ill-feelings emanating from the domination and exploitation of the non-Moslem groups, the Kirdi, by the less numerous Moslem Fulbe.[51] In fact Ahidjo appeared to have allowed this injustice for fear of hurting the dominant Moslem Fulbe families. Today in this part of the country the non-Moslem groups remain antagonistic to the Fulbe.

The consequences of memories and mourning deriving from traumatic experiences of ethnic, tribal and regional antagonisms are better seen in the plural party politics in Cameroon today. At the dawn of new multipartyism in Cameroon in the 1990s, three main political parties emerged: the SDF, the UNDP and CPDM.[52] The three groupings reflect regional tendencies. The SDF with headquarters in Bamenda in the Northwest Province draws a majority of its supporters from that province and from the other Western provinces, where related ethnic groups are found.[53]

These people supported John Fru Ndi, fondly called ni Fru as a matter of ethnic attachment not ideological appeal. Fortunately for Fru Ndi, the people of his ethnic and regional extraction are many, and quite migrant in their culture.[54] They therefore quickly spread the party to all the areas where they are found in the national territory, thus giving the party a picture of a wide national spread. In this way they were able to win some non-tribesmen to the party. But many of these non-tribesmen who became the militants of the SDF were the masses. The elite in high-ranking positions in the country remained sceptical, due to memories of ethnic sinecures and patronage that have characterised the body politic of the country since independence.

From the memory of the experiences of Ahidjo, Foncha, Muna, Biya and other previous politicians, the expected trend is that he who wins the presidency wins for his family, tribesmen and regional supporters. Other Cameroonians would only be considered for peripheral positions. In fact the critics of Fru Ndi claimed that the shadow government he created in 1992 had only his tribesmen in major positions[55] despite the support he appeared to enjoy from the masses of other parts of the national territory. It is widely believed by analysts even within the SDF that Fru Ndi was robbed of victory in that election because he did not have the support of the elite corps of the military, judicial and the civil society outside his tribesmen.[56] The reason for this lack of support is two-fold. Firstly there was the fact that many of these people were Biya's men, and secondly there was the fear that Fru Ndi would replace them with his own tribesmen.

The traumatic memories of tribalism that have characterised politics and appointments in Cameroon will continue to plague Cameroon's democratic process for long unless serious efforts are made to reverse the situation. Like the SDF, NUDP´s headquarters is in the home province of founders, at Garoua, headquarters of the north province. The majority of its adherents come from that province because they perceive it as an attempt to revive Ahidjo's politics and policy in Cameroon. This was the reason why they quickly replaced its first Christian chairman Samuel Eboa, by a northern Moslem chairman, Maigari Bouba Bello.[57]

The CPDM is the ruling party. It was first known as the CNU. In principle every Cameroonian was its member. Its headquarters was therefore the national capital, Yaoundé. And because it is headed by the southerner Paul Biya, at the rebirth of multiparty politics it was perceived as the party for the southerners, especially the ethnic Beti people. It was however not long before the ethnic and tribal bigotry fired Cameroonians to make the creation and running of political parties in Cameroon a mere joke. Of course, the multiplicities of parties in the country appeared to have worked in favour of the ruling CPDM party because it fragmented and weakened the opposition.

A major political problem in Cameroon today is how to unite the many opposition parties of various ethnic and tribal inclinations behind a single candidate in the upcoming presidential elections.[58] And it is in the interests of the CPDM to keep them as divided as possible.[59] In fact, one could state without fear of contradiction that CPDM government promotes ethnicity in Cameroon despite its obvious negative effects on national unity. This makes it difficult to build a national political culture that can enable the electorate to choose their leaders freely. In other words, the syndrome of traumatic memories of the harmful effects of tribalism, ethnicism and regionalism have eaten deep into the fabric of Cameroon's body politic and seems to be perpetuating itself to the detriment of the growth of democracy.

Conclusion: Suggestions

It is clear that the deep-rooted memories of ethnic division and oppression have led to far-reaching and negative repercussions on the country's political, economic and social development. This situation holds in Cameroon as in Chad, Central African Republic, the Congo and other multi-ethnic states in Africa. The struggle to build strong nations from these ethnic entities is not easy, especially when political leaders encourage ethnic bigotry. The way out is to adopt the following policies:

Build and nurture nationalism: The building of strong nations out of the numerous ethnic entities that make up the states in central Africa requires selflessness, vision and relentless effort. Nationals of multi-ethnic states like Cameroon should be free to move and settle in any part of the national territory. The citizenship of any administrative entity—province, division or council— should be automatic to nationals who have settled and done business in an area for five years. The concept of indigenes should be discouraged in national political life. In fact the government should give nationals who create development projects and businesses that transcend ethnic and regional boundaries encouragement and protection. Civic education programmes for school should put more emphasis on pragmatic ways of encouraging nationalism. The youth must grow up with the deep conviction that the nation needs them, and cares about their welfare and wellbeing.

Create harmony among ethnic entities: Conscious effort should be made to create understanding and love among the ethnic groups that have a history of recurrent conflict and hostility. This can be done by the resettlement of ethnic entities in a manner that creates healthy interaction and cooperation among them. The more cosmopolitan Cameroonian rural settlements become, the less antagonistic these groups will be. The enjoyment of common amenities—pipe-borne water, electricity, telephone, medical facilities, roads, and so on could create a sense of resilient unity among them. Thus broad-based development would reduce ethnic bigotry and consequent conflict and promote nationalism and love among the nationals. The government should strive to build 'bridges', not walls, between hostile ethnic entities as was the case in the Bali-Meta hostility in the 1980s where the authorities built a wall to separate the two warring entities. A truth and reconciliation strategy remains a wonderful weapon to use in defusing traumatic memories.

Improve the political culture: The law on the creation of political parties that insists on all of them reflecting a national character by transcending ethnic and regional boundaries should be strictly applied. In fact the multiplicity of parties reflects the multiplicity of ethnic entities and is an indication that the law is not rigorously applied. It should be possible to insist as it is in Nigeria that any president of Cameroon must not only obtain the majority of the total votes but also those of a majority of the provinces. Key political appointments like provincial governors should be elected by the citizens concerned. And all elections should be transparent, free and fair so as to ensure that the will of the majority prevails.

Improve the governance of the country: Memories of traumatic experiences that engender conflict among ethnic entities and political groups are a sign of the absence of good governance. It is because a particular ethnic entity considers itself denied development that it starts blaming another, especially the one benefiting. Poverty and the absence of governance breeds underdevelopment, misery and faction. In such circumstances people evoke the past to guide their present actions. Traumatic conflict evoked by relationships are a sign of poor governance and are inimical to development.

Decentralise Administration: The merging of numerous ethnic entities in to a nation requires bringing them together under a common administration. But when this centralisation is carried to an extreme, the result is the absence of administration and development in some of these entities.

While a candidate in Nigeria cannot win a presidential election by drawing votes just from one region, in Cameroon such provisions do not exist in the present electoral code.[60] However, the measure governing the creation of political parties in Cameroon stresses that they should not be restricted to one ethnic entity.[61] But that is only on paper. The implementation of the measure is far from conforming to the principle. In fact, few parties are truly national parties in terms of their militants. The Cameroon Democratic Union (CDU) of chairman Adamu Ndam Njoya is based only in his home division of Noun, in the Western Province of Cameroon – the wonderful leadership qualities of the chairman[62] notwithstanding.

This article is far from arguing that we should practice collective amnesia. That would be moving from one extreme to another. Oral traditions based on remembered history of various peoples in societies where writing was late in coming are today a major source of their history and must be encouraged. To negate it is to estrange such peoples. The history of Cameroon is the history of these entities put together as well as the collective history of all of them when they started journeying together in the enterprise of nation building. Nation builders must discourage tendencies that allow memory and mourning to lead to regional coalitions, and that foster tribal and ethnic bigotry that can only hinder national cohesion. Cameroon still needs a major effort in this direction.

Notes

1. Ali A. Mazrui, *The Africans: A Triple Heritage* (London BBC Publications, 1986), p. 270.
2. John D. Hargreaves, *Prelude to the Partition of West Africa* (London Macmillan, St. Martin's Press. 1963), p. 199.
3. In many of these African States, persons still consider themselves not as belonging to a state but more to an ethnic tribal entity.
4. Kofi Anyidoho, *The Pan African Idea in Literatures of the Black World* (Accra: Ghana Universities Press 1989), p. 9; Ayi Kwei Armah, 'The African Heritage series', Remembering the Dismembered Continent (Video), and discussion with fellows at the African Humanities Institute programme, University of Ghana, Legon, 26 January 1998.
5. Mark W. Delancey and Dike Delancey, *Historical Dictionary of the Republic of Cameroon*, Third Edition, African Historical Dictionaries, No. 81 Lanham, Maryland and London, The Scarecrow Press, Inc. 2000), p. 1.
6. Ibid., p. 2.
7. William Nditor Akem, 'Colonial Impact on Indigenous political institutions: A Case Study of Nweh Politics', a Post Graduate Diploma Dissertation in the teaching of History (University of Yaoundé, 1981) pp. 49-68.
8. Interview with Nkamacha, Buea, 17 April 2003. He is a notable of the royal family of Lebang who left Lebang some years ago and is now residing at Bue. He is about 75 years old.

9. Stanley Peter Nzefeh, 'A History of Lebang Fontem 1850-1950' (Mimeo, 1990) p. 65.
10. The most recent conflict between Ndungatet and Lewoh which took place in 2002 and resulted in bloodshed, originated from a quarrel between two individuals from the two groups over farm land.
11. Christraud Geary, 'Things of the Palace A Catalogue of Bamum Palace Museum in Foumban (Cameroon)', Wiesbaden; 1983, p. 60; and passim; *Etudes Camerounaise* No. 25-26, 1949 (Institut Français d'Afrique Noire Centre Camerounaise Mai-Juin 1949), p. 17.
12. George Atem, 'The Fontem Kingdom: A brief history and tradition of Lebang people' (Mimeo, 2000).
13. In the 1980s when S.T. Mua (Meta) was still the speaker of the national parliament of Cameroon, government allegedly had to build a wall to prevent the Bali people from farming on Ngembo (Meta) land.
14. Michael Ndobegang Mbapundah, 'Grassfield Chiefs and Political Change in Cameroon. (1884 - 1960)', Ph. D. Dissertation (Boston University, 1985), p. 103.
15. Ibid.
16. E.S.D Fomin, 'Multiparty Municipal Administration and corruption in Cameroon', Paper presented at APAD-ASC conference 22-25 May 2002, African Studies Centre, Leiden; The Bishops of Cameroon, 'Prayer against Bribery and corruption in Cameroon', Hand bills.
17. Richard Joseph, *Gaullist Africa. Cameroon under Ahmadou Ahidjo*, Enugu, Fourth Dimension Publishers 1978) pp. 54-64; Delancey and Delancey, *Historical Dictionary of the Republic of Cameroon*, p. 18.
18. Richard Joseph, *Gaullist Africa*, p. 49.
19. It was only in the 1990s that the outlawed UPC took advantage of the reintroduction of multipartyism in Cameroon to reorganise but it is still to regain its popularity and influence.
20. Albert Mukong, *Prisoner without a Crime*, Editions NUBIA, London, Calvert's press, 1990, pp. 33-37; Delancey and Delancey, *Historical Dictionary*, p. 199.
21. This explains why the foreword to the Cameroon rights and freedoms texts of 1990 by Professor Augustine Kinchou Kouomegni, the then Minister of Information and Culture, is entitled 'The Era of Liberty and Democracy'.
22. Mokung, *Prisoner without a Crime*, p. 32.
23. Henry H. Fussong, 'Catechism of the Southern Cameroons Questions', (upcoming 2003), p. 33.
24. Ibid.
25. Mukong, *Prisoner without a Crime*, p. 1; N.N Mbile, *Cameroon political story: Memories of an Authentic Eye-Witness* (Limbe, Presbyterian Printing Press, 1989) p. 147.
26. Paul Biya, *Communal Liberalism*, (London, Macmillan Publishers), pp.111-121.
27. In the 1992 Presidential Elections, both the Social Democratic Front (SDF) and National Union for Democracy and Progress (UNDP) Parties whose candidates were the main contenders used this effectively to campaign against Paul Biya, the CPDM Candidate.

28. Paul Biya, 'Opening Speech of the 10th Ordinary congress of the CNN', in Bamenda, Fresh impetus, speeches by National President (Bamenda: C.P.D.M 21 March 1985), pp. 7-13.
29. Delancey and Delancey, *Historical Dictionary*, p.xxxv.
30. John Fru Ndi, 'We want grassroot democracy', Interview in *Cameroon Life* Vol. 1 no 7. January 1991 (Mutengene, Alpha Communication S.A. Cameroon), pp. 8-13.
31. Ibid.
32. During the last legislative and Council Elections of 30 June 2002, the author of this paper saw SDF Parliamentarian in Lebialem Constituency, Dr. The Hon. Michael Ndobegang, use many such songs for his campaign.
33. The Cameroon Electoral Code, revised in 1997, shows that administrative officers, all appointees of government, are active at all levels of the organisation of elections in Cameroon.
34. Interview with M.M. Ndobegang, former SDF MP of Lebialem constituency. He explained that in the 1996 Legislative elections SDF won 43 seats in parliament.
35. Interview with Mr. Sylvester Ngemasong, head of SDF Council election list in Alou Council Lebialem, Buea, 2003. He said the SDO Lebialem physically tortured him and some of his supporters and his victory was seized.
36. Fossung, 'Catechism', pp. 24, 27; 'SCNC Communiqué of 7 October 1995', signed by Ekobang Elad, as chairman of SCNC.
37. Fossung, 'Catechism', p. 29.
38. Ahidjo started the process in 1966 with the introduction of the unitary state and Biya concluded it in 1984 when he changed the name of the country from the United Republic of Cameroon to the Republic of Cameroon. Chief Gorgi Dinka protested against the change and was arrested and detained for several months without trial. He lives today in exile.
39. The writings include SCNC communiqués, speeches and publications by SCNC leaders – Henry Fossung, Mfor, Nfor, Ekotang Elad, etc.
40. This is discussed commonly in many newspapers in Cameroon, notably *The Post*, 4 November, 2002, April 7, 2003, and *The Herald*, 11 December, 2002.
41. The Author witnessed the episode.
42. Fussong, 'Catechism of Southern Cameroons questions', p.v.
43. Fussong, 'Catechism', p. v.
44. *The Messenger* No. 17, Thursday December 2002 gives facts and figures on Anglophone Marginalisation on p. 44; 'SCNC Communiqué of October 7, 1995', signed by Sam Ekotang Elad as chairman, stresses this point.
45. Don Sisai, 'The Other Side of the Capital Flight', *Cameroon Life* May, 1992, p. 29;
46. The talk about a single opposition presidential candidate is rife in Cameroon today and many parties are positioning for it.
47. When Ahidjo resigned in 1982, he handed power to Biya constitutionally but tribal and regional antagonism was at the root of the problem between them.

48. Field work in Metaland, 1984-1988. There is a wonderfully well-built road from Bamenda to Batibo through Bali as part of this road project from Bamenda to Mamfe.
49. S. T. Muna was one of the first collaborators of Ahidjo in Anglophone Cameroon. He held many high positions in government and the National Assembly of Cameroon till he retired in 1977.
50. Interview with Professor Leke. Ivo Tambo, Buea, 10 May 2003. He was the coordinator of Lewoh water project when interviewed.
51. Mark W. Delancey, *Cameroon Dependence and Independence* (Boulder, Westview Press Inc. 1989), p. 97.
52. In the 1992 Presidential Elections the thee parties CPDM, SDF and UNDP came 1st, 2nd, and 3rd according to official results.
53. The main ethnic groups include the Bamileke, Ngemba, Bafut, Nso and Bali.
54. Fru Ndi comes from Bafouchu in Mezam division.
55. Interview with Henry Fussong, Buea, 14 May 2002. He was the campaign manager of Ndam Njoya in those elections.
56. Interview with Martin Nkemngu Buea, 10 April 2003. He is a member of SDF National Executive Council (NEC).
57. This was the first congress of the party held at Garoua in 1992. The north became its chief until other ethnic loyalties created other smaller parties and splinters of the NUDP.
58. *Camnews magazine* No. 001 1998 bemoaned this multiplicity and ethnically rooted parties, for now only parties in the Northern provinces have come out to express the desire and wish to put one opposition candidate against Biya.
59. It will be recalled that the CPDM under Biya has been in power for the past twenty years.
60. Cameroon Electoral Code, 1997, revised Edition.
61. *Cameroon rights and freedoms: Collection of Recent Texts* (Yaoundé, SOPECAM, 1990), Section 9, sub 1, p.58.
62. Adamou Ndam Njoya was quite appreciated by progressive Cameroonians when he was Minister of National Education under Ahidjo from 1977–1980.

References

Akindés, Francis, 1996, *Les Mirages de la Democratie en Afrique Subsaharienne Francophone*, Serie de livre du CODESRIA, Paris: Karthala.

Armah Anyi Kwei, 1998, 'The African Heritage Series: Remembering The Dismembered continent', Video and discussion with fellows of the African Humanities Institute Programme, University of Ghana, Legon, January-March.

Atem, George, 2000, 'The Fontem Kingdom: A Brief History and Tradition of Lebang People', Mimeo.

Atemnkeng, Ndobegang, N., 1987, *Our Cultural Heritage I. Lebang Chiefdom*, Limbe: Mooremac Press.

Benjamin, Jacques, 1972, *Les Cameroonais Occidentaux, La Minorité dans un Etat Bicommunicataire*, Montreal: Presse de l'Université de Montreal.

Boh, Herbert, 1994, 'In the shadow of Gummen, AAC Adopts; Bamenda Proclamation', *Newslink* Vol. 1 No. 5, 2 May.

Bwuham, Philip, 1996, *The Politics of Cultural Difference in Northern Cameroon*, Edinburgh: Edinburgh University Press.

Change Cameroon, Le 11 October 1992, Autopsie d'une election présidentielle controuversée, Yaoundé: Editions C3, 1993.

Constitution, Internal Rules and Regulations, Standing Orders of the Convention of the Social Democratic Front (SDF), adopted 16 February 1990, and amended 31st July 1993.

Delancey, W. Mark and D. Delancey, 2000, *Historical Dictionary of the Republic of Cameroon, African Historical Dictionaries*, No. 81, Lancham, and London.

Delancey, W. Mark, 1989, *Cameroon: Dependence and Independence,* Boulder and San Francisco: Westview Press.

Etudes Camerounaise, *Revue Trimestrielle*, Tome II, Mars-Juin 1949, No. 25-26, Institut Francais d'Afrique Noire, Centre Cameroun.

Eyoh, Dickson, 1998, 'Conflicting Narratives of Anglophones Protest and politics of identity in Cameroon', *Journal of Contemporary African Studies* 16, No.2: 249-76.

Fokum, Hilary Kebila, 'Memorandum on the Anglophone problem', *The Messenger* No. 7 No. 2, p. 4.

Fomin, E.S. D., 1994, *A Handbook of Essoh-Attah Chiefdom*, Bamenda: Patron Publishing House.

Fomin, E.S.D., 2002, 'Multiparty Municipal Administration and Corruption in Cameroon', APAD-ASC conference paper, Leiden, 22-25 May.

Fonchingong, Tangie Nsoh, 1998, 'Multipartyism and Democratisation in Cameroon', *Journal of Third World Studies* 15, No. 2 (Fall): 119-36.

Fossung, N. Henry, 2003, Catechism of the Southern Cameroons Question, Upcoming.

Friedrich Ebert Foundation, 1996, 'L'Opposition dans LCS Parlements Africains. Actes du Seminaire Parlementaire regional Sur: 4 Role, droit et responsabilités de l'Opposition dans les parlements Africain', Ouagadougou, 15–16 Nov.

John, Willard R., 1970, *The Cameroon Federation: Political Integration in a Fragmentary Society*, Princeton, NJ: Princeton University Press.

Joseph, Richard, 1978, *Gaullist Africa: Cameroon under Ahmadu Ahidjo*, Enugu: Fourth Dimension Publishers.

Kofi, Anyidoho, 1989, *The Pan-African Idea in Literatures of the Black World*, Accra: Ghana University Press.

Mukong, Albert, 1989, *Prisoner without a Crime*, Paris: Nubia Press.

Ndifor, Akepu William, 'Colonial impact on indigenous political institutions: A case study of Nweh Politics', a post Graduate Diploma Dissertation in the teaching of History, University of Yaoundé.

Nkwi, Paul Nchoji and Francis B.Nyamnjoh, eds., 1997, *Regional Balance and National Integration in Cameroon: Lessons Learned and the Uncertain Future*, Leiden: African Studies Centre.

Nnoli, Okwudaba, 1990, *Electoral Politics in Nigeria*, Enugu: Fourth Dimension Publishers.

Olaniyan, Richard, ed., 1982, *African History and Culture*, Lagos: Longman Group.

SOPECAM, 1990, *Cameroon Rights and Freedoms. Collection of Recent Texts*, Yaoundé: SOPECAM.

Tafor, Ndzang and Atangcho Alexander, 1991, 'What does Fru Ndi Want', Interview, *Cameroon Life Magazine* Vol. 1 No. 7 January. Mutengene: Alpha Communications SA Cameroon 1991.

Tolen, Aaron, 1997, *The Electoral Process in Cameroon,* Yaoundé: FEMEC.

Wache, K. Francis, 1991, 'How Idyllic Transfer of Power Turned Sour', *Cameroon Life Magazine* Vol. I No. II September.

10

Tribulations of a Democratic Transition: The Cameroonian Experience

Valentine Ameli Tabi

Preliminaries and Theoretical Perspectives

The collective experience gathered by Cameroonians during the past dozen years confirms indeed Sorensen's celebrated dictum that 'there is no royal road to democracy'.[1] A look through the memory lane of the democratic trajectories of most African countries and before now, European as well, reveals that the path to democracy is filled with thorny bushes and thickets of bamboos.

The path to democracy or transition to democracy, otherwise known in political science jargon as democratisation, is the movement from authoritarian rule to a democratic form of government.[2] The concept of modern democracy has seen many definitions crowding around it. To understand it better, we borrow from two great authors their conceptualisations of the practice namely, Larry Diamond and Joseph Schumpeter. The former opines that democracy involves a substantial level of individual and collective competition for public office among the citizens, the existence of regularly scheduled elections from which no citizen of legal voting age is excluded and the acceptance of, and the respect for, the currently universally held freedoms and the sanctity of human dignity (Diamond 1988:14).[3] The latter on his part takes democracy to mean an 'institutional arrangement for arriving at political decisions in which individuals acquire the power to vote by means of a competitive struggle for the people's vote'.[4]

It is trite to state that democratisation in Cameroon has been a huge disappointment. Like in many human stories ours has been one replete with intrigue, deceit, greed, hypocrisy, prevarication and betrayal. In the face of the frustration engendered by the democratic stalemate coupled with the country's limping economy, many despondent citizens especially intellectuals and youths are fleeing the country while the rest of the citizens have either gone into resignation and prayers or been obliged to turn to the ruling party to be 'praise singers' as the sole means left to them for survival.

This paper is an attempt to explain why Cameroon's democratisation process which took off very enthusiastically, eliciting much support from the citizenry as a whole, suddenly turned out to be a chimera. Furthermore, we examine what prospects there are for the resurrection of this noble enterprise.

Background to Multiparty Democracy

The history of Cameroon's transition to democracy which began some fifteen years ago with President Paul Biya's accession to the throne has been painstakingly analysed by many researchers and scholars on Cameroon politics.[5] Suffice it here therefore to give just a bird's eye-view.

If we have to give to Caesar his due then we must begin by saying President Biya started off his presidency with the slogans 'liberalisation and democratisation' as well as 'rigour and moralisation'.[6] He moved to concrete reality by organising internal municipal and legislative elections within the ruling Cameroon People's Democratic Movement Party (CPDM), in which many party stalwarts bit the dust of defeat. Meanwhile the president made sure that his own position was unchallenged. So others could face elections but not him; giving the impression that he was a kind of patriarch. By the time the eastern wind of democratic change started blowing across Africa therefore, Cameroonians had psychologically been conditioned to a certain form of democracy. However, given the heavy repression they had experienced under Biya's predecessor Ahmadou Ahidjo, people were very eager for real change. Like Mikhail Gorbachev in the former Soviet Union, Biya's changes turned out to be superficial. Little wonder then, the advent of full multiparty politics in 1990 met with a lot of enthusiasm nationwide despite some desperate attempts from one-party enthusiasts to turn back the hand of the democratic clock – which proved futile.

If Cameroonians in their vast majority embraced democracy this does not mean they all viewed it from the same perspective. Each sub-national, ethnic, religious group or otherwise saw something different accruing to it as a result of the restoration of free speech and legal political competition.

It must be underscored here that underlying the concept of democracy is the belief that all citizens are now elevated to the status of equals in terms of rights as well as obligations. This in turn energises hitherto suppressed groups, relegated to the background of political and economic development, to present their case or bring forward their grievances in order to eventually seek redress.

This was exactly the Cameroonian experience at the dawn of democratisation in the early 1990s.

Democratisation and the Elusive National Unity Issue

If democratisation of political life in Cameroon has its positive side in terms of the increased participation of citizens in state affairs, a greater degree of respect for human rights, an increasingly free and vocal press etc, it has its ugly side as well. This is because as we have seen elsewhere, as political liberalisation has the tendency of provoking a backlash in that it reawakens sub-national religious, ethnic regional or linguistic sentiments that had been long held in abeyance by the one party repressive regime. Dramatic happenings in the former Soviet Union where glasnost and perestroika were introduced by Gorbachev, events in the former Yugoslavia after the end of the iron rule of Marshall Tito, genocide in Rwanda, war-lordism in Somalia and the Democratic Republic of Congo (DRC) and the growing separatist threat in Cameroon to name just these few examples, are daily reminders of the dangers of a precipitated and unplanned transition to democratic rule.[7] In all of these cases sub-national groups availed themselves of the new political openings and tried to cast away the shackles of serfdom by demanding an equal place on the master's table, even went a step further to advocate the creation of an independent state for their peoples.

As adumbrated earlier, peoples and individuals alike may expect different outcomes from a democratisation process. While some groups wish to see the redress of economic grievances, others may want the granting of an autonomous status to their region. Yet others may want to see equity in the distribution of appointments, development projects, contracts, etc. We shall essay to demonstrate in this paper that at the dawn of the democratic transition in Cameroon, many groups were ready with various agendas and wishes regarding the political system.

A presentation of the expectations and relations among the major groups in competition is found below. Thanks to the resurgence of political liberalisation ushering in press freedom, there are no more taboo subjects. Henceforth no crucial issue of national import escapes the scrutiny of the press; very conscious and jealous of its new-found liberties. We look first at the relations between the two linguistic groups, before considering that between the ethnic groups.

Anglophone/Francophone Relationship and the Democratic Transition

Present day re-united Cameroon is the offspring of an agreement midwifed in Foumban in 1961 by delegates from the then former Southern Cameroons or West Cameroon and the Republic of Cameroon or East Cameroon. Following the terms of the accord, the French-speaking and English-speaking parts of the country were to live as separate autonomous entities under the umbrella of a federal union. However, under circumstances akin to the Ethiopia/Eritrea case, the Foumban agreement was jettisoned in a hastily announced and organised referendum in June 1972, full of procedural irregularities[8] that left the voters with no choice in the real sense of the word. This highly dramatic political event has been the subject of much scholarly writing.[9] As a result of the great controversy the issue has raised, it is today the favourite topic for conversation among the anglophone intellectual elite especially, and has almost been transformed into a national sport as well.

Anglophones like other minorities elsewhere in the continent saw the advent of democratisation as the opportuned moment to submit their case for the revisiting of the Foumban agreement which provided guarantees and security to the continued existence of their cultural values and perception of the world or way of life.[10] The argument has been that only a federal arrangement can provide adequate protection for groups living side by side in the same territorial bloc and marked by primary affinities.[11]

The demand for a special status within the Cameroon state for Anglophones has been received angrily by the majority francophone largely out of envy and jealousy because of the political and economic benefits that may accrue from such an arrangement. Some francophone ethnic groups such as the Pahouin – also known as Beti, Bassa, Kirdi, Bamileke and others – have asked for the same status for their groups as if to counterbalance and water down the claims made by anglophones. The Anglophones, comprising about 65 ethnic groups and/or tribes, then feel minimised and downgraded to the equivalent of any one of Cameroon's hundreds of tribal groups.

Yet the Anglophone clamour for special status through a federal arrangement persists and shows no sign of abating. The Social Democratic Front (SDF), the main Anglophone-led political party in the country has taken up[12] the case for a federal state in Cameroon. This is not without consequences though as the position has estranged it from many of its Francophone supporters, mostly the Bamileke, the immediate Francophone neighbours of the Anglophones and who have a substantial emigrant population in English-speaking provinces of the North West and South West.

What is positive in it all is that this Anglophone/Francophone antipathy has not degenerated into a violent clash so far, unlike the situation which has obtained in many African countries with societal dichotomies, such as Nigeria, Tanzania, Rwanda, and Burundi. Anglophone and Francophone political activists have behaved in a civilised and gentlemanly fashion thus far, which has led to the suspicion harboured by many that the charges of marginalisation and neglect laid by the former against successive Francophone-led governments in Yaoundé are unsubstantiated or very marginal at best, and as such epiphenomenal. Like one Francophone told me, anyone who claims that Anglophones are marginalised should prove that Cameroon's current prime minister is not an Anglophone.[13]

Lastly it must be stated here clearly that the Anglophone/Francophone rift is a delicate issue because of its inherent potential for the disintegration of the Cameroonian state. Historically Anglophones who inhabit the western region of the country used to be a self-governing political entity in a specific geographical location prior to independence and re-unification. The potential to resurrect memories of the past and stage a political revival of the Southern Cameroons in the face of the political atomisation of the Anglophone in a largely Francophone-dominated political set-up always lurks in the air. This is more so given the emergence of secessionist groups with the objective of restoring the Southern Cameroon's state, an initiative which has already registered its first official deaths in Kumbo North West province on 1 October 2001.[14]

We now tackle a new aspect of the national question – the ethnic element.

The Problem of Ethnic Cleavages

Just as in many contemporary African states, Cameroon is home to about 200 extant ethnic groups and/or tribes speaking different tongues.[15] The clamour by groups for their own share of the resources available to the state for distribution is not a novel occurrence. What has been peculiar in the Cameroonian situation is that as a reaction to the foiled coup of April 1984[16] which was as an ethnic attempt to stage a political come-back by the Fulanis, President Biya closed ranks and henceforth turned increasingly to members of his own ethnic group, the Beti, as a power conservation measure. Thereafter, the ethnicisation of politics and the politicisation of ethnicity became so flagrant.[17] that it created a backlash. As other groups were outspoken about state tribalism, the Betis became fearful of their future should they completely democratise and let go their last instrument for self-preservation – political power at the helm of the state. It is therefore clear that the 1984 attempted coup caused Biya to renege on his initial liberal political agenda and this has taken, and still continues to take, its toll on our democratisation.

We examine the ethnic issue using some of the major groups of the country and their relations vis-à-vis other groups as well as with the political process.

Relations between the Bamileke and others

The Bamileke of the western grassfields constitute the largest single ethnic group in Cameroon.[18] Though they live under several autonomous chiefdoms and the name Bamileke is actually a generic term, their dialects and mode of life are similar.

The Bamileke are a highly migrant and enterprising people who are never tired of taking opportunities in their new abodes. Due to their dynamic and enterprising spirit they have been very successful as businessmen, academics civil servants, farmers and what have you. This group is comparable to the Ibos of Nigeria or the Jews – at least in terms of their urge for achievement and mobile nature. As a matter of fact, they are found everywhere in the country where they are involved in all kinds of activities, from petty jobs to the largest income-generating activities. Tables 1 and 2 illustrate their strength in the two major cities of Douala and Yaoundé.

Table 1: Population of Douala (in percentage)

Ethnic groups	1947	1956	1967	1973	1976
Douala	49.2	19.5	15.0	12.1	10.5
Bassa	15.9	17.0	18.0	19.3	20.7
Beti	17.4	16.6	11.0	10.2	9.5
Bamileke	17.4	25.0	39.0	42.2	47.0

Table 2: Population of Yaoundé (in percentage)

Ethnic groups	1957	1962	1964	1976
Bamileke	14.4	21.2	18.9	27.8
Ewondo	24.6	18.6	20.2	25.2
Eton	10.6	10.7	9.9	10.0
'Mbamois'	5.4	7.4	7.0	6.9
Bassa	10.4	7.2	8.7	9.4

Source: Jean-Louis Dogmo, *Le Dynamisme Bamileke*, Thesis, Paris, 1979, p.733.

The highly mobile nature of Bamileke people has earned them the name of 'invaders' and their great successes, especially in the sphere of business, have made their hosts envious and even jealous. Thus the several incidents that have throughout history opposed members of this group to their host communities, some very bloody.[19] In Cameroon ethnic stereotyping the Bamileke are often portrayed as money-mongers and land grabbers.[20]

Since the colonial era unto this day the Bamileke have always been seen as a threat[21] to the wielders of political power in Yaoundé because of their demographic weight and economic resilience. Even today, the syndrome remains as there is a morbid fear within the ruling political circle that the Bamileke are a menace to their power and that any attempt at genuine democratisation is tantamount to handing power to them – in which case they will combine political with the economic power they already possess and totally dominate the country, some argue.[22] Attempts to slow down the pace of democratisation, or even freeze, it have been interpreted as a move to stop Bamileke political advance as well as that of their Anglophone allies. To many a political observer at the start of the multiparty era, the attitude adopted by the Bamileke would be very determining in influencing the democratisation process. When the vast majority of them joined the opposition SDF it was interpreted by the ruling ethnic group, the Betis, as a ploy to exploit their English-speaking cousins, especially those of the Bamenda grassfields, in order to seize power. Consequently, the appearance in Cameroon's political vocabulary of the neologism the 'anglo-bami' alliance – that is, the union of Anglophones and Francophones of the grassfields. To counteract it the regime then put in place enormous political and economic resources in order to split, and undermine the alliance through creating a counter group known as the 'Sawa'[23] movement said to bring together all the coastal tribes whose ancestors were believed to have emerged from the oceans.

Bamileke/Anglophone co-operation has faced several challenges in recent times and seems to be on the rocks. It will not an overstatement to say it is increasingly becoming a fading alliance – if the twin elections of June 2002 are anything to go by. This is not unconnected to the coming into being of the Southern Cameroon's National Council (SCNC) and its vocal claim to the specificity of Anglophones as a people with a peculiar identity and specific problems. This state of affairs has alarmed many Bamileke who support the alliance with Anglophones. Henceforth, there are strong indications that members of this union will have to part ways so as to allow each group to fly with its own political wings in trying to forge its own political future.

The collapse of the alliance is neither surprising nor is it difficult to comprehend in the opinion of analysts.[24] Anglophones and Francophones are socialised differently, which means whether we are 'sawas' or 'grasslanders' we may have a common past but our destinies will be different. Since our socialisations are varied we end up internalising not only different languages (French and English) but different norms, values, mentalities as well as the cultural models associated with the languages, for, after all, no language exists ex nihilo, but is the offspring of a particular culture and *weltanschauung*.[25] As long as the citizens of a country do not read and speak the same language, have different educational experiences (read different textbooks, literatures, histories, have different heroes etc), their terms of reference will differ and there will often be a dearth of consensus in several aspects of national life.[26] The Cameroonian experience since the re-birth of political pluralism lends much credibility to this assertion.

It is clear that at the beginning of democratisation the Bamileke had their peculiar concerns. They hoped to see the advent of a peaceful, stable and predictable political atmosphere for the flourishing of business activities, less discrimination on the basis of tribe, and more recognition given to merit and equal opportunities for all. They wished in short to see a country in which no citizen would be regarded as a foreigner in any part of the country they chose to settle – an obvious concern for anyone involved in business. This means that the idea of federalism fervently defended by their Anglophone political allies does not sit well with the Bamileke who are spread nation-wide. Sooner or later the policy of federalism was going to put the two groups on a collision course. While the workings of federalism favour groups that are concentrated in given geographical locations in terms of autonomy or self-government rights, it works against the interests of groups that are very dispersed and constitute minorities in several regions. This is one of the major problems facing the Bamileke today, namely, that wherever they settle and begin to prosper the local inhabitants, as it should be expected out of the natural instinct of envy, start erecting protective measures which discriminate against them. This is the likely scenario that obtains in a federal arrangement that is poorly worked-out and this scares the group.

Muslim/Non-Muslim Relations in North Cameroon

The three northern provinces contain about 30 percent of the country's population.[27] With the Islamic holy wars or Jihad of Othman Dan Fodio, the northern region came under Islamic influence. The Fulani, also known as Fulbe, became islamicised while the rest of the northern tribes, pejoratively given the generic name 'Kirdi', meaning pagans or heathens, by the Fulani refused to submit to the dictates of the new religion imposed by the sword. The Kirdis who constitute the majority group in North Cameroon are either Christians or animists. However, as history was to make it, Cameroon's first post-independence President, Ahmadou Ahidjo, was a Fulbe. No sooner had he acceded the supreme magistracy of the country than he immediately sought to broaden his political base. To this effect he wanted to present the entire population of the North in the eyes of the rest of the country as constituting as single group strongly united under the banner of Islam.[28]

The non-islamicised ethnic groups had to grapple with the problem of assimilation for as long as Ahidjo continued in power.[29] When democratic openings set in almost a decade after the end of Ahidjo's reign, the Kirdis had started organising themselves under their own political leaders and sought to put an end to Fulani and Islamic domination.[30] The ruling CPDM government was also very instrumental in promoting the Kirdi cause, especially when it realised it could make political capital out of the region, pitting Kirdis against Fulanis who are mostly in the rival National Union for Democracy and Progress (NUDP), the biggest indigenous political party in the northern region. It is in this light that we can best comprehend the creation of many administrative parties[31] in the North, the several appointments[32] to cabinet posts made to the benefit of the elite originating from this region, the most underscolarised in the country. The start of democratisation, consequently, saw the Kirdis at daggers drawn with their former political masters, the Fulbe, whom they blame for all their woes ranging from socio-economic stagnation to educational and political retardation since the beginning of the entire post-independence era.

Pahouin Relations with Other Groups

The term Pahouin, Beti, or Fang is generally used to cover the ethnic groups that people most of what we know today as the Centre, South and parts of the East provinces of Cameroon. This group, which is very conscious of its privileged relations with the regime in place under Paul Biya, saw democratisation as a conspiracy directed against them intended to oust the ethnic group from power. In this light the normal reaction was to defend itself in the face of the Anglo-bami democratic onslaught masterminded by the SDF party.[33] All attacks or criticism levelled against the government in power regarding tribalism, embezzlement of public funds, poor handling of the economy, waste, human rights abuses etc, at the dawn of multipartyism by a newly constituted and buoyant private press were interpreted rightly or wrongly as a personal assault on the ethnic group as whole. Individual members of the group then thought it necessary to create various associations and movements in order to fight back in defense of the Pahouin ethnic nation which now became more important than the national fatherland under the circumstances, against the tribal enemy and bête noire, the anglo-bami. This consequently plunged the country into a bizarre sort of modern tribal showdown, thereby tribalising the whole democratisation enterprise.[34]

It must be underscored that though the private press did much in exposing wrong-doing in high places in its early formative years, it definitely contributed in no small way to ethnicising politics and creating a sense of insecurity in the minds of the incumbents who thought that in the event of their losing power their lives, and those of their families and kinsmen, could be threatened by the new occupants of political power. How far the lack of moderation and accommodationist outlook on the part of African oppositionists has led to the retardation of democratisation is anybody's guess. The bottom line however is that when there is a high level of mistrust between an in-coming and an out-going political elite, the latter cannot easily cede power to the former.

This in a nutshell was the state of relations among the main groups at the beginning of the democratic transition. Our next task is to analyse how this has impacted on the rules of the democratic process.

Establishing the Rules of the Democratic Game (modus operandi)

Against this background of linguistic and ethnic competition, it has been difficult to evolve a set of equitable rules to regulate elections in Cameroon thus far. The fear that power could revert to somebody in the opposite camp is strong among the current power holders.

There is no gainsaying that most African elections, for the same reasons evoked here, have been held according to rules and under conditions that no reasonable person would consider fair to all the competing teams. Because of this Michael Chege has described them as 'highly flawed'[35] Most sitting governments abuse the powers of incumbency in several ways; fixing unilaterally the calendar of electoral events, allowing the biased registration of voters and the subsequent manipulation of voters registers, control over the returning officers and voting operations etc. In some instances, the ruling party's desire to determine the outcome[36] of the election has been so manifest that opposition parties have preferred to boycott it.[37] For an election to be considered free and fair though, the outcome should be fairly uncertain to all competitors.[38] Again on the abuse of incumbency, in Cameroon government often proceeds on the eve of elections to the transfer or redeployment of district officers, prefects, governors and even ministers. Those who contributed in winning previous elections for the party – even fraudulently – are promoted, those who could not 'doctor' election results in their areas of jurisdiction are punitively transferred to the suburbs or relieved of their posts. Administrators in opposition strongholds are often on the hot seat with the threat of demotion hanging over their heads like the fabled sword of Damocles since it is more difficult to manage elections here to the ruling party's favour.[39] Sometimes the party in power gerrymanders constituencies in their favour through the creation of new administrative units and constituencies in areas likely to vote for it. Also the criteria for the allocation of parliamentary and council seats are often manipulated so that a smaller region in terms of population may at the end of the day have more representation than a bigger one.[40]

Another weapon in the government's electoral arsenal is the judiciary. It is not a body independent of the executive as of now [41], but it participates in the management of elections. The vote counting operations at the level of the divisions are presided over by magistrates as provided for by law.[42] Given that the judiciary is still an arm of the executive, it is often seen to be meddling in electoral politics in an obvious attempt to protect its own interests through serving its master. Certainly it is due to the important role magistrates play in determining the outcome of elections or in fixing election results – a role second only to the military in sustaining the regime in power – that recently magistrates were accorded handsome pay rise and various allowances. This has been interpreted as an attempt to buy the consciences of judges because of their nuisance value.

The thread that runs through all of Cameroon's electoral laws[43] is the omnipotence and omnipresence of the Ministry of Territorial Administration in election matters. The contention here is not that the administration should not run elections but that the manipulative influence of the administrative bureaucracy is enormous since it is not an independent and neutral body. When we know that most African administrations are basically run by members of the ethnic group in power that completely dominates it, thanks to tribalism (and Cameroon is no exception) we easily side with the argument that an independent management body is indispensable for the conduct of any credible election that could confer legitimacy on the winners. This will be difficult to come by if the national question is still on the table as it is in our present case.

As usual, in reaction to both internal and outside pressure to reform its electoral laws, the government created a body called the National Elections Observatory[44] (NEO), not to organise but to 'observe and supervise'[45] elections. The twin elections (both legislative and municipal) of 30 June 2002 reveal that NEO's role in electoral matters is definitely marginal. Since the body has no jurisdiction over the electoral operations themselves, they can only make recommendations based on what they observe to the competent administrative authority [46] to redress the electoral irregularity in question. In fact there is no evidence that the June 2002 elections, the first that NEO observed, enjoyed more transparency than previoius ones since the start of the democratic transition; notably those of 1997 and 1992. Instead the verdict at the polls shows that we are probably moving towards a new form of authoritarianism[47] and a record voter apathy.[48] For instance, the results in the legislative body saw the ruling party winning over 80 percent of the seats, precisely 149 seats out of a total of 180, as compared to the 116 it gained in 1997. Its principal challenger, the SDF, won 22 seats as against 43 it had in 1997. The NUDP won only one seat, unlike in 1997 when it won 13. The CDU managed to conserve its 5 seats in the party leader's native region.

The same trend was observed in the council elections where the ruling party won 85 percent of the 337 available councils. It increased the share of councils it controls from 219 in the 1996 elections to 286 in 2002. In contrast, the SDF fell from 62 councils in 1996 to 36 in the 2002 poll, the NUDP fell from 29 councils in 1996 to barely 3, the CDU fell from 9 to 8, the UPC from 5 to 3 and the MDR from 5 to 1.

All in all, it could argued convincingly that elections in present day Cameroon by and large are simply a symbolic routine meant to please western aid donors and human rights groups but certainly not to select political leaders.

Conclusion and Future Perspectives

Democratisation in Cameroon is obviously passing through a crisis period. For over a decade now there has been no indication that the transition to democracy is becoming consolidated, with major disagreements persisting on basic issues directly affecting the political future of the country. The emergence of Anglophone nationalism as earlier predicted by Bernard Fonlon[49] nearly forty years back, is today a stumbling block to any meaningful advance in the area of democracy. Presently doubts are being cast on the loyalty[50] of Anglophones as they claim the right to live with their own specific identity in a state where the majority is Francophone. When we add this obstacle to the several ethnic micro-nationalisms that abound we realise that serious difficulties lie ahead. Thus regionalism and ethnicity have become political issues that threaten to torpedo the Cameroonian democratic boat.

To address these issues which are not new to the human race, we may draw inspiration from the solutions that have been adopted by the old democracies such as Canada, Switzerland, Germany, Great Britain, Belgium and others. Some amount of decentralisation, federalism, self-government rights, poly-ethnic rights[51] and special representation rights[52] may come into play, depending on the circumstances of the sub-national groups cohabiting. When these measures are put in place and mutual confidence is restored we may then proceed confidently to enact equitable rules for genuine democratic competition.

It is no exaggeration to state that so far we have experienced what Huntington and Moore describe as 'exclusionary elections'– call them liberal-machiavellian elections – where the overall objective of the government is to prevent the authentic manifestation of popular wishes while maintaining a liberal facade.[53]

Notes

1. G. Sorensen, *Democracy and Democratization*, Boulder, Colorado, Westview Press, 1993, p.39
2. D. Potter et al., eds., *Democratization*, Cambridge, Polity Press, 1992, p.3.
3. L. Diamond, *Political Culture and Democracy in Developing Countries*, Boulder, Colorado, Rienner, 1993, p. 431.
4. J. Schumpeter, *Capitalism, Socialism and Democracy*, London, Allen & Unwin, 1976, p. 269.
5. See notably, M. Banock, *Le Processus de Démocratisation en Afrique, le cas camerounais*, Paris, L'Harmattan, 1992; N. Mbarga, *Ruptures et Continuités au Cameroun*, Paris, 1993; M. Kamto, *L'Urgence de la Pensée*, Yaoundé, Mandara, 1993, E. Mbuyinga, *Cameroun/Kamerun, La Transition dans l'Impasse*, Paris, L'Harmattan, 1994.
6. P. Biya, *Communal Liberalism*, London, Macmillan, 1987.
7. G. Sorensen, op.cit., p.41.
8. The most important irregularity was that the procedure of revising the federal constitution, which called for a concurrent majority of Anglophone and Francophone MPs, was carefully shoved aside by Ahidjo. Some say it was the desire to control oil just discovered in the Anglophone region that prompted the hasty revision.
9. N. Susungi, *The Crisis of Unity and Democracy in Cameroon*, Abidjan, 1991; A. Mukong, *The Case for the Southern Cameroons*, CAMFECO, USA, 1990; E. Mbuyinga, *Tribalisme et Problème Nationale en Afrique Noire*, Paris, l'Harmattan, 1989; L. M. Nkoum-Me-Ntseny, 'Dynamique de Positionnement Anglophone et Libéralisation Politique au Cameroun', *Cameroonian Political Science Review*, Vol. 1, Feb. 1996, pp. 68-100.
10. See on this head the Federal Constitution of 1 September 1961.
11. This position was adopted by the All Anglophone Conference (AAC 1) in the Buea Declaration of April 1993, p. 29.
12. See SDF election manifesto for the 30 June 2002 twin elections.
13. As one of the measures to placate the Anglophones it is almost a constitutional custom since the 1990s to appoint the PM from Anglophone Cameroon.
14. This was during the 41st anniversary celebration of the independence of Southern Cameroons as part of the Federation of Nigeria.
15. D. Lembezat, *Le Cameroun*, Nouvelles Editions, Latines, Paris, 1965 and in the opinion of anthropologists such as Prof. Nkwi.
16. H. Bandolo, *La Flamme et la Fumée*, Yaoundé, Sopecam, 1985.

17. M. Krieger, 'Cameroon's Democratic Crossroads', *Journal of Modern African Studies*, 32, 4 (1994): pp. 605-28, Collectif: Pour Changer le Cameroun, *Le Cameroun Eclaté? Anthologie des Revendications*, 1992, pp.540-67.
18. Estimated at about 20 percent of Cameroon's population. J .L. Dogmo, *Le Dynamisme Bamileke*, Thesis, Paris, 1979, p.1082.
19. The most bloody was the inter-tribal clash between Bamileke settlers and the local inhabitants, the Bakossi of Tombel, South West province in 1966.
20. J.P. Fogui, *L'Intégration Politique au Cameroun*, Paris, LGDJ, 1990, 1957.
21. R.A. Joseph, 'Economy and Society', in R.. A. Joseph (ed.) *Gaullist Africa, Cameroon under Ahmadou Ahidjo*, Enugu, Fourth Dimension, 1978, p. 158.
22. A line of thinking which is common currency in most Yaoundé-based newspapers published by indigenes, such as *Le patriote*, *L'Indépendant* and others.
23. M. Tatah, *Constitutionalism, Press and Factional Politics: Coverage of Sawa Minority Agitations, Réforme Constitutionnelle*, Yaoundé, Friedrich Ebert, 1996, p. 182.
24. Debates we engaged in as fourth year students in Yaoundé university were to the effect that the modern educated generations would share and deal more with members of their linguistic group than with their tribal folks on the other side of the linguistic divide.
25. A German word for way of life or cultural model.
26. The much heralded convergence of interests between Anglophone and Francophone grassfield people on the one hand and Anglophone and Francophone sawas on the other was never seen during the constitutional talks of the mid-1990s aimed at drafting a democratic grundnorm for the country. Instead it was clearly observed live on television cameras that there were basically two opposing camps at the Yaoundé talks, namely, a Francophone unitarist camp that defended a unitary draft constitution and an Anglophone federalist camp that supported a federal draft constitution. For reasons that are obvious the Anglophone cabinet ministers in President Biya's government decided to sit on the fence. There was no other constitutional draft proposal espousing the Bakweri, the Bassa Bamileke, Pahouin, Fulani or Toupouri philosophy on what form the modern nation-state should take. Yet we are told these groups matter as much, if not more, than the two principal linguistic communities in the country, i.e Francophones and Anglophones.
27. M. Banock, op. cit.; also see 1986 Census Results, Directorate of Statistics, Ministry of Plans and Regional Development, Yaoundé.
28. R.G. Nlep, *L'Administration Publique Camerounaise*, Paris, LGDJ, 1986, p. 215.
29. See D. Dakole *Libre Derrière les Barreaux*, Paris, Jaquar, 1993.
30. M. Banock, op. cit., p. 35; *Le Messager*, No 42 of January 1992, p. 42.
31. Examples of such parties include, the 'Parti National pour le Progrès' (ANP) of Antar Gassagay, the 'Alliance Nationale pour la Démocratie et le Progrès' (ANDP) of Hamadou Moustapha, the 'Mouvement pour la Défense de la République' (MDR) of Dakole Daissala etc.
32. Some of the key cabinet posts held today by northerners are in the hands of non-muslims such as the post of Speaker of the House, President of the Economic and Social Council and Defense.

33. M. Banock, op. cit., p. 35.
34. See *Le Patriote*, No. 87 of 4 October 1991, *Challenge Hebdo*, No 39, July 1991; Mbarga N, *Ruptures et Continuités au Cameroun*, op.cit.
35. M. Chege, 'Between Africa's Extremes', *Journal of Democracy*, Vol. 6, 1 (1995): 48.
36. W. Boek, *How to Establish a Democracy or Improve the One You Have*, College of Democracy Press, Arlington, Virginia, 1993, p. 35.
37. Opposition parties boycotted the 1992 legislatives and the 1997 presidentials in Cameroon for these same reasons.
38. See W. J. M. Mackenzie, *Free Elections*, London, Allen & Unwin, 1958, p. 168.
39. In the constituency of Dschang in Menoua division of the West province, after the June 2002 elections, the minister of towns, Mbafou Claude, a local elite and later the Prefect of Dschang, Muluh Takweh lost their posts because of poor management of elections in an opposition stronghold where super vigilante militants exposed several incidents of 'ambulance voters'.
40. The South province, for example, is the smallest in the country with a representation that is proportionally higher than other provinces.
41. Even though the 1996 revised constitution of Cameroon promises to elevate it to the status of an independent power, in Article 31.
42. Law No. 92/020, op. cit., Article 40 (1).
43. The Laws are: Law No. 92/010 of 17 September 1992, laying down conditions governing the Vacancy of and Election to the Presidency of the Republic; Law No. 92/020 of 16 December 1991 relating to the Election of Members of Parliament, and Law No.92/002 of 14 August 1992 relating to the Election of Municipal Councillors.
44. Created by Law No. 2000/016 of 19 December 2000.
45. Article 6 of Law No. 2000/016 of 19 December 2000.
46. Article 12 of same law.
47. M. Kamto, *Pouvoir et Droit en Afrique Noire*, Paris, LGDJ, 1987, p. 490.
48. Many are reluctant to vote because they think the whole talk about democratisation is a hoax.
49. B. Fonlon, 'Shall We Make or Mar?', in *Abbia, The Cameroon Cultural Review*, Special Edition, March 5, 1964.
50. J.G. Gros, 'The Hard Lessons for Cameroon', *Journal of Democracy*, Vol. 6, No. 3, 1995, p. 117.
51. President Ahidjo instituted admission quotas in all competitive entrance examinations into state professional schools following Decree No.82/407 of 7 September 1982. Also see his interview in *Cameroon Tribune* No.2377 of 18 May 1982. This is similar to the notions of positive discrimination, preferential hiring or benign quotas in the USA.
52. See generally, L. Arend, *Democracy in Plural Societies*, op. cit., P. Kaiser, 'From "Imagined Community" to "Multicultural Mosaic": The Politics of Difference in Tanzania', *African Journal of Political Science*, Vol. 6,1, June 2001, p. 98.
53. S. Huntington & C. R. Moore, eds., *Authoritarian Politics in Modern Society*, 1975: 15.

11

Protection against Human Rights Abuses in the Central Africa Sub-region: The Case of Children

Margaret Ayike

Introduction

The concept of human rights provides a way of thinking about events. It is a device for thinking about the real, and expressing our thoughts.[1] The concept raises difficulties which stretch well beyond cases of extreme cruelty and injustice. It is commonly believed that human rights and democracy are mutually supportive or related to each other by definition. The Vienna declaration of 1993, for example, asserted that democracy and human rights were 'inter-dependent and mutually reinforcing'.[2] The relations between the two are however quite complex. Similar values such as the respect for the dignity of the individual may form the basis of both human rights and democracy. Democracy may also be, empirically, the best form of government for protecting human rights, although some electoral democracies fail to protect economic and social rights while some authoritarian regimes do so quite well.[3]

In the above light, I wish to situate this study within the struggles for democratisation and quest for democratic renewal in the sub-region through the protection of the Children's Human Rights. For the purpose of this study, by children here will be every human being under the age of 18 years unless maturity is attained earlier under national law.[4]

Children Human Rights are routinely denied the basic protection that most states and private individuals take for granted: the right to an education, to enjoy freedom of movement, freedom from torture, freedom from discrimination and protection from armed conflict. Children's human rights are the blocks with which we build a human rights culture in societies and secure human rights for future generations.[5]

Children around the world suffer appalling abuses. Too often, street children are killed or tortured by police. Children as young as seven or eight are recruited or kidnapped to serve as soldiers in military forces in countries like the DRC and Rwanda. Sometimes as young as six years old, children are forced to work under extremely difficult conditions often as bonded labourers.

They are imprisoned in inhumane conditions, at times in cells with adults. They are often brutalised by guards or not protected from assaults by other inmates. Refugee children, often separated from their families, are vulnerable to exploitation, sexual abuse or domestic violence.

Ironically, in the care of the state, children are often subjected to abuse and mistreatment – orphaned and abandoned children are housed in appalling institutions where they suffer from cruelty and neglect; many die.[6] For many students, life in and outside of the classroom is intolerable – at the hands of peers and teachers, many children suffer acts of discrimination, abuses, sexual violence, and harassment.

In many countries, teachers are allowed to use corporal punishment on children. Children are discriminated against in education because of their race or ethnicity. Children orphaned or otherwise affected by HIV/AIDS are discriminated against and often are left to fend for themselves.

In the past, this huge and largely voiceless population has fallen through the cracks in the international human rights arena. Traditional children's humanitarian groups have focused mainly on vital survival and developmental projects, and have rarely addressed other human rights concerns because they could not afford to antagonise host governments. Human rights groups have focused chiefly on the rights of adults. As the human rights movement was founded out of the concern for political dissidents, it has sometimes overlooked those ofchildren, whose persecution is unrelated to their views.

Thus, the convention on the rights of the child (CRC), puts children's rights on the world's agenda; it is the most widely rectified treaty in the world. Adopted by the United Nations General Assembly on November 20, 1989, the convention promises children around the world the right to life, liberty, education and health care.

The above instrument provides protection to children in armed conflicts, protection from discrimination, protection from torture or cruel, inhuman or degrading treatment or punishment, protection with the justice system, and protection from economic exploitation, in addition to many other fundamental protections. Despite the convention's near universal ratification (only the US and Somalia have not ratified it),[7] children are still denied their basic rights.

To guarantee the human rights of children is to invest in the future. Children's rights are the building blocks for a solid human rights culture, the basis for securing human rights for future generations. Also, as human beings, children are entitled to all the rights guaranteed by the Universal Declaration of Human Rights

(UDHR) and the various treaties that developed from it. But children also need special protection and care from adults since they are targeted simply because they are dependent and vulnerable.

However, for countless children around the world, these promises have been broken.[8] The armed conflicts that have raged in all quarters of the world have produced appalling abuses of children's rights. Hundreds of thousand of children have been pressed into service as soldiers. Millions have become refugees - displaced from their homes, often separated from their families with their future and safety uncertain. Street children on every continent endure harassment and physical abuse by police. Even schools, intended to promote the healthy development of children, may be the site of abuse. In some countries, the use of corporal punishment by teachers has resulted in injury and even death. In others, gay and lesbian students endure harassment and violence by their peers, while school authorities fail to intervene.

Millions of children have no access to education, work long hours under hazardous conditions, or languish in orphanages or detention centres where they endure inhumane conditions and daily assaults on their dignity, in violation of their rights guaranteed to them under the convention.

The Central African sub-region, on which this study is based, is not exempted from the abuses and violence on children cited above, owing to its specific characteristics. I concentrate therefore on analysing the situation of crisis, reforms and reconstructions in the Central African sub-region.

In order to create an appropriate atmosphere of analysis to the above problems, our working hypothesis will be that the state of children's Human Rights in the Central African sub-region has been exacerbated by the general instability that characterises the region, although pertinent efforts have been made to remedy this situation.

The Situation Regarding Children's Human Rights in Central Africa

Central Africa like other parts of the world is prone to human rights abuses on children. These abuses are perpetrated by the state, individual or community in which the children are living. The state does this through 'state violence against children' and the individual and community do so via exploitation, as will be examined below in detail. It should be noted that, in whatever form it is manifested, it remains a Human Right abuse, hence degrading to humanity.[9]

Children and Armed Conflict

War is an every day reality for millions of children. Some have never known any other life; they have grown up in the midst of civil war, guerrilla insurgency, or the long-term occupation by a foreign army. For others, the world is suddenly turned upside down when invasion or ethnic cleansing forces them onto the road as refugees or displaced persons often separated from their families. Untold thousands have been killed, disabled or orphaned. Many more have died or suffered from starvation or malnutrition, or lack of clean water, sanitation and medical care. Witnessing brutal deaths and being surrounded by violence, fear and hardship traumatises many. And hundreds of thousands of children around the world are obliged to participate in the killing where they are used as child soldiers.

Children are not always the accidental victims of the carnage. Security forces and armed oppositions groups, either in retribution or to provoke outrage in each other's communities, kill some deliberately. Some, mostly girls, are singled out for sexual abuse. Many are killed and tortured because of where they live, or because of the politics, religion or ethnic origins of their family.

The use and maltreatment of children in armed conflicts are great violations to the children's Human Rights as stipulated in the international instruments protecting the right of the child.[10]

Child Soldiers

The use of children as armed personnel is another form of child abuse widely perpetrated in the Central African sub-region. Children recruited by both armed forces and armed opposition groups, and exploited as combatants. Many children have been forced to join by intimidation, including threats against families or abduction. Others volunteer, sometimes because they want to fight, sometimes because their families are destitute, and sometimes because they themselves are homeless and seeking food, shelter and security.

Most get only minimal training and equipment before being thrown into the firing line of an adult war. Casualty rates among children are generally high because of their inexperience, fearlessness and lack of training, and because they are often used for particularly hazardous assignments, such as intelligence work or planting landmines. In Colombia child soldiers are sometimes called 'Little Bees', because their size and agility enables them to move quickly and 'sting' their enemies.

A 1996 United Nations report on the impact of armed conflict on children raised international concern about the plight of children in war, prompting varying initiatives to end the use of child soldiers and other wartime abuses. The number of children killed every year by antipersonnel mines has dropped in the wake of massive efforts to end the use of the weapon and the adoption of the 1997 Mine Ban Treaty.[11] The adoption for the statute for the International Criminal Court holds out the hope of ending of the impunity of those who recruit children under the age of 15 in armed conflicts and target schools for attack.[12] The protocol to this convention insists now on 18 years as the minimum age to recruit children in armed conflicts.

More than 300,000 children under the age of 18 are thought to be fighting in conflicts around the world, and hundreds of thousands more are members of armed forces who could be sent into combat at any time. Although most child soldiers are between 15 and 18 years old, significant recruitment starts at the age of 10 and the use of even younger children has been recorded. Amnesty International (AI) has drawn attention to human rights abuses in the context of child recruitment both by governments and armed opposition groups in countries such as Angola, Burundi, Columbia, Democratic Republic of Congo, Rwanda, Sierra Leone and Uganda.[13]

In Burundi dozens of children are in prison accused of collaborating with the armed opposition. For some of these children contact with the opposition forces consisted of having being forced to carry weapons or undertake other duties. None has been tried and at least one was only 12 years old when he was arrested.

In northern Uganda, thousands of boys and girls have been abducted by the Lord's Resistance Army (LRA), and forced to fight against the Ugandan Army. The children are subjected to a violent regime. Those caught trying to escape are killed or tortured and both boys and girls are brutalised by being made to kill other children. LRA commanders own abducted children, with girls allocated to commanders in forced marriages and effectively held as sexual slaves.

There are a number of reasons why those under 18 should be excluded from military service. In most countries 18 years is the legal voting age and the age which marks the formal transition from childhood to adulthood, with the assumption of adult legal and moral responsibilities. Children who become combatants before they gain emotional maturity can suffer devastating psychological effects. Casualty rates among child soldiers who are innately less cautious than adults tend to be high and children are less likely than adults to survive battlefield injuries. Girl soldiers are generally expected to provide sexual services as well as to fight and so suffer the additional risk of sexually transmitted diseases, HIV/AIDS, pregnancy, childbirth or abortion. Participation in armed conflicts is necessarily 'hazardous' work which jeopardises the health, safety and moral development of children, and as such is contrary to article 32 of the CRC.

Refugees and the Internally Displaced

The Central African sub-region equally faces the problem of refugees and internally displaced, which becomes a major human rights challenge. Each year armed conflicts force many thousands of children to flee their homes in search of refuge. Sometimes they go with their families, sometimes alone, many get separated on the way. Their routes to safety are often dangerous.

Many children flee because of the abuses directed at them. Children may engage in political activities, such as joining demonstrations, distributing leaflets or attempting to organise in their schools and workplaces. This is often enough to get them detained and tortured. In many countries, just being a student is dangerous, as schools and colleges are suspected of being hotbeds of radical opposition to the government.

Eight years of brutal internal armed conflict in Sierra Leone have forced hundreds of thousands of civilians, many of them children, to seek refuge in neighbouring countries or in other parts of Sierra Leone. Children have not been spared the atrocities of the conflict: many have been killed, deliberately mutilated or maimed, others abducted and forced to fight with the rebel forces. Girls have been raped and forced into slavery. Many of the refugees and displaced are unaccompanied children who become separated from their parents after being abducted by rebel forces, or after their parents were killed or abducted in attacks on their towns or villages.

Following the rebel incursion into Freetown in January 1999, UNICEF registered some 3400 children as missing: by mid-May 1999, only about 500 had subsequently been traced and reunited with families.[14]

Also many thousands of displaced children have lost both parents and are left in charge of families and households. Children in displaced persons' camps inside their own country are seldom able to carry on with their schooling, and are often subjected to forced recruitment in the armed forces, and to exploitation and sexual abuse.

Those children who are forced to flee across international borders and thus recognised as refugees, have formal guarantees of protection: government parties to the CRC and to the 1951 UN convention (UN refugee Convention) and the protocol relating to the state of refugee are obliged to give them protection and security. Unfortunately this guarantee does not often translate into better treatment.

Juvenile Justice

The rights of the child to special care and assistance are being disregarded by the very institutions that should be protecting them. Children often suffer neglect, abuse and violence in the administration of juvenile justice which is contrary to article 19 of CRC. When children are picked up and questioned by the police, they are frequently beaten and humiliated. Their legal rights are often ignored: their parents are not informed, of their whereabouts; they are held in degrading conditions, and often have to share cells with adults.

Some are denied the right to fair trial, and are given sentences that disregard the key objective of juvenile justice: the child's rehabilitation and reintegration into the society. For the vast majority of children, the reality is not reintegration and special care, but punishment, intolerance and greater marginalisation.

Yet when children come into conflict with the law, it is most often for minor, non-violent offences; usually theft, and in some cases their only 'crime' is that they are poor, homeless and disadvantaged. Children forced to live on the streets are particularly vulnerable to arbitrary arrest and ill-treatment. Many survive by begging, petty crime or prostitution, activities which bring them regularly to the attention of the police. Some are detained and ill-treated simply because they are easy prey; others are arrested under laws which make destitution, vagrancy and begging criminal offences.

The CRC sets out the fundamental principles which should guide the treatment of all children who come into contact with the law. In common with the laws of most countries, the CRC prohibits torture and cruel, inhuman or degrading treatment or punishment (Article 37 of CRC). Yet legal safeguards are not enforced. In many countries, young women and girls taken into custody by the police are vulnerable to rape and sexual abuse which is an abrogation of article 34 of CRC.

Also the reality is that many children in detention are not accorded even basic minimum safeguards. Children are detained without charge or trial, denied access to lawyers and relatives, and are tortured and equally ill-treated to obtain confessions. Where children are held without access to relatives or legal counsels, the risk of physical abuse increases dramatically. All the countries in this sub-region are sites of the above abuses on children, therefore, actions have to be taken in order to reform and reconstruct the democratisation process here.

It should be noted that the best interest of the child must be the guiding principle behind all procedure and justice systems affecting children. Their overriding aim must be to protect and promote children's fundamental rights and to give young offenders the greatest possible chance of reintegrating into society.

Children in the community and family

In ratifying the CRC, governments committed themselves to protecting all the rights of the child - social and economic, as well as civil and political. Under the CRC, children are not only protected from abuses of state power but from all forms of physical or mental violence or abuse while in the care of 'parents', legal guardians or any other person who has the care of the child, including schools. The CRC affirms that every child has the right to an adequate education and standard of living. It establishes the right of the child to be free from sexual abuse and exploitation, and the illicit use of drugs. It commits states to protecting children from economic exploitation and work that may that interfere with education or damage their health.

Delivery on this commitment is an enormous challenge. Some governments have taken worthwhile initiatives, ranging from legislation against bonded labour to human rights education, with varying degrees of implementation and success. But this cannot excuse the way state officials help to perpetuate a wide range of abuses against children in the community and family, either through active collusion and complicity or through tacit toleration or acquiesence.

A spectrum of abuses faced by children in the family and community ranges from ill-treatment in institutions to violence in the family, from child trafficking to child-bonded labour. The vulnerability of children to such abuses often depends on other aspects of their identity such as gender, ethnicity or economic status. This is a powerful reminder of the indivisibility of human rights as stipulated in article 2 of the CRC.

The denial of one set of rights leads to the abuse of others. Children denied an education because they are girls or because they are poor and forced to work are condemned to a cycle of maginalisation, poverty and powerlessness that involves further violations of their civil, political, economic, social and cultural rights.

In what follows I will be looking more closely at human right abuses by non-state actors, including business and private institutions and at the state's role in failing to prevent such abuses.

Abuses in private institutions

Many children are abused in institutions such as schools and orphanages, that are supposed to look after their needs. Even when the abuses become widely known, the authorities appear unwilling to take decisive actions to protect the children.

Bonded and Exploitative Child Labour

Children all over the world are hard at work. The ILO 1995 estimate put the number at 250 million for the developing countries,15 and the Central Africa sub-region is not excepted. Such labour usually take place in fields and sweat shop factories, in mines, building, or brothels and especially in private homes. They often work in dangerous and unhealthy environments and are deprived of the rights promised them in the CRC such as health, (article 24), education (articles 28-29), recreation (article 31), and even the childhood itself. Children grow up illiterate, unskilled and prone to crime. Many are sold or forced into labour by their parents or families.

Child labourers are often employed in rural communities, many as bonded labourers. Some are sold to a rural landlord to work against a debt incurred by the family. Others are born into bondage simply by being the child of a bonded labourer who works in the family unit to pay off a family debt.

For many children this is the only work they can find, while in some societies children from poor families are placed in another home by their parents in return for cash. Child domestics may be forced to work long hours for little or no salary, often endure permanent or long term isolation from their families and friends, and rarely have the chance to attend school. An unknown number suffer rough treatment at hands of their employers, sometimes including severe beatings. The majority of the 250 million child workers internationally are involved in domestic labour.16

The issue is complicated. Not all child workers are abused, and there is an ongoing debate about the degree to which children should be allowed to contribute to their families economically. Some argue that prohibiting child labour completely would increase the economic deprivation of extremely poor families who often depend on money brought in by children for their basic needs. Others say that removing children from some industries will only force them onto the streets or into more dangerous and exploitative forms of work. There is no easy answer to this. Under the CRC, the 'best interest of the child'17 should be the primary consideration in all discussions affecting them. In addition, child labour often become a critical link in the cycle of deprivation and disadvantage that feeds other abuses. As a minimum, governments must ensure that child workers are protected; including by regulating children's working conditions, eliminating small children from the work place and ensuring that those who abuse child labourers are brought to justice.

Unlike child soldiers, child labourers prevail in countries which have relative political stability, or at least are not at war. Countries like Cameroon and Gabon are not at war but they harbour a good number of child labourers, which is an abuse of children's human rights. All the countries in this sub-region suffer from a prevalence of child labourers irrespective of whether they are embroiled in violent conflict or not.

Child Trafficking and Sexual Slavery

Every day across the world a miserable cargo of women and children is being trafficked across well-beaten paths. The illegal and highly profitable transport and sale of human beings for the purpose of exploiting their labour is a human rights abuse with global dimensions.[18] In any given year, many thousands of women and girls around the world are lured, abducted or sold into forced labour, forced prostitution, domestic service or involuntary marriage.

Organised groups kidnap girls and sometimes boys, often very young, and sell them into prostitution, domestic servitude or bonded labour. Smugglers take advantage of the economic vulnerability of young women from disadvantaged and marginalised groups, luring them with the promise of jobs or acquiring them from their impoverished families. The number of very poor children being sold into prostitution is on the increase, apparently because of the preference for virgins and the fear of AIDS. A significant number of trafficked children end up being detained by the authorities on grounds such as prostitution. Many remain in detention for indeterminate periods, as they have no money for bail or to make the journey home.

Trafficking within the Central African sub-region takes broadly two forms: internal and external. Internal trafficking is within a country; from rural to urban zones (Cameroon). External trafficking is a trans-border phenomenon. This form of smuggling in humans operates between countries within the African sub-region and even beyond.

Female Genital Mutilation

Female genital mutilation (FGM) is the surgical removal of parts of the genital organs. It is generally performed by traditional practitioners with crude instruments. It is painful, terrifying and traumatic. Most of the victims are young girls, usually between the ages of 4 and 10, although in some cultures, FGM is carried out in infancy or on newly married women. Long-term physical effects include permanent damage to the genital organs and mild to severe impairment of normal body functions, including the sexual ones, and can even be a cause of death. The psychological trauma is impossible to quantify.

FGM is practised in some 29 countries in Africa and in minority communities in other parts of the world. It is estimated to have afflicted well over 100 million women and girls. Some two million African girls are believed to undergo FGM each year. There is a complex web of interrelated cultural factors behind FGM. Its practitioners see it as a necessary right for initiation into womanhood and integration into the culture, without which a woman cannot marry. But it is increasingly opposed by women and men in Africa and elsewhere as a systematic form of violence against women and girls and a denial of their fundamental rights.

Street children

An estimated 100 million children live and work on the street – begging, peddling fruit, cigarettes or trinkets, shining shoes, often resorting to petty theft and prostitution to survive.[19] Some of them have family links, but many others have been abandoned, rejected, orphaned or have run away from home because of abuse or poverty.

These children sleep in parks or doorways, under bridges or in abandoned buildings; many are addicted to drugs. They often use inhalants such as glue, which are cheap and easily accessible, but which cause irreversible brain damage, as well as a host of physical debilities.[20] Very few street children enjoy the standards guaranteed by the CRC, which much be 'adequate for the child's physical, mental, spiritual, moral social development'.

Street children often fall victim of 'social cleansing' campaigns, in which local business owners pay to have them chased away or even killed. Many are victims of abuse, sometimes murder, by police and other authorities who are supposed to protect them. Amnesty International has documented violence against street children in many countries. Most countries in Central Africa harbour a large number of street children, including Burundi, Cameroon, RDC, and Rwanda.

The situation regarding child abuse sketched above illustrates the troubling extent to which the international community has failed children. These issues selected for attention here are not exhaustive but represent those which have been the focus of human rights investigation and advocacy over the past decades.

Factors Influencing Children's Human Rights Abuses in the Central African Sub-region

There are many factors that cause children to be abused in this sub-region to the extent that this article has already documented. Some of these factors are discussed below.

Natural Resources

Central Africa is the African sub-region most highly endowed with natural resources.[21] It holds the biggest expanse of tropical forest and in the Congo basin, the largest water reserve on the continent. In addition to the 'Geological Scandal' dormant in the DRC, major exploited resources include precious minerals (gold, diamonds, and some platinum), petroleum, bauxite and iron ore, as well as copper, cobalt, timber, hydroelectric power, uranium and natural gas. The presence of such resources can lead to an internecine conflict as various groups struggle to obtain a share of the spoils. It should be noted that children's rights are most violated in conflict-ridden areas like Chad, DRC, and Angola where there is an abundance of natural resources.

Demographic Factors

The sub-region contains nearly 100 million people,[22] spread unevenly across the region and within each country, between areas of high density (like Rwanda or Burundi), and those of low density like Sao Tome and Principe, Equatorial Guinea or even the DRC. On the whole the population is predominantly young, with approximately half the population in the 0–14 age bracket. Thus, because of the high infant population, the states, communities and families become unable to cater for the need of children. Hence the phenomena of child labour and numerous street children.

Poverty

Despite its vast natural resources, the Central African sub-region is generally poor. Gabon with an adjusted real GDP of USD 3641 per capita is the 'richest' of all countries in the economic community of central African states (ECCAS). Rwanda by contrast, is ranked second among the poorest countries of the world with only USD 352 per capita.[23] On the other hand, the sub-region's large population makes it potentially a large consumer market. But since regional integration is yet to gain ground, production is not very developed in every sector and country. The disparity between these countries in the region becomes a source of conflict and violence, hence child abuses.

Trade restrictions hamper the development of the market for consumer goods between the member-states of the sub-region. Forced to fend for themselves, local producers have generally taken things into their own hands, even if it means violating existing government regulations on regional trade. Smuggling, illicit exports and migration continue to increase unabated between Cameroon and Gabon, Gabon and Congo, the DRC and CAR, across the Congo River or in the Luanda area of the Congo-Angola border. This situation creates the opportunities for children to be involved in production, to be trafficked in several forms, and hence the abuse of their human rights.

In addition, the lack of a clear and sustained government commitment to promote sub-regional cooperation is not limited to economic issues. It is also evident in peace and security matters. According to the United Nations Standing Advisory Committee on security question in Central Africa, recurrent political crises and military hostilities have kept the sub-region 'continuously in the headlines for nearly 40 years'.[24] Child abuses have become rampant in an area where political and economic security are so strikingly absent.

Internal and Interstate Violence

The sub-region has witnessed a proliferation of internal and interstate violence. On account of cynical remarks about the inability of the sub-region to handle its numerous problems, one is often led to believe that nothing important ever happens here in the area of conflict management. The lack of conflict management mechanisms puts children's human rights in in even greater jeopardy.

The Geo-strategic Profile of Central African States

Nearly 60 percent of Central African countries (CAC) are currently either in a state of war or under precarious political and security conditions. Only four countries can boast of relative peace (i.e. the absence of war) and political stability. But here, too, political and ethno-regional tension persists, while material conditions have not improved much for the majority of the population. Therefore children who are most at risk because most vulnerable, become the most affected by the various forms of abuse.

A major cause of the gross violation of children's human rights in the sub-region remains the huge movement of refugees and of soldiers fleeing from war. This factor in particular has led to the increased rate at which children are trafficked and taken into child labour within and beyond Central Africa. For instance, Cameroon harbours a good number of refugees from DRC, Rwanda, Burundi and Chad.

Amnesty International in Bujumbura recently published a new report on poverty, isolation and ill treatment, Juvenile justice in Burundi,[25] which highlights the multiple abuses children are suffering at the hands of the law. The armed conflict and related human rights and humanitarian crisws in Burundi have particularly affected children. Their most basic civil, political economic, social and cultural rights have been routinely and massively violated by government security forces as well as by armed political groups. Children in detention are a sign of a human right crisis in Burundi and should not be forgotten. Burundi's prison population is predominantly male and adult and, relatively speaking the number of children in detention in Burundi is quite small. Out of a prison population of approximately 9000, some 160 are under the age of 18, of which most are boys. Child detainees however are spared none of the abuses inflicted on the adult detainees. They are arrested in violation of arrest and detention laws, some are tortured, some detained for long periods of time without trial, often in conditions amounting to cruel, inhuman and degrading treatment. The majority are detained with adults and are vulnerable to sexual abuse and exploitation. Few benefit from the assistance of a lawyer.

In March 2002, Amnesty International delegates visited six of Burundi's prisons as part of its research into the plight of child detainees in the country. The report included reference to cases such as that of Mossi Rokondo,[26] who was arrested in November 1999 at the age of 14 in Bubanza province, on suspicion of links with an armed political group. He is still awaiting trial three years later. Joseph Masabirie, then aged 15, was arrested in southern Burundi in May 2000 by soldiers on suspicion of belonging to an armed political group after failing to produce any identification. He was reportedly beaten on his legs and the back of his head and neck and stabbed on his right arm while in the custody of the gendarmerie.

Amnesty International also gathered information on hundreds of cases in which children, even babies, have been shot, bayoneted or beaten to death with impunity by members of the armed forces. Over fifteen children were extra-judicially executed in rural Bujumbura and Bubanza provinces between January and 2002. Scores of new extra-judicial executions including those of several children have taken place since.

However, the above are not the only cases of abuses in these aspects in Central Africa. There are others, but of which facts were difficult to be reached.

Institutional Actions to Prevent and Eliminate Human Rights Abuses on Children

Several institutions are active in the attempt to protect the human rights of children. In this part of the paper, I will refer to these efforts. They will be discussed under two broad headings: efforts at the sub-regional level and efforts at the international level. In analysing these efforts, distinctions will be made between the activities of state actors and of non-state actors, in order to reform and reconstruct the Central African sub-region from child abuses, hence promoting human rights and the democratisation process.

Inter-governmental efforts at the sub-regional level

The Sub-regional Centre for Human Rights and Democracy in Central Africa

This Centre was created to promote human rights and democracy in the sub-region. It works through the reinforcement of national and regional institutional capacities. It equally reinforces the capacity building of civil society at all levels. The Centre has been active in terms of the following activities: the organisation of training seminars in the techniques of lobbying and counselling regarding human rights, HIV/AIDS, racism, xenophobia and intolerance.[27]

It also offers internship programmes in the domain of human rights and makes subventions available to training institutions and coalitions of NGOs which are eligible in terms of the framework of the project. Many countries have already benefited from the activities of this Centre in one way or another, especially Equatorial Guinea, The Republic of Congo, and Cameroon.[28]

The Centre has also facilitated the adoption of the following perspectives in the 'Declaration De Malabo', in the domain of media, human rights and democracy:[29]

- The training of journalist with regard to human rights and democracy.
- The promotion at the sub-regional level of a network of women journalists specialised in the domains of human rights and democracy.
- Support to states and to the viability of community radio,
- Support for the creation of organs of the press by women and for women,
- Support for the production and the popularisation of programmes on questions linked to human rights and democracy, and
- Support for the creation and functioning of a sub-regional network of specialist journalists in the domain of human rights and democracy and to create social points.

The Centre also takes an interest in promoting peace and security in the region. For example, it took part in the sub-regional seminar in Brazzaville on the implementation of the UN action programme with a view to preventing, combating and eliminating the illegal commerce in light arms. It was also present at the 19th ministerial meeting of the UN Permanent Consultative Committee for Security Questions in Central Africa.[30]

The Supreme Council for Peace and Security in Central Africa

Alternatively called Le Conseil supérieur de Paix et de Sécurité de l'Afrique Central (COPAX), this initiative was created at the Yaoundé Summit on 25th February 1999.[31] This initiative came as a result of the decision by the heads of state and governments to establish a legal and institutional framework to promote and strengthen peace and security in the sub-region.

COPAX was established under the auspices of the UN Standing Advisory Committee for Security Questions in Central Africa, grouping all the eleven member states of the Economic Community of Central African States (ECCAS), the Secretary General on 20 May 1992, Pursuant to the resolution of the General Assembly.[32]

COPAX is thus a security mechanism and has a dual mission. First, it aims to prevent, manage and resolve conflicts in Central Africa. Second, it will undertake all and any necessary actions that can deal effectively with political conflict and lead to the promotion, preservation and consolidation of peace and security in the sub-region (Article 2). Further, it develops confidence-building measures and encourages arms limitation and development.

Non-Aggression Pact

Nine ECCAS members signed this initiative in Yaoundé on 8 July 1996. It is one of the major steps in Inter-State Cooperation on peace and security in Central Africa. ECCAS members, in order to reaffirm their commitment to inter-state cooperation on peace and security, took the responsibility to refrain in their mutual relations from the threat or use of force or aggression, either against the territorial integrity or independence of other states, or in any other manner inconsistent with the charter of the OAU.[33]

Early Warning Mechanism (EWM)

EWM was created out of the need for Inter-State Security Cooperation in Central Africa. For the first time at the Yaoundé Summit of 8 October 1996, the heads of state and governments of the sub-region decided to create an EWM for Central Africa in Libreville, Gabon. At a meeting in Libreville on 8 May 1997 over the political crisis in Zaire, the political leaders agreed on the necessity of creating an Inter-State Security Mechanism and Cooperation for the Prevention and Management of Conflicts in the sub-region.

The mission of EWM is three-fold.[34] First, it will regionally monitor the political, socio-economic and security situation throughout the sub-region. Second, it will identity all sources of tension and detects those that appear likely to degenerate into political conflict. Third, it will be expected to keep political leaders informed about potential sources of conflict and assist in implementing preventive measures decided by the region's leaders. Among three Units that it operates, the third would specialise in humanitarian and refugee assistance.

A Sub-Regional Parliament

The idea of a sub-regional parliament entered the discourse on peace and security in the sub-region for the first time at the conference on democratic institutions and peace in Central Africa.[35] In his opening statement at that Conference, President Teodoro Obiang Nguema Mbasogo of Equatorial Guinea made as impassioned defence of the linkages between democracy, peace and social justice.[36] He argued that peace and security could not be achieved without giving the people (including children) social justice, which is lacking. In conclusion, he proposed the establishment of a 'Sub-regional parliamentary assembly responsible for protecting the interests of the people'.

The sub-regional parliament is intended as a political framework to harmonise peace, security and economic measures, and to generate the political will to bring together the peoples of the Central African sub-region through their representatives. It is seen as a pre-eminent platform for the promotion of democratic values and practices, as well as the creation and dissemination of a culture of tolerance and peace among the people of Central Africa.

Multilateral Efforts at the International Level

The International Labour Organisation (ILO)

The ILO, which is an organ of the UN, is a specialised agency in the domain of labour, including child labour. The ILO has adopted many conventions to this end, notably Convention No.138, 1973 on the minimum age for child labour, child soldiers and other related abuses. Also, Convention No. 182 of 1999 enumerates the types of labour that a child below 18 years of age should not perform (Article 3) because they constitute abuse of children's physical, psychological and educational development. And last, Convention 184 of 2001, on safety and health in agriculture, defines the types of agricultural labour which children should not be engaged in, since that would be tantamount to an abuse of their rights (Article 1).

Second, in terms of institutional efforts, the ILO has a Bureau for the Central Africa sub-region. This Bureau has established a Multidisciplinary Team for Central Africa,[37] otherwise called 'Equipe Multidisciplinaire Pour l'Afrique Central' (EMAC). This organ is constituted from governments, non-governmental organisations, and partners in development. These actors collaborate in diverse domains, in order to combat the multiform abuses of children in this sub-region.

EMAC is therefore a sub-regional strategy by ILO, which was created to serve a double purpose. Firstly to bring its technical expertise closer, in order to rapidly respond to the abuses incurred on children. Secondly, it takes into consideration the specific characteristics of the Central Africa sub-region, promotes research on solutions and furthers cooperation among countries. This initiative also assists countries of the sub-region to adopt national plans of action to target human rights abuses on children. According to this body, national projects are encouraged which aim at the following:

- Basic education;
- Health and social protection;
- Apprenticeship and professional training;
- Leisure, sport, culture;
- Orientation, counselling, and welcoming children and young people and informing them how to solve their specific problems.

These projects created in urban and rural zones will lead, it is hoped, to social reconstruction in the post-conflict period, the reconstitution of social ties, the construction of peace at the elementary level, and hence contribute to the achievement of economic progress. The ILO collaborates closely with UNICEF in this domain.

Action by the International Community

To the international community, 'Humankind owes the child' the best it has to give.[38] To guarantee the human rights of children is to invest in the future. Children's rights are the building blocks for a solid human rights culture, the basis for securing human right for future generations. Children are entitling to all the rights guaranteed by the Universal Declaration of Human Rights (UDHR) and the various treaties that have developed from it.

The international community has an obligation to protect children from abuses. To this end, the community through the UN has taken the following actions to protect children's human rights.

First, the 1959 UN Declaration of the Rights of the Child set out 10 principles, which provided a powerful moral framework for children's rights, but which were not legally enforceable.

Second, the Convention on the Rights of the Child (CRC) was adopted by UN General Assembly in 1989, and entered into force the following year. Since then, the CRC has been ratified by every single UN member state in the world, except Somalia – which has had no central government able to do so – and the USA.

One of the guiding principles of the CRC is that the 'best interests of the child' should be a primary consideration in all decisions or procedures related to the child (Article 3). The rights contained in the CRC fall into four broad categories.

- Subsistence rights, including the right to food, shelter and health care.
- Development rights, which allow children to reach their fullest potential, including education and freedom of thought, conscience and religion.
- Protection rights, such as the right to life, and to protection from abuse, neglect or exploitation.
- Participation rights, which allow children to take an active role in community and political life.

The CRC elaborates rights according to the special needs and perspectives the child. It is the only human rights treaty that covers the full rights of children, stressing their indivisible nature and interdependence. By virtue of its comprehensive nature and universal ratification, the CRC stands as a landmark for the international consensus on the basic principles of the universality and indivisibility of all human rights. One of the key differences between the CRC and other treaties is that it recognises that rights must be actively promoted if they are going to be enforced. Article 42 imposes a responsibility on governments to make the CRC widely known to adults and children alike.

Amnesty International (AI)

AI is an international non-governmental organisation acting as a watchdog for human rights. AI has often highlighted individual cases of children who have been the victims of human rights violations such as torture, ill treatment or extra-judicial execution. But too often, AI's work on children has been incidental to its core research, and its campaigns have often been invisible in AI coverage of human rights violations in the adult sphere. In recent years, AI's membership forums have recognised the need for AI to increase work on children and adapt its research and accompanying strategy so that it can play a wider and more constructive role in promoting and protecting children's rights.

AI, guided by the framework of the CRC, develops its work on children around three key themes: Juvenile Justice, Children in Armed Conflict, and Children in the Community and Family.[39] By concentrating its efforts in these areas, it can combine its traditional strengths with a new field of work affording it a possibility to make a real contribution. AI's basic principal mode of action is by reminding states of treaties to protect the rights of the child. Equally, it engages other children's rights organisations like Save the Children in concerted action in support of human rights protection more generally. The value of the contribution of AI in the Central African sub-region can not be over-emphasised, especially the role it has played in denouncing human rights abuses in children in countries like the DRC, Rwanda, Chad, Burundi and Angola.[40]

Conclusion

The discussion above has attempted to highlight the problem of the abuse of children's human rights, a stumbling block for the Central African region in its struggle for democratisation. Our main preoccupation in this paper was to examine to what extent leaders and the community of this sub-region have taken action to redress 'the plight of children'. Much have been done to minimise child abuse in the region, both at national, sub-regional and international levels. The concern now remains regarding the implementation and operationaliation of the acts, instruments and institutions, in order to prevent and ultimately eliminate human rights abuses on children within and beyond this region.

Notes

1. Michael Freeman, *Human Rights: Key Concepts*, Polity Press, 2002, p.2
2. Ibid., p. 71.
3. Chun, L., 'Human Rights and Democracy: the case for decoupling', *International Journal for Human Rights*, 5(3), 19-44.

4. UN Convention on the Rights of the Child, 1989, article 1.
5. Amnesty International, 'Children's Human Rights: The Future Starts Here', http:/ www.amnestyusa.org/children/chr.html.
6. Human Rights Watch, December 2001 report, http://www.hrw.org/child.
7. Ibid.
8. Human Rights Watch, 'Promises Broken: An Assessment of Children's Rights on the 10th Anniversary of the Convention on the Rights of the Child, December 1999', http://www.hrw.org/campaigns/crp/promise.
9. Casa Alianza, 'Human Rights Violations, State Violence Against Children', presented by Bruce Harris, Executive Director Latin American Programmes, Casa Aliens, http://www.Casa-alianza.org.
10. UN Convention on Rights of the Child, 1989, Article 36 and 37 ILO conventions N 182, 1999 on Worst forms of child abuse Art. 3.
11. http://www.hrw.org/campaigns/crp/promises/op.cit.
12. UNCRC, 1989, Article 38.
13. http://www.amnestyusa.org/children/future-3.html.
14. http://www.amnestyusa.org/children/future_3.html.
15. ILO *Child Labour Briefing Material: The Problems*, Geneva, 2000, p. 2.
16. http://www.amnestyusa.org/children/future-4html.
17. UN CRC, 1989, article 3.
18. Peter Stalker, 'The No-Nonsense Guide to International Migration', *New internationalist*, 2001, and p. 57-62. See also United Nations (2000), General Assembly. Document A /55/383. Available at: www.undcp.org/palermo/convmain.html.
19. http://www.amnestyusa.org/children/future_4.html.
20. Heather Parker Lewis, *Also God's Children: Encounters with street kids*, Ihilihili Press, 2001.
21. Musifiky Mwanasali, 'Politics and security in Central Africa', *African Journal of Political Science* (1999), Vol. 4 No. 2, p. 89.
22. Ibid.
23. UNDP *Human Development Report 1997* (New York and Oxford: Oxford University Press, 1997), pp.146-148.
24. United Nations Standing Advisory Committee on security questions in Central Africa. UN Concon for Peace and Security in Central Africa. (NY: UN, 1997). p.1.
25. Amnesty International, 'Poverty, Isolation and ill-treatment. Juvenile Justice in Burundi', 24 September 2002, http://www.reliefweb.int/w/rwb.nsf.
26. Ibid.
27. Centre Sous-Régional Pour les Droits de l'Homme et la démocratie en Afrique Centre, Bulletin des Droits de l'Homme et de la Démocratie N° 9 Mai-Août 2003, p. 6.
28. Ibid., pp.7-8.
29. Ibid., pp.10-11.
30. Ibid., p. 5.

31. Eight Head of States and Government and one vice-president, participated in the Summit and signed the decision establish a security mechanism for Central Africa. Rwanda and Angola did not attend the Summit.
32. UN, General Assembly's Resolution 46/37, which was adopted at the forty-sixth session in December 1991, for central Africa. This Resolution welcomed the initiative taken by ECCAS member States with a view to developing Confidence building measures, disarmament and development in their ub-region, in particular, by the creation under the auspices of the UN, of a Standing Advisory Committee on Security Questions in Central Africa.
33. Musifky Mwanasali, op. cit., p. 98.
34. Ibid., p. 99.
35. UN Standing Advisory Committee on Security Questions in central Africa. Subregional Conference on democratic Institutions and peace in Central Africa. Conference report. (UN, 1999) The Conference was held in Bata, Equatorial Guinea, May 1998.
36. Musifky Mwanasali, op.cit. p. 102.
37. Ibid., p. 105
38. UN, Declaration of the Rights of the Child., 1959.
39. http://www.amnestyusa.org/stoptorture/children/drc.html.
40. Amnesty International USA, *Children's Human Rights: The Future Starts Here*, op cit.

References

Amnesty International, Children Human Rights: The Future Starts Here.

Bulletin du Centre Sous-Regional Pour les Droits de l'Homme et la Démocratie en Afrique Centrale, No. 9 mai - août 2003, p.6.

CASA ALIANZA, Human Rights Violations, 'State Violence Against Children', presented by Bruce Harris, Executive Director Latin American Programs.

Chun, L., 'Human Rights and Democracy: The Case for Decoupling', *International Journal of Human Rights.*

Heather, P. L., 2001, *Also God's Children: Encounters with Street Kids*, Ihilihili Press.

Human Rights Watch, December 2001 Reports.

Human Rights Watch, 1999, 'Promises Broken: An Assessment of Children's Rights on the Tenth Anniversary of the Convention on the Rights of the Child', December.

ILO, 2000, *Child Labour Briefing Material: The Problems*, Geneva.

ILO Convention No. 182, 1999 on Worst Forms of Child Labour

Freeman, M., 2002, *Human Rights: Key Concepts*, Polity Press.

Musifiky, N., 1999, 'Political And Security in Central Africa', *African Journal of Political Science*, Vol. 4, No. 2.

Rapport Général, Equipe Multidisciplinaire Pour L'Afrique Centrale (EMAC): Atelier Tripartite sur l'Interdiction des Pires de Travail des Enfants en Afrique Centrale, BIT, Douala Cameroun, 1999.

Stalker, Peter, 2001, 'The No-Nonsense Guide to International Migration', *New Internationalist.*

UN Convention on Rights of The Child, 1989
UN Declaration of the Rights of the Child, 1959.
United Nations General Assembly, Document A/55/383, 2000.
UN General Assembly Resolutions 46/37, adopted at the 46th Session in December 1991 for Central Africa.
UNDP, Human Development Report 1997 (New York and Oxford: Oxford University Press, 1997).
UN Standing Advisory Committee on Security Questions in Central Africa. UN Concern for Peace in Central Africa. (New York: UN, 1997).
UN Standing Advisory Committee on Security Questions in Central Africa. Sub-regional conference on Institution and Peace in Central Africa. Conference Report (New York: UN, 1999).

Websites

http://www.amnestyusa.org/children/chr.html
http://www.undcp.org/palermo/convimain.html
http://www.hrw.org/children
http://www.hrw.org/campaigns/crp/promise
http://www.casa.allianza.org/
http://www.amnesty usa.org/stoptorture/childrendrc.html

12

The Vicissitudes of Cameroon Civil Society in the 1990s: What Lessons for the Central African Region?

Susanna Yene Awasom

Introduction

The 1990s will go down in recorded history as one of the tumultuous eras in contemporary history, comparable in several respects to the violent decolonisation struggles of the 1950s. In response to the global and domestic environment, Cameroon civil society was galvanised and electrified into action to expand the domestic space and ensure a peaceful and lasting requiem for monopartyism. Civil society forces were actually at the forefront for the campaign for democratic development. When one pauses a moment to take stock of this eventful decade, one may question what was actually achieved in concrete and visible terms.

This chapter critically traces the itinerary of Cameroon civil society in its quest for political pluralism and change in the 1990s. I argue that a vibrant civil society in Cameroon incarnated by student movements, octogenarian female groups (Awasom 2002), churches, the Cameroon Bar Association, traders and so on emerged in the 1990s to clamour for multipartyism and a new political order. But few have been able to become sustainable as we turn the century and fewer still will be able to survive without developing shared partnership beyond their national confines in the future. The conclusion advocates a rehabilitation and reactivation of the moribund Cameroon civil society as an insurance for checks and balances and good governance through painstaking political education and support by national and international stakeholders.

This paper is divided into the following principal sections. First, it looks at the components of the Cameroon civil society. Second it examines the domestic and in the global circumstances that reactivated and energised civil society in Cameroon. The author then proceeds to examine the politics of confrontation that took shape in the organisation of Ghost Towns and Civil Disobedience Campaigns and the outcome of such strategies. Lastly, the article explains the waning and eclipsing of civil society in the context of elections and the enveloping of a political landscape by an all-pervasive attitude of political apathy and disaffection.

Components of Cameroon's Civil Society

The crisis of the African state in the 1990s was paralleled by the resurgence of vocal civil societies bent on opening and expanding the political space. Celestine Monga (1998: 4) recognises the ambiguity of defining precisely what civil society actually means and defines it simply as 'new spaces for communication and discussion over which the state has no control'. So groups, organisations and personalities that pursue freedom, justice and rights of citizenship and good governance against authoritarian states constitute civil society. The civil society groups that concern us must be clearly identified in this study to avoid any ambiguity.

The first group included student organisations and trade unions that re-emerged as vocal opponents of the government in response to a severe deterioration in services at the lone University of Yaoundé, the lack of professional jobs for university graduates, and the overall deterioration of the economy (Konings 2002). Women's organisations, especially the Takumbeng, were very prominent during the civil disobedience campaign and after the organisation of the October 1992 presidential elections (Awasom 2002).

Religious groups and organisations also emerged as vocal elements of civil society. The Catholic and Protestant church officials raised critical voices against the deteriorating state of affairs in Cameroon. As the call for a national conference in Cameroon intensified, Bishop Ndongmo, from his exile in Canada, indicated his willingness to chair such a conference, if given the opportunity.

The Cameroon Bar Association contributed significantly in the expansion of the democratic space. It organised nation-wide protests against the arrest of Yondo Black, its former President, and this single act gained public sympathy for the campaign and emphasised the need for a more plural society.

An important component of the resurgence of civil society in Africa was the formation and expansion of opposition political parties, particularly after the discrediting of the single party model of the former USSR at the end of the 1980s. The nascent opposition parties sought to compel the Biya regime to convene a national conference.

The Domestic and Global Environment for the Emergence and Reactivation of Civil Society in the 1990s

The economic crises that affected Cameroon from the mid-1980s intensified by lay-offs and the freezing of employment led to a general disillusionment with the Biya regime. However, the collapse of Sovietism in 1989 that represented a model and rationalisation of a monolithic political order for African despots had a shattering effect on proponents of the one-party state in Africa. In the last edition of *Jeune Afrique* in 1989, Diradiou Diallo had already predicted that the profound democratic upheavals in Eastern Europe and the resultant East-West Détente would sooner or later inevitably affect Africa. These events quickly pervaded the African continent through the media, transistor radios, televisions, video cassettes, telephones, Internet, e-mails, faxes etc. (Aina 1996).

The collapse of Sovietism also gave way to a unipolar world with the US standing as the sole superpower. The West and international donor organisations gave an extra push to democratisation by linking any further economic assistance to Africa to democratic reform and good governance (Fofana 1997: 142; Gibbon 1993). It is against this background that African political regimes, which were largely monolithic, were compelled to adopt plural democracy. Put differently, external conditionalities created room for a rise of a vibrant civil society, which championed the cause of plural democracy.

Benin republic was the first victim of the rising wave of democracy. Mathieu Kerekou's self-proclaimed Marxist-Leninist regime was facing a serious economic crisis that created serious liquidity problems. The suggested way out of it was the holding of a sovereign national conference which resulted to a transition from a one party to a multiparty state. The Benin example quickly spread to Gabon, Zaire (Democratic Republic of Congo) and Côte d'Ivoire (Banoc 1992: 12-16). These events were widely commented upon in Cameroon, particularly in the private print media, and had a direct impact on Cameroon civil society.

Cameroon became a one party state in 1966 following the amalgamation of the Union Camerounaise, the Kamerun Democratic Party (KNDP), the Cameroon People's National Congress (CPNC), and the Cameroon United Party (CUC) (Bayart 1973; Ngoh 1996: 240-243). In 1985, the single party, the Cameroon National Union, was transformed into the Cameroon People's Democratic Party (CPDM) under Paul Biya. The Biya government resisted the nascent democratic simmering against a background of pressures from civil society.

Lawyers launched the first blow on Cameroon's monolithic political structure. Yondo Black, the former President of the Cameroon Bar Association, analysed the political situation in Cameroon and came to the conclusion that the country was ripe for multipartyism. He was therefore among a select group including Albert Mukong, Tekam Michel, Njoh Njoh, and Ekani Anicet who held a clandestine meeting on 23 January 1990 to examine the prospects of introducing multipartyism in Cameroon. The group constituted itself into the National Coordination Committee for Democracy and Multipartyism in Cameroon and proceeded to the drafting of a document to serve as a basis for introducing multipartyism. According to the document, the absence of human rights, the undemocratic nature of Cameroon institutions, and the plunder of the nations resources, necessitated multipartyism in Cameroon. The authors of the document appealed to all Cameroonians to mobilise against the one-party dictatorship and in favour of a plural democracy (Mukong 1992: 117-156). The document leaked into the hands of the secret police and by 27 February 1990 the entire group had been arrested.

The arrest made headlines as the international media blasted it on the airwaves. The government was fast to defend itself by declaring that the group had held a series of seditious meetings during which people were incited to revolt against the Head of State. The entire Cameroon Bar Association was mobilised by its President, Ben Muna, to defend the arrested activists as their own contribution to the defense of human rights in Cameroon. The presence of Yondo Black, the former President of the Cameroon Bar Association, was an additional rallying cause for Cameroon's lawyers. The importance of the arrest of the Yondo Black group lies in the fact that it set in motion a series of events that culminated in the reintroduction of multipartyism in Cameroon.

The Cameroon Bar Association embarked upon an indefinite strike that paralysed the Cameroon judicial machinery, starting from 28 March 1990, making the speedy and equitable trial of Yondo Black and his companions a condition for the call-off of the strike. Cameroon lawyers, as a class, had therefore transformed themselves into a social movement which, in Amadiume's view, took initiatives that were anti-government and overly political (Amadiume 1995). The government was cornered into opening the trials on 3 April 1990 against a background of unprecedented national and international press coverage. News coverage of the Yondo Black affair concentrated on the fact that the Cameroon government's problem was its stubborn refusal to accept multiparty democracy.

The charge against the government for opposing multiparty democracy was embarrassing at a time that Cameroon's neighbours were all undergoing a transition from a one-party to a multiparty system. The government was so embarrassed by the charge that it was forced to issue a statement which pushed civil society into actually introducing an alternative political party. In defending itself against the charges, a Cameroon government statement over radio and television on 13 March 1990 stated that the arrest of Yondo Black and his companions was not related to their desire to form a political party, which was legally allowed by the Cameroon constitution. The statement further added that the government had not obstructed anybody from forming a political party. The Yondo Black group was accused of offences against the penal code. They had held clandestine meetings during which they fabricated and circulated tracts in which they treated the government with contempt and incited Cameroonians to revolt against the government (*Cameroon Tribune* 13 March 1990).

When the government statement was issued stating that multipartyism was constitutional and allowed in Cameroon, John Fru Ndi, a bookshop owner in the North West Provincial town of Bamenda and Professor Siga Assanga, a lecturer in the University of Yaounde, were emboldened to form an alternative political party. They deposited a dossier at the Governor's office and received a receipt for the formation of a political party. They slated 26 May 1990 as the date for the launching of the party. This action sent a powerful signal of the intention of civil society to break the one-party monopoly of power.

The government party, the Cameroon's People's Democratic Movement (CPDM), organised a series of anti-multiparty demonstrations which included in its ranks the members of the National Assembly, Generals and Colonels of the Armed forces, Chairmen and Directors of parastatals, and the Lord Mayor of the Yaoundé Urban Council. In a televised speech to the nation on 9 April 1990, President Biya assured the demonstrators that he had understood them and that the only genuine problem in Cameroon was the economic crisis that was ravaging the nation and the others were simply diversionary maneuvers (*Cameroon Tribune,* 10 April 1990). The tug of war between civil society and the government had just begun.

The sincerity of government commitments to multipartyism was soon put to the test when John Fru Ndi announced the imminent launching of an alternative political party on 26 May 1990. The government panicked and ferried thousands of well-armed troops into the North West Provincial capital of Bamenda. The government dubbed the launching of the political party as illegal and proceeded to lock up the stadium where the party was supposed to have been launched. John Fru Ndi went ahead to launch his party, the Social Democratic Front (SDF), on 26 May 1990. An estimated crowd of over 20,000 participated in the launching at an improvised site at Ntarikon Park. Six youths lost their lives from the bullets of soldiers after the launching (Konings and Nyamnjoh 1997: 215).

Students of Cameroon's University of Yaoundé complemented the efforts of lawyers and opposition activists in expanding the political space. Students involved themselves in the dance because of 'their long-standing grievances about the deteriorating conditions of life and studies' on campus (Piet 2002: 179). The severe economic crises and the subsequent Structural Adjustment Programmes only aggravated a very difficult situation. This compelled the government to drastically to cut the budget of the University, stop scholarships to University students and freeze the recruitment of graduates in an already over-sized public service. Students were clearly an abandoned, lost generation as prospects for them were bleak. The scapegoat for their predicament was taken to be the authoritarian regime and they supported the transition to democracy as a necessary precondition for change to a society in which they stood to be beneficiaries. This explains why students marched in Yaoundé in May 1990 following the launching of the SDF1[1].

While the international media gave intensive coverage to Cameroon's difficulties in adjusting to a multiparty culture, government media attempted to justify why Cameroon had to adopt a gradual approach to multipartyism, and branded John Fru Ndi and his SDF as 'undesirables' and 'enemies in the house'. A succession of anti-multiparty demonstrations continued to be organised by government. However, pressure from international donors and France compelled the Cameroonian authorities to bow to multipartyism.

During the Franco-African Summit at La Baule, President Francois Mitterand stressed the importance of multiparty democracy for African development and promised to make it the cornerstone of France's African policy. The Cameroon government therefore proceeded to legalise multipartyism in Cameroon on 9 December 1990, six months after the launching of the SDF. This legalisation of multipartyism was accompanied by the introduction of a certain degree of freedom of communication and association, including the holding of public meetings and demonstrations (SOPECAM 1990). Consequently, several political parties, pressure groups, human rights organisation and private newspapers were established in Cameroon. The government-owned *Cameroon Tribune* newspaper of 9 January 1991 published a list of 41 registered political parties, which today amount to more than 180.

Essentially, the context of the resurgence and reactivation of civil society composed of lawyers, students, and opposition activists was both domestic and international. The declining economic situation coupled with external conditionalities of linking economic assistance to political pluralism and liberalisation strengthened the resolve of Cameroonian civil society to expand the nation's political space.

The Vibrancy of Civil Society and the Quest for a New Political Order

After the introduction of multipartyism, the nascent opposition parties had to pursue the expansion of the democratic space to correspond to their vision of a truly democratic society. Their struggle consisted of seeking a revision of the electoral laws and the constitution of Cameroon to correspond with the new democratic age, and the organisation of a sovereign national conference *à la beninoise*. The opposition logic of holding a sovereign national conference was to ensure a smooth and an unimpeded transition from a monolithic to a pluralistic order. The aim of the conference was to set up a transitional government at the expense of the Biya regime, which would be empowered to revise the constitution and electoral codes of all elections in Cameroon and design a general electoral calendar. In the euphoria of their found liberty, the opposition vociferously and ceaselessly called for a sovereign national conference, and they were supported by many sympathisers, especially students and victims of the Structural Adjustment Plan, including civil servants and retrenched workers.

The Biya administration might have been compelled by forces beyond its control to concede to multipartyism but it resisted the idea of relinquishing power through a sovereign national conference. Biya argued that the idea of such a conference was unconstitutional and did not correspond to Cameroonian realities His supporters, including Archbishop Jean Zoa of Yaoundé, argued that the word national conference did not exist in the dictionary while the renowned philosopher, Marcel Towa, considered the use of the term national conference as dangerous, unacceptable and unconstitutional (*Cameroon Tribune*, 16 May 1990).

During the April meeting of the politburo of the ruling CPDM party on 23 March 1991, President Biya decided personally to address the issue of a sovereign national conference. He categorically rejected it as having no constitutional basis and as being untenable. Meanwhile, in April, students demonstrated in favour of a conference. The social climate continued to deteriorate and on 11 April 1991, Biya announced the convocation of the National Assembly to adopt a number of laws, which would correspond to the spirit of the 'advanced democracy' that had been introduced in Cameroon. During the extraordinary session of parliament held between 18 and 22 April 1991, a number of constitutional modifications were made towards the deconcentration of power, with the creation of the post of Prime Minister. It was decided that early parliamentary elections would be held at the end of the year instead of April 1993 as earlier planned.[2] The government claimed that sovereignty emanated from the people's duly elected representatives and not political formations that did not enjoy any political legitimacy. A law was enacted granting general political amnesty, particularly to those who were involved in the April 6 1984 coup d'état against the Biya administration.[3] (*Cameroon Tribune,* 23April 1990) Parliament was meeting against a background of nation-wide demonstrations for a sovereign national conference and bloody confrontations between the forces of law and order and demonstrators.

Whatever concessions the government made, they tended to incite rather appease the opposition who considered the measures as palliative and escapist. What the nascent opposition insisted on having was a sovereign national conference, pure and simple. The Biya administration for its part put up a ferocious resistance to the idea of a sovereign national conference, which would erode the ruling party's prerogatives. The intransigence of the Biya government and the expectations of the opposition forces created a situation of protest and tension, which was reminiscent of the chaos that characterised the decolonisation phase in Cameroon history.

The opposition devised the ghost town and civil obedience strategy to compel the Biya regime to concede to the idea of a sovereign national conference. This strategy emanated from the bitter experience of Cameroon civil society with Cameroon's security forces. Each time demonstrations were organised, they were brutally dispersed by Cameroon's forces of law and order, through the use of tear gas and sometimes live grenades and bullets, causing several victims. Owing to the casualties that often accompanied confrontations with government forces, an opposition leader, Mbuoua Massock, came up with the idea of ghost towns and civil disobedience campaigns, which were initially known as 'franc jeu'. His idea was that the ghost town and civil disobedience campaign would have the capacity of mobilising the masses to the opposition cause with a minimum loss of lives. At the initial stage, the campaign hinged on two fundamental issues: civil disobedience and non-violence. Tracts were distributed to hawkers, taxi men, bus drivers, and traders amongst others, as a method of reaching the masses regarding the opposition programme. Mboua Massock's first ghost town campaign was in Douala in the month of March 1991 and he successfully brought activities in that town to a halt through the mobilisation of taxi drivers and the sensitisation of the population. The Douala population were instructed through tracts to stop paying taxes and utility bills. Commercial vehicles were asked to ground all activities (*Le Quotidien*, 29, 30, 31 May 1998). This type of protest had the advantage of mobilising the population to disobey the government while minimising casualties from direct confrontation with the government. Mbuoa Massock's successful experiment with the civil disobedience campaign set a model for the opposition nation-wide. His success caused the security forces to detain him.

The opposition parties, now working in coalition as a unit under the name of the National Coordination of Opposition Parties (NCOOP), unanimously adopted the ghost town strategy as an instrument of extracting political concessions from the government. For over nine months, the opposition forces took the Cameroon nation hostage as they immobilised activities through their civic disobedience campaigns and were generally obeyed by the masses that anticipated changes through them from which they would benefit. The civil disobedience campaign gradually died out after the convening of the Tripartite Conference on 30 October 1991 between the Government, civil society and independent personalities, to look for ways of establishing a consensus on the political future of Cameroon. After much negotiation, the Tripartite delegates signed the Yaoundé Declaration on 13 November 1991. The opposition agreed to suspend the civil disobedience campaign while the government accepted lifting the ban on public meetings. Most importantly, the government promised to grant a moratorium to tax payers who had suffered from civil disobedience operations. Opposition activists arrested and not yet charged were immediately released.

On 17 November 1991 the Tripartite Conference came to an end with the signing of the Tripartite Accord between the parties. But the civil disobedience instrument in the form of ghost towns came to stay as a political weapon and heritage of Cameroon. It is estimated that over 400 Cameroonians lost their lives in the hands of the Cameroon armed forces during the civil disobedience campaigns. The economy was seriously affected yet the masses followed the opposition activists in their struggle for a more promising society.[4] But the opposition did not achieve the convening of a sovereign national conference despite all the sacrifices they made and this had implications for the prospects of the masses adhering to future calls to participate in civil disobedience.

The Progressive Waning of Civil Society and the Remaining Lone Voice

The vibrancy of civil society was a reflection of domestic and external support. As long as the masses and the international community backed civil society groups implicitly or explicitly, their energisation and survival could be guaranteed. Political developments after the ushering in of multipartyism in Cameroon in 1990-1991 witnessed the gradual decline of civil society.

During the first multiparty elections in March 1992, the opposition SDF party championed a boycott of the elections by a group of radical opposition parties on grounds that the Biya regime had refused to revise the electoral code to permit fairness and transparency. In the SDF's perceived stronghold of the North West, South West, West and Littoral provinces, the boycott was largely adhered to and this allowed the majority of non-boycotting voters to give their vote to opposition parties, which emerged with a majority of seats at the expense of the CPDM governing party. Even though the results of the elections gave victory to the opposition (the first and last of its kind) the CPDM was able to woo the Mouvement pour la défense de la République (MDR) and the Union des Populations du Cameroun (UPC) to join it in government (Nyamnjoh 1999: 103). The boycotters stayed out of parliament and remained as the extra-parliamentary opposition until 1997 when they decided to join the race.

The opposition SDF and its radical camp decided to join the campaign for the presidency in October 1992 and performed admirably. Cameroon's Supreme Court responsible for the declaration of the results of the presidential elections declared a narrow win of Paul Biya over John Fru Ndi. In the Anglophone North West and South West Provinces and in the Francophone West and Littoral provinces, Fru Ndi pulled 86 percent, 52 percent, 68 percent and 68 percent of the votes cast respectively, against 8 percent, 21 percent, 12 percent and 14 percent for Paul Biya (Sindjoun 1994: 21-44).

Earlier polls had indicated that the opposition candidate, Fru Ndi was winning. When the Supreme Court declared Paul Biya victor with 39.5 percent against 35.5 percent for Fru Ndi (Sindjoun 1994: 34) after a protracted vote count of over a fortnight, Fru Ndi rejected the verdict and proceeded to proclaim himself president-elect. The population of Fru Ndi's constituency went on a rampage and a state of emergency was imposed on Bamenda that lasted for over two months. Fru Ndi's claims of election fraud were substantiated by the US National Democratic Institute, which accused Paul Biya of poorly organising the elections (Awasom 2003: 220-222). This external appreciation of the elections was important because it questioned the legitimacy of Biya's victory, but it demoralised the masses who had sacrificed so much during the ghost town operations and state of emergency, without effecting any political change.

Subsequent elections were demoralising owing to their deliberately poor organisation, and as a result an attitude of apathy and disaffection pervaded the political landscape in Cameroon. The 1996 local government elections, the first since the reintroduction of multipartyism in Cameroon in 1990, were a sham. There were 336 local government constituencies for Cameroon's 123 registered political parties. However only 37 opposition parties were able to present candidates to run for the council areas (Fonchingong 1998: 125). It was in the interest of each contesting party to present candidates in as many constituencies as possible as an image building and propaganda strategy, and the major opposition parties like the SDF and the UNDP understood this. The government CPDM declared its readiness to contest in all the constituencies while the opposition SDF filed in candidates for 243 local government areas to the surprise of the government (*The Herald*, Jan. 1-4 & 11-14, 1996). What is important to note here is the government harassment of the opposition through the disqualification of opposition candidates and the inability or impotence of the opposition to effectively challenge the government, with negative implications for the morale of the masses. The SDF was allowed to run in only 112 local government areas instead of the 243 it had intended (*L'Expression* Jan. 23, 1996). The grounds for election violence had been prepared especially in constituencies where there was an overwhelming sympathy for the opposition. In the Mbanga local government area, for instance, the heavy deployment of security forces did not deter angry opposition forces from disrupting the polls because the opposition list was not allowed to contest the elections. Yet, the Cameroon Radio Television later announced a heavy turn out at Mbanga and the overwhelming victory of the government list (*L'Expression*, Jan. 23 1996).

Government manipulation starting with the registration processes to the proclamation of final election results also characterised the May 1997 legislative elections which the CPDM was said to have won by 116 seats as against 64 for the opposition (Nyamnjoh 1999: 103). As usual the opposition protested but had no viable means of addressing the situation. It is against this background of an unfavourable electoral law and practice that the opposition insisted on the total revision of the rules of the game. The opposition therefore boycotted the October 1997 presidential elections in which Paul Biya obtained 92.57 percent of the vote cast. The 2002 parliamentary elections saw the expected overwhelming victory of the government party under the existing electoral laws.

The impotence of civil society can be explained by the fact that the opposition can no longer mobilise the masses to its cause as it did in the early 1990s. They have come to learn from experience that demonstrations have never yielded the expected dividends in Cameroon. They have therefore adopted an attitude of wait and see. Perhaps the only voice or action that constitutes a cause for concern to the government is that of the Christian churches. Through the voice of Christian Cardinal Tumi, the Catholic Church has consistently criticised the Biya administration for its litany of election malpractices.

Conclusion

Civil society in Cameroon, like its counterparts in the Central African region and elsewhere in Africa, was at the forefront of the transition from a monolithic to a plural political order. It was vibrant in the early 1990s when lawyers of the Cameroon Bar Association, students, the private sector entrepreneurs like John Fru Ndi and the nascent opposition parties caused a political earthquake in Cameroon through their activism. The lawyers paralysed the judiciary in defense of human rights and in a bid to accelerate the trial of the Yondo Black group. The opposition SDF party was formed in that context and was combated by the regime's one party ideologues. The government finally succumbed to plural democracy owing to both internal and external pressures, especially Francois Mitterand's La Baule declaration. Once the opposition saw the light of day, it unsuccessfully struggled for over nine months to force the hand of government to agree to the idea of a sovereign national conference as the ideal forum for the designing of equitable laws that would govern all elections in Cameroon. The vibrancy of the civil society did not however outlast the first half of the 1990s.

Civil society lost its vibrancy owing to the disillusionment of the masses with their failure to access power through the voting process, and their unwillingness to involve themselves in further futile political agitation. The government has held civil society at bay through a series of methods, the most significant being their fostering of a generalised political apathy and resignation through the instrumentalisation of ambiguous electoral rules and regulations (Awasom 1998), which make regime change almost impossible. The immobility of civil society removes checks and balances and paves the way for monolothism to thrive. The future of democracy in the Central African region depends on the activation of the internal and the international support systems of civil society.

Notes

1. It must be pointed out that student politics in the 1990s was soon polarized along ethnic lines as the 'Beti' students felt the 'Anglo-Bamis' were bent on unseating their kinsman from power (*cf* Konings 2002: 179-204).
2. The last legislative elections in Cameroon were held in 1988 and fresh elections were actually scheduled for 1993.
3. Hundreds of Cameroonians, most of whom originated from former President Ahmadou Ahidjo's northern province were involved in an abortive coup d'etat against President Biya in 1984 and were incarcerated in several prisons in Cameroon.
4. It is estimated that the slow down at the port of Douala cost the government a lost of revenue of 5 billion francs per day and within the span of the ghost town the government lost over 900 billion francs cfa (*Le Quotidien*, 29, 30, 31 May 1998).

References

Aina, T. A., 1997, *Globalisation and Social Policy in Africa. Issues and Research Directions*, Dakar: CODESRIA.

Amadiume, I., 1995, 'Gender, Political Systems and social movements: A West African Experience', in Mahmood Mamdani & Ernest Wamba-dia-Wamba (eds.) *African Studies in Social Movements and Democracy*, Dakar: CODESRIA.

Awasom, N.F., 1998, 'Ambiguous Laws as Sources of Violence in Cameroon in the Era of Globalisation: An Appraisal of the Implementation of the Council (Local Government Electoral Code and the 1996 Constitution', Unpublished Paper.

Awasom, N. F., 2003, 'Anglophone/Francophone Identities and Inter-Group Relations in Cameroon', in R.T. Akinyele (ed.) *Race, Ethnicity and Nation-Building in Africa: Studies in Inter-Group Relations*, Ibadan: RC Rex Charles Publications.

Awasom, S. Y., 2002, 'A Critical Survey of the Resuscitation, Activation and Adoption of Traditional African Female Political Institutions to the exigencies of Modern Politics in the 1990s: the Case of the Takumbeng Female Society in Cameroon', Paper presented at CODESRIA's 10th General Assembly, Kampala, Uganda.

Banoch, M., 1992, *Le Processus de Démocratisation en Afrique : le cas Camerounais*, Paris: L'Harmattan.

Bayart, F., 1973, 'One-Party Government and Political Development in Cameroon', *African Affairs,* 73: 125-144.

Cameroon Tribune, 13 March 1990, 10 April 1990, 9 January 1991, 16 May 1990, 23 April1990.

Fofana, M.B., 'Is there any Organic relationship between Good Government and Development?', in *Institut Africain pour la Démocratie*, Dakar: Editions Démocraties africaines.

Forchingong, T. N., 1998, 'Multipartyism and Democratization in Cameroon', *Journal of Third World Studies,* 15 (2): 119-136.

Gibbon, P., 1993, 'The World Bank and the New Politics of Aid', *The European Journal of Aid,* 5 (1): 36-62.

Jeune Afrique, no 1507 de 1989

Konings, P., 2002, 'University Students Revolt, Ethnic militia and Violence during Political liberalization in Cameroon', *African's Studies Review*, 45 (2): 179-204.

Konings, P. and Nyamnjoh, F., 1997, 'The Anglophone Problem in Cameroon', *The Journal of Modern African Studies*, 35 (2): 207-229.

La Nouvelle Expression, January 23, 1996

Le Quotidien, 29, 30 and 31 May 1998

Monga, C., 1996, *The Anthropology of Anger: Civil Society and Democracy in Africa*, London: Lynne Rienner.

Mukong, A., 1992, *My Stewardship in the Cameroon Struggle*, Bamenda: Nooremec Press.

Nyamnjoh, F., 1999, 'Cameroon: A Country United by Ethnic Ambition and Difference', *African Affairs*, 98: 101-118.

Ngoh, V., 1996, *History of Cameroon Since 1800*, Limbe: Presbook.

Sindjoun, L., 1994, 'La Cour Supreme, la compétition électorale et la continuité politique au Cameroun', *Africa Development*, 19 (2) : 21-44.

SOPECAM, 1991, *Cameroon Right and Freedoms: Collection of Recent Texts*, Yaoundé: SOPECAM.

The Herald, January 14 and 11-14, 1996

13

Rethinking Political Will and Empowerment as Missing Dimensions in Post-Conflict Reform and Reconstruction in the Central African Sub-Region

John W. Forje

Probing the Rationale of the Technology of Violence

The profound changes of the past decades have left us in no doubt that traditional power politics and diplomacy are not, on their own, capable of delivering sustainable peace. Yet because modern warfare is so destructive of lives and resources, and so unpredictable in its effects, merely reacting to events is no longer an option. The search is on for new forms of intervention that can restore the peace, happiness, security, hope and confidence to the suffering silent majority.

Looking back into history, it is certainly relevant to recall that Africa in general, and the Central African sub-region in particular, have witnessed some of the most brutal and oppressive forms of colonial exploitation played in Africa. The technology of violence reached its peak at the dawn of independence. A new era of terror was established which changed the geopolitics not only of the sub-region but the entire continent.

The Central African sub-region has not only known some of the worst and most prolonged forms of political instability in Africa's post-independence history; the region has also experienced a series of genocides, of which the 1994 events in Rwanda were simply the most spectacular and tragic but by no means the last, as recent and ongoing events in the war ravaging the Democratic Republic of Congo (DRC) indicate. Apart from Cameroon which can be classified as an island of peace in a turbulent sub-region, chaos and not coherence reigns. The geo-strategic advantages enjoyed by the sub-region, coupled with the immense mineral wealth and other natural resources it harbours, as well as the huge hydro-power and agricultural potential, have made it important in the reflections and calculations of the Pan-African movement. For this same reason the sub-region is high on the political and military agenda of imperialists interests intent on gaining access to and controlling its vast wealth. Conflict over natural resources has had its impact on the region. A clear correlation can be perceived between persistent political instability in the region and the unceasing colonial and neo-colonial machinations for the control of these resources.

As an evidence of the chronic instability and the huge toll it has exacted, one only needs to recall the number of military coups, successful or unsuccessful, that the sub-region has known. The civil wars already fought in the region and those underway; the number of United Nations Peace-keeping and other diplomatic missions that have been constituted so far, the widespread availability of light weapons for the prosecution of conflicts; the repeated cases of massacre and genocide inflicted on the civilians; the massive refugee problems arising from conflicts in the sub-region; the humanitarian emergencies that continue to reach the area; and repeated experiences of invasions by mercenaries and foreign armies, inject fear, uncertainty and despair among the people.

Meanwhile, the nature of conflict has shifted. There is a gradual but significant shift from crisis to reform and reconstruction. We see fewer inter-state wars and more civil conflicts, although some of these civil wars exert an inter-state influence. And we observe the growing importance of non-state actors in fomenting or preventing conflict. Today civil society is playing a more significant role as natural allies working for crisis prevention, reform and reconstruction at different levels in state building - a role that was denied them the morning after the granting of independence. However, mobilising and coordinating such an alliance is not easy due to the various vested interests. Once you get it right, your coalition may be powerful enough to indeed prevent conflict. Get it wrong and the problem may get worse.

CODESRIA's 30th Anniversary Conference celebration beginning with the different regional conferences highlights the need for conflict prevention and nation-state construction. It opens new avenues for researchers to further discover how complex nation-state building can be, and thus map out ways and means to promote peace and development within divided communities.

On the other hand, governments are beginning to welcome cooperation with non-state actors. 'We, the people', in whose name the United Nations was originally set up, are finally taking our place at the table. The success of 'we the people' builds on deepening democracy as the golden rule in the prevention of crisis, as well as it constitutes a golden opportunity for reform and reconstruction in order to consolidate rapid and sustainable development and political stability.

The strengths and limitations of the approach have yet to be properly evaluated. The problems of integration and coherence intrinsic to new forms of diplomacy that build on inclusion not exclusion are yet to be grasped by society.

What is important to note is that cleavages between clans, tribes and nations constitute a seriously disruptive force in domestic and regional politics. Sensitive border disputes - one the troubling legacies of colonialism - which more often than not erupted into armed conflict, continue to be a major problem in the region. So do population pressure and the economic crisis due to mismanagement. Mismanagement and the lack of sustained attention by governments, have often transformed major urban centres into breeding grounds for poverty and insecurity, eroding the country's social capital and undermining the very competitive assets it needs to improve the quality of livelihood of the people and integrate fully into the global economy.

Many of the countries in the region continue to experience a widening gap between rich and poor segments of their respective societies, a rise in urban and rural unemployment or underemployment, and a deepening of mass poverty and corruption.

The burden of coping with these problems in what we see as 'reform and reconstruction' lies with the countries of the sub-region themselves: outsiders will continue to shape the environment within which their tasks of nation-building must proceed; their actions weighing heavily on the chances for accelerating growth and averting impending crisis. However, the important step lies with the people to address their predicaments from the standpoint of collectivity and inclusion.

The determination of the colonial powers in Central Africa to safeguard their interests and influence through various neo-colonial machinations, including the promotion of different divide-and-rule tactics, and the reduction of the area to a playground of the super-powers at the height of the Cold War, meant that across the sub-region, the transition to and after independence occurred in highly conflictual contexts. These contestations which were to be woven into the fabric of domestic politics had the consequence of weakening state and governmental capacity over time. To regain its power and authority and ensure its political legitimacy the state converged on deploying an authoritarian governance system which has taken hold in the region. This constitutes what could be seen as the challenge of nationalism/self-determination.

The Challenge of Self-determination and Post-modernity

The challenge of self-determination was a call for nationalism. Nationalism is first and foremost a state of mind or an act of consciousness. In the words of Hans Kohn, 'nationalism demands the nation-state. And the creation of the nation-state strengthens nationalism'. The struggle for self-determination did not lead to nationalism; in other words, the tribes in Africa have not evolved into nations. As such the tribes duly encased themselves in sovereign states, or at least in states intending to be sovereign; instead, these states one after another, have torn each other to pieces.

Within this framework, the strategic agenda of nation-building that was close to the heart of the founding fathers—'seek the political kingdom and all would be added to it'—suffered. The challenges of state-building necessary for the advancement of the post-independent processes could not be handled by a neocolonial setup. The common and collective interest had been replaced by individual interest. The 'politics of the belly' (Bayart 1993) took the upper-hand and the state started its descent—a descent which has made its landing extremely difficult as can be seen by the presence of too many weak and fragile states in Africa.

Seeking the political kingdom expressed the central maxim of which the truth appeared self-evident; once independence was attained by colonised territories, no matter under what conditions, 'the road to freedom and development would be theirs to follow' (Davidson 1992:163). African countries did not follow the envisaged path mapped out during the self-determination struggle. Neo-colonialism took the upper hand. The might of the technology of violence and mobility to which the Democratic Republic of Congo was subjected under the very eyes of the United Nations turned the Central African sub-region in a battlefield. The politics of the Cold War era did not make it easy for the newly independent territories and the newly created continental organisation, the Organisation of African Unity (OAU). The same scenario is being repeated today as US President Bush's War on 'Global Terrorism' hardly facilitates the transformation of the OAU into the African Union (AU).

Acceptance of the post-colonial designed nation-state implied acceptance of the legacy of the colonial partition of the continent, of the moral and political practices of colonial partition, and of the moral and political practices of colonial rule in its institutional dimensions. This acceptance constituted a handicap which to some extent was foreseen by some of the leaders like Nkrumah. For example, he noted that 'there is a great risk in accepting office under this new constitution which still makes us half-slaves and half-free'; adding that there would be a great need for 'vigilance and moral courage to withstand the consequent temptations of temporary personal advantage'. This was because 'bribery and corruption, both moral and factual have eaten into the whole fabric of our society and these must be stamped out if we are to achieve any progress' (Davidson 1964:86).

The independence of African states was accompanied by conflicts including genocide or 'ethnic cleansing' such as in Rwanda in 1994 or the ongoing 'slow genocide' in Burundi. One can also look at the effects of Nigeria's Civil War of

1966–1970. The problem of violent internal conflict in the sub-region is acute. As of late 2000–2001, internal conflicts raged in Congo-Brazzaville, Democratic Republic of Congo (DRC), Rwanda, Burundi, Chad, Central African Republic, with Cameroon facing instability as witnessed in the secessionist agitation of the Southern Cameroon National Council (SCNC). These developments underline the nature of 'weak states' and the absence of a strong state capacity.

A strong state as noted by Migdal (1998:12) Skinner (1978), and Jackson (2002) exists as a 'hegemonic idea', accepted and naturalised in the midst of the population so that they 'consider the state as a natural as the landscape around them; they cannot imagine their lives with it'. On the other hand, weak states are mirrored by a set of opposite characteristics. In addition, they face serious problems of legitimacy, expressed through very low political participation rates, high levels of disengagement or 'exit' by significant sectors of the population, a reliance on coercion to ensure compliance, unstable politics, social cleavages, and the total centralisation of power by a tiny ruling elite.

Because of the unpreparedness in spite of the determined belief in the politics of 'self-determination', and backed by the forces of the hidden agenda of the departing colonial powers, a weak rather than strong state formation emerged after independence, giving birth to 'fragile politics' and leading to an internal incoherent political system constantly manipulated by the external environment. The consequence was exclusive politics, political centralisation and authoritarianism fanned by an elite corps that deprived the state of the relative autonomy necessary to effect meaningful reform and ensure genuine democracy. The one-party system which was meant to rally and reinforce the 'self-determination' struggle was deployed to facilitate the policies of exclusive politics. It is not surprising that countries within the sub-region invariably lack cohesive national identities. National loyalties are often expressed in ethnic or sub-national terms, which destroy the social, economic, political and cultural fabric of the society. The aftermath is that 'the hegemonic idea of statehood is missing or only weakly present with the modern state structure in Africa forming little more than a thin carapace' (Cornwell 1999:62, Jackson 2002:39).

The establishment of weak states either by design or neglect by both the departing colonial masters and the neo-colonial elements, creates varying levels of institutional incapacity and a frequent inability by governments to implement their policies. In addition institutional weakness furthers both the causes and consequences of the ongoing economic and political crisis faced by the region, thereby making states vulnerable to external conditionalities, which is the direct result of their internal fragility. To reform and reconstruct, the countries of the Central African sub-region must understand and address the underlying and proximate causes of internal conflicts. Above all, it is necessary to destroy the ethnic, clientelist, and patronage politics that has eaten deep into the social fabric of society. The politics of identity are often a strategy of first choice for many weak state elites. As noted by Boone (1994:111), ethnic politics have their roots in the contradictions inherent in the exercise of state power by colonial and neo-colonial authorities. It is common in the region to see how the politics of 'ethnocracy' are quickly established once a new leader is in office. Many cases abound in the region in illustration of this situation. For example, in Cameroon Ahidjo relinquished power in 1982 only for the new President to quickly replace the cohorts of the former leader with his own tribesmen. In the Central African Republic (CAR), General Kolingba quickly established a governance system built on ethnocracy, but in 1993 the new President, Ange Felix Patasse, took revenge by excluding Kolingba's people in favour of his own tribespeople.

Coping Strategies: The Challenge of Reconstruction

Decolonisation as it turned out only implied the transfer of power—which above all was a transfer of crisis. The new state inherited a crisis of social disintegration. Colonial rule had wiped out the social structure and basis of the people in the name of civilising the uncivilised. The new state was left with a state of deepening structural malfunction. Neo-colonialism did not make the situation better; rather it reinforced the forces underlying this malfunctioning. The cynical political calculations of the departing colonial masters and the neo-colonial custodians of power had a common agenda. And it was this agenda that plunged the region into a state of unresolvable political and economic crisis.

It should be noted that the quest for self-determination was challenged by the politics of assimilation. The Central African sub-region was under the total hegemony of big brother France. France's African Policy was constructed on the notion of assimilation as the climax of the civilisation mission which was to lead to modernity. While the politics of assimilation was seen as a betrayal of national sovereignty, the emerging governing elite nevertheless converted this into a new form of hegemony—that of transferring state property into personal/private poverty; of an ethnic grouping constituting the state, and the creation of a family dynasty as the legitimate source of succession. The sovereignty of the people was greedily hijacked. The politics of exclusion replaced that of inclusion. The entire region was subject to turmoil. It has yet to recover from the backlash of greed: creating the political strategic, economic and cultural ambiguities that cut across the sharply demarcated boundaries of 1884 imposed by external powers.

The politics of assimilation created a new power and authority, with the legal sovereignty of the country resting on the individual and not the people as the custodian of the state and its institutions. Successive constitutions transferring power simply bent to the winds of momentary or monetary pressures and perpetuated the single party system. Contradictions emerged and persisted following the return to multi-party politics which opened a new Pandora's box of ethnic hegemony and cleansing. The demise of the single party could be seen as internal imperialism and dispossession. The current custodian lost all the privileges, prerogatives and authority of state power in a new setting. The new era saw the clamour for democratic liberties, and a spreading demand for a politics of democratic participation and partnership with all the different actors.

A new contradiction between despair and hope was overwhelmingly present as could be seen in the warring clans of Burundi and Rwanda, the Democratic Republic of Congo (former Zaire), Central African Republic, Chad, The Peoples Republic of Congo, and others. In Cameroon the return to multi-party politics unleashed old provincial or regional differences, ethnic cleavages between the North and South, between the Beti hegemony and the rest of the country, between the Anglophone and Francophone, which were exacerbated beyond all good sense. People from other parts of the country resident in the Beti land were chased, molested or killed for not belonging to the party of the 'son of the soil'. The absence of participatory democracy created a situation of a 'rapidly faltering regime'. A decade or more after the return to mass participation in the political process the divide between the haves and have-nots continues to widen.

The politics of inclusion is yet to penetrate significantly into the new body politic. Without this penetration there is no guarantee that a culture of tolerant consensus, a culture able to promote a politics of self and sustainable development, is going to be possible. Reform and reconstruction should build on a democracy that embraces the politics of participation, self-commitment and inclusion. In short a process of deepening democracy, cultivating and nurturing a culture of democracy and good governance. The states within the sub-region will have to operate more as a vehicle of liberation and social justice than as a mechanism for repression and division. The state must act as a bridge between the aspirations of different forces and interest groups if the events of the past are not to be repeated.

Of course, the state system will increasingly be torn between two logics - the individual and the common interest, between national sovereignty and neo-colonialism/post imperialism, or between two forms of interdependence. The one institutionalises the principles of identity, autonomy, community and inclusion, the other in practice negates those principles by clinging to the increasingly elusive notion of ethnic hegemony.

The challenges are great but can be overcome provided the political will exists and is extended beyond the confines of ethnic and tribalistic frontiers. There is no doubt we may therefore expect a deepening contradiction between emerging processes of decentralisation and democratisation within and between societies and the intensified centralisation and bureaucratisation of economic and political life. It is not out of place to state that as of now the state pretends to act as a passive or neutral agent in societal conflict. On the whole, its actions have often favoured systemic or anti-systemic forces, depending on the interests of those in positions of state power and the structural relationship between the state on the one hand and civil society and the international division of interests on the other.

The sub-region is caught within the twin trends of democratisation and globalisation. The two processes are occurring simultaneously and must be addressed. The two processes impact on each other and tend to be vehicles for the internationalisation of domestic conflict as well as the localisation of international conflict. The Cold War conflict has been replaced by the US 'War on Terrorism'. Either countries are on the side of the United States, or they are considered as terrorists states - what President Bush terms 'rogue states'. The American engineered Global War on Terrorism breads fertile grounds for African leaders lacking domestic political legitimacy. The twin trends of democratisation and globalisation and their corollary, domestic fragmentation, exclusion, social injustice and the absence of the rule of law, weaken the conceptual and practical foundations of state sovereignty. They do so in various ways: (i) By challenging the notion that state authority is exercised exclusively or even primarily within clearly demarcated boundaries; (ii) by calling into question the claim that within its territory the state's authority is unlimited and indivisible; and (iii) by suggesting a growing disjunction between state and civil society, between political authority and economic organisation and between national identification and social cohesion (see Camiller and Falk 1992). A redefinition of the role of civil society and of its incorporation into the mainstream body politic is imperative.

The rapid retrieval of lost states is even more difficult - if not impossible. Most weak and collapsed states are immersed in, or just emerging from, bitter internecine conflict. The people of the sub-region are burdened with a heavy task of reconciliation and consensus. Given the fact that politics in the region since independence have been highly charged with exclusion, suspicion and mistrust, new bridges across the dividing lines must be constructed to heal the wounds through the politics of 'inclusion, confidence, trust and quality output of the state machinery' in addressing the needs of society, not just a select few. A major task here is that of building capability, confidence, and ensuring security to both life and property.

Redefinition and Rehabilitation of Civil Society

The state, by disassociating its activities from those of civil society, the path for crisis, chaos and instability was set. The quest for self-determination and the granting of independence demanded greater involvement of civil society in order to ensure an effective and cohesive emerging nation-state, and to ensure that nationalism, self-determination remained the determining factors for social cohesion and national unity.

Unfortunately the trends of state and civil society after the attainment of independence diverged, giving way to neo-colonialism, chaos and state collapse, for example, Somalia, Congo, DRC, Burundi, Rwanda, Sierra Leone, Chad and others. As Africa became the breeding ground for military coups, clientelism and corrupt governments, a neglected and passive civil society watched hopelessly, with the international community, especially the two super powers, calling the shots.

The prevalence of individual interests above common and collective interests backed with the centralisation of the state and the integration of the national economy into the world economy made it increasingly difficult for national society to preserve its integrity. One of the greatest failures of the state in the post-colonial era was the exclusion of civil society in the governance process. This disjuncture is interesting. One would have expected that the emergence of the single-party and of its marriage with state bureaucracy would have strengthened the role of civil society in the governance process. This was not the case. Apparently, civil society was sidelined or succumbed to 'belly politics', or the state and political party machinery were too powerful and excluded civil society from meaningful participation. The consequences of this disjuncture is the what can best be described as 'failed states', 'weak states', 'captive states, and 'collapsed states' that littered the continent. Only recently has civil society been making a substantial re-entry into the governance process. One positive consequence of this new marriage is the gradual transition to a new concept and functional role of civil society, a new polity cultivating a renewed sense of wholeness, with no clearly demarcated boundaries set by state territoriality or statist notions of national identity.

The move towards partnership, participation and responsibility-sharing between state and civil society and other actors creates a new political framework that best can move the nation forward. Without coherence between the different actors, the current situation of collapsed or failed states cannot be adequately and meaningfully addressed. Camiller and Falk (1992) state that 'civil society acquires a clear meaning grounded in a multiplicity of overlapping allegiances and jurisdictions where the traditional, the modern and the post-modern coexist, where local, regional and global space qualify the principle of nationality and redefine the context of community. The recovery of local and regional identities may encourage new expressions of autonomy and democratic practice and at the same time facilitate the emergence of a cosmopolitan global culture'.

The conceptualisation or redefinition of civil society as an integral part of the development process constitutes an inherent part of the triangular concept of partnership, participation and responsibility-sharing in the process of reform and reconstruction (PPRS). The reconstruction of the politics of inclusion, and the acceptance of cultural pluralism as an asset in organising society cannot be underestimated in the twin trends of democratisation and globalisation.

Central to the reconstruction process lie the inherent forces of technological change that equally impact on the democratisation and globalisation process. Apart from reforming the political landscape, total reconstruction will require the indispensable application of technology. Particularly significant here is the deployment of information and communication technologies (ICTs) in accelerating the democratic and globalisation processes. The impact of the transformation in information technology is not restricted to communication. The new technologies are contributing to the evolution of a technological political and economic system, which may in part be characterised as a 'regime of permanent innovation'. The new technology of knowledge gives rise to at least three structural considerations in the process of reform and reconstruction:

i) The rapid structural change occurring in the technology of communication and genetic engineering are helping forge a concept of an accessible national community, thus taking away the monopoly of information held by the state. A new accessible national community is in the making and able to link with others in all parts of the world, thus creating a new vibrant civil society. National governments are forced to communicate with a more enlightened civil society and citizenry. A new political landscape has been created due to widespread ICTs.
ii) Major structural changes in the global market pose another powerful challenge to the concept of the national community. Information technology and globalisation are creating a brave new world; and the region has to exploit the advances in science and technology to construct a new society and be part of the emerging globalised and democratised world. In addition, production is being 'dispersed and deterritorialised'.
iii) The economic impact on the environment leads in some respects to the strengthening of state power, hence the image of the national community. But that image can only realised and strengthened through the increasing technological advances of genetic engineering and ICTs, whose intensity and scale of production and consumption have also led to the development of transnational environmental effects. All these developments provide a sharp demonstration of the limits to the state's ability to regulate crucial aspects of the environment and other related development activities. A message is also sent to the state to forge a new partnership with civil society to sustain the supposed virtues of democratisation, globalisation and development.

Politics of Deconstruction to Reconstruction

One thing is clear, the state has to deconstruct (delink) itself before reconstruction (relinking) can effectively and meaningfully take place. Deconstruction implies relinquishing authoritarianism, the notion of 'Presidents for Life', the fanning of ethnic hegemony or ethnic conflicts in order to stay in power, and the other vices that have characterised the state since the attainment of independence.

Reconstruction demands transparency, accountability, the rule of law, social justice and inclusion. However, the movement towards a post-democratisation and post-conflict Central African sub-region, and Africa as a whole, calls for a determined political will that places common interests above all other interests. The state has to de-link from the past in order to re-link to the present and to construct a better future.

The crisis that has plagued the sub-region highlights the relentless process of authoritarianism and greed which is compounded by an increasing distrust of foreign forces that undermine national structures. Foreign hegemony must be contained. This attitude is not taken kindly by the neo-colonial state and its foreign partners.

But contemporary post-independent Africa of the 21st century requires civil society 'gaining power' by capturing control of the legislature, armed forces and the executive. The state has to delink itself from centralised, top-down governance, and to reconstruct through participatory democracy with civil society ensuring a bottom-up approach. It must be admitted that half-a-century after the official demise of colonialism, the task will not be easy, given the image of state power, authority and its monopoly of institutions and resources. But reconstruction cannot be possible without deconstruction of the existing system. The effectiveness of a new nation-state rests on the ability of the existing state structures to deconstruct, rethink and reconstruct a new political agenda. Only through this process can the nation-state deal effectively with a bewildering array of vital issues plaguing it. Old recipes for change, such as deploying military might to resolve purely social problems, are no longer effective in a post-democratisation era.

By de-constructing the state will enhance its chances of political legitimacy. In all, post-structuralist perspectives invite a radical deconstruction of the process by which state power is constructed and legitimised. If the region is to build a strongly constructed society, the politics and techniques of the Baobab tree must be given a chance to construct a 'nation-ness' spirit based on the narratives of inclusion, participation, partnership and responsibility-sharing, and in so doing permit national and global problems to be addressed in a more constructive, consensual and innovative context.

Whether that political will exists in the project of deconstruction is a serious matter that could make or mar the sub-region, but one that must be seriously resolved for the region to move forward. The countries within the region must close the gap that exists between the state and civil society and to explore other forms of democratic decision-making as part of the process of enhancing the democratisation process. Curbing the state of crisis that has ravaged the sub-region has to be addressed; and this should begin with de-constructing the current state form.

Of course, the challenges are not friction-free. First it requires a level of individual consciousness; the development and strengthening of the 'politics of identity'. Second the de-construction and reconstruction of subjectivity is a political project extending beyond each person. It has to be through a sense of collectiveness, partnership, participation and responsibility-sharing including equitable sharing of the wealth of the nation. Third, there is the need to harness a nation- and world-wide consciousness which understands that to locate the individual politically in a world that is increasingly globalised and democratised implies developing structures and systems which permit him/her to map their actions and understanding within a perspective of both the nation and the world.

The Politics and Techniques of the Baobab Tree

Looking at the state of art of crisis, reform and reconstruction in the Central African sub-region, the observation in the light of this paper is that tribes and nations and lesser bands rise and fall on the strength of their leaders support from civil society and on the ability with which their leaders carry out their responsibilities of office – seeking first the good of the people, not of self. We cannot of course, underestimate or bypass what the impact, influence and consequences of the international community have been in shaping the contestations which were woven into the fabric of domestic politics, especially as most of these countries attained independence at the peak of the Cold War Conflict.

What were the consequences in weakening state and government capacity over time? What has been the response of civil society to the changing circumstances of nation-building that was at the heart of the nationalist independent movements? To what extent did the aspiration of self-determination suffered serious setbacks due to the geo-politics of the East-West conflict? Civil society acquiescence helped form or reinforce the diabolic agenda of the western industrial-military complex in the new states. The sub-region suffered serious setbacks in the face of the challenges of state-building necessary for the advancement of the post-independence process.

The hidden agenda by and large engineered the widening gap between state and civil society. This destroyed the hopes for the construction of a solid framework for citizenship and sense of belonging that could better accommodate the diversity of the peoples as well as recognise their ability across inherited colonial boundaries. The technology of violence and mobility were placed at the disposal of leaders who had signed an unholy pact with the agenda of the west, to intensify the deployment of violence, patronage and ethnic divides and exclusion. Instability and chaos, not freedom, coherence and unity reigned, leading to what could be described as the 'tragedy' of the Central African sub-region. Colonial rule was ensured in a disguised form.

Armed with this unholy weapon of destruction and constructed on the politics of patronage and ethnic divides as a second source of power, the tentacles of corruption were institutionalised and fanned both by external and internal forces. The prevailing state of instability and corruption in the region is largely a result of the clamorous yet empty life its leaders seek to lead. Having lost their sense of direction, the employment of foreign forces helped shaped their dictatorial attitude to carry out the responsibilities incumbent on foreign mercenaries.

The state of crisis and conflicts in the region could be seen through leaders seeking to gain office and stature by political manoeuvring, casting aside personal standards of excellence in achievement and high expectations for unity. Political leadership in the Central African sub-region is based on weakened foundations and shallow loyalties. There has to be a reversal of attitude and approach for reform and reorientation to take place. In other words, a new era of concerted political will must emerge and be made concrete. Ethnic diversity must not be seen as a liability. Rather, diversity should be used as vital asset in the development and nation-building processes.

While we are a young nation as a unity of tribes, we have strong traditions that tie us mystically together. We must use this delicate alliance as a basis for powerful bonds that better serve our collective destiny. Leadership, responsibility, social justice, equality and the rule of law must prevail and guide the people. The way forward should be entrenched within the genuine framework for struggles for democratisation and the content of the quest for democratic renewal.

When we see the state of crisis in the sub-region, reform and reconstruction remain a clarion call for all to be part of the evolving democratic governance. We have to appreciate the realities of the problems plaguing the people, or the region will continue to depreciate. The problems of the sub-region could be viewed as misery caused by malice and incompetence, or greed could be blamed for the prime failure of governments that stepped into the vacuum created by the departing colonial masters. But they were not the cause - they were the effects. The cause was to be found elsewhere. In fact in the politics and policies of 'assimilation', 'the failure of our rulers to re-establish vital inner links with the poor and dispossessed of this country' (Achebe 1988:130-31) reinforced an already bad situation.

The failure of post-colonial communities to find and insist upon means of living together by strategies less primitive and destructive than rival kinship networks, whether of 'ethnic' clientelism or 'its camouflage in no less clientelism multiparty systems' (Davidson 1992:291) led to the calamities of the Nigerian Civil war, the Burundi–Rwanda genocides, and countless military coups across the continent. The politics of exclusion has taken over from that of inclusion, making the governance system fail. Both capitalism and socialism have remained the prerogative of a small minority. The absence of both political and moral legitimacy underscores the content and dimension of the plight of the people.

Decades of bureaucratic dictatorship under the control of monolithic party systems have bitten deeply into capacities for self-government and democratic governance. As a result most Africans since independence ceased to be able to be participants in governing themselves. As Olowu (1989:13) states, 'institutions that were established to promote participation, such as parliaments, political parties, local governance and independent print media, have either been legislated out of existence, or transformed into institutions which are clearly dominated by their executives'.

Reconstructing the continent will require building the political legitimacy of the governing parties and political leaders, and creating a level playing ground for all. In this regard, a return to the African politics of the Baobab Tree is highly recommended. (The African Baobab is one of the world's hardiest trees, thriving in even the most arid environment. It is also the tree under which some Africans have traditionally met to decide issues of common interest.) It is envisaged that through the dialogue of partnership, participation and responsibility-sharing (PPRS) a new politics of minds and capacities will emerged, a politics that might at least be able to control the real problems of the sub-region, indeed, the entire continent and begin to solve them. Africa has to weather the storm or compromise through the techniques of baobab tree democracy. It is not imported democracy seen as if it were a patent medicine to be uncorked and poured at will. Maybe it is this uncorked western democracy or the 'rule from the West' misused and misunderstand that failed to deliver the goods for post-independent Africa. Failure could be perceived also from the perspectives that the colonial powers had promised a simulacrum of the west's governing conditions but went beyond to put their economic interest far above the welfare of the local population.

The policy of destruction or downgrading of the continent's own political and cultural institutions—the baobab tree—which to a large extent regulated and provided a control mechanism over public officials as well as sanctioned important public executives – destroyed forms of democratic behaviour and direction, and led to a loss of a confident sense of possessing and exercising real control over their own way of existence. Restoring the institutions and practices of past governance systems is now a problem. The sub-region, like the entire continent, finds itself wandering in the wilderness of underdevelopment, uncertainty and instability. An image has been created in which there is nothing in Africa's past that could be useful to Africa's future.

Reform and reconstruction must be able to resurrect the lost institutions of the past to construct the present in order to hand a better present and future to later generations. This reform and reconstruction exercise must depart and build on democratic governance. More democracy and political will remains vital in the reform and reconstruction processes. It is vital that reform and reconstruction must involve mass participation in the political process. It is only through the politics of democratic participation and equitable sharing of the nation's wealth that genuine and sustainable development can be attained.

The collapse of the apartheid governance system in South Africa, the return to multi-party politics in many of the states within the region, and the removal of the 'black man's burden' and other legacies of colonial dictatorship, personality cults, the scourge of the HIV/AIDS pandemic, coups, poverty, corruption and mismanagement are beacons for a new era for democratic governance. From Cape to Cairo, from Banjul to the Horn, a new political dispensation is on the horizon that should provide a new guide map by which to address the puzzles and complexities of nation-building through an inclusive political accommodation. Inclusive politics builds a strong state with the 'willingness and ability of a state to maintain social control, enure societal compliance with official laws, act decisively, make effective policies, preserve stability and cohesion, encourage social participation in state institutions, provide basic services, man and control the national economy, and retain legitimacy' (Dauvergne 1998:2).

Reform and reconstruction imply moving forward in a holistic and concerted way by reshaping the present in order to create a better future. I have in this paper sought to construct an alternative model with no illusions that old habits die hard. Those currently benefiting from the spoiled system will not give up easily. But for how long will individual and personal interests prevail over the common and collective interests of the majority? However, my more modest concern and aim has been to go through the crisis, reform and reconstruction processes of the sub-region and the continent with the normal framework of conventional political analysis. In doing so, an attempt has been made to identify several key trends in the emerging patterns of national, continental and global life. Admittedly, it has not been possible to predict the future but rather to see more clearly the direction in which the process of reform and reconstruction can best be shaped and meaningfully attained. We can only advance a sketch of possible trends which include:

i) Trends relating to the institutional fabric of the society. Given the increasing diversity, complexity and interaction, these should not be seen as liability but as asset on which to construct a healthy society, free from conflict, wars, underdevelopment, corruption, poverty and abject misery.
ii) The failure of the nation-state to make adaptive responses to an increasing fragile sub-regional environment that can be characterised as ticking time-bomb.
iii) Resolving the crisis and embarking on reform and reconstruction in the Central African sub-region requires good governance which should create and ensure the legitimacy of government, which depends upon and derives its sources of strength from the existence and functional practice of participatory process and the consent of those who are governed. Governments must be able to formulate appropriate policies, make timely decisions, implement them effectively and deliver services. There must be respect for human rights and the rule of law to guarantee individual and group rights and security, to produce a framework for economic and social security and to allow and encourage all individuals to participate. There needs to be accountability of both political and official elements of government

for their actions, depending upon the availability of information, freedom of the media, transparency of decision-making and the existence of mechanisms to call individual and institutions to account.

iv) In strengthening associational aspects of society, collective citizen action is the 'actor'. The state complements this with its facilitator role, which is crucial to building and nurturing collective citizen action.

v) In enhancing the participation of citizens, the state has to play the role of an active promoter. By engaging themselves in the public arena, citizens complement the 'promoter role' of the state.

vi) The Central African sub-region like all other parts of the continent needs a 'new consensus'. Creating that new consensus requires at least three conditions to be fulfilled - a strong State and a strong civil society; a deepened' democracy and democratic culture; and an enlarged role for citizens.

Ways Forward: An Agenda for Change

This paper argues that the state and the skills of leadership maintain a strong grip over the process of political, economic and social transformation, and are decisive in determining whether that development is sustainable. In all, the potential of the state and the leadership to leverage, promote, and immediate change in pursuit of collective ends is unmatched.

Development in the sub-region is indicative of the inappropriate use of power, lack of vision and a state of high-intensity greed. There is a strong urge to change track, reforming policies and institutions so as to improve the state's effectiveness and to advance national unity and development. Why are the states in the region in desperate situations? And why do these states not attempt to reform and reconstruct themselves? Politics and leadership quality provide much of the answer. However, it is not simply a matter of democracy versus authoritarianism. The leaders and people of the sub-region and the continent at large need to go far beyond those broad concepts of political organisation to understand the incentives that inspire state institutions to function better. The spirit and forces that propelled the struggle for self-determination must not be lost nor derailed. That spirit has to be put back on track.

The people need to put collective and common interests above individual and narrow interest which have so far directed activities in the society; they need constantly to understand the economic, social, cultural and political interests that favour development, and how these can be harnessed to bring about the policies and politics of inclusion and sustainable development. The realisation of these fundamental goals rests on a number of inter-related issues.

i) Efforts to restart development in countries with ineffective states and institutions must start with institutional arrangements that foster empowerment, partnership, participation, accountability, transparency, participation, partnership, responsibility and benefit sharing, confidence building, social justices and impartiality.

ii) Focusing limited state capability on the basics is a badly needed first step in a wide range of countries within the sub-region and in Africa in general.

iii) Improving state capability is not simply a matter of mere technical assistance. It takes the right incentives of matching role with capability, genuine actions, and empowering the people.

iv) Reinvigorating the state's capacity to subject the state to more rules and restraints and greater competitive pressure, and making it more transparent, open and attractive to all in order to better construct an active and vibrant civil society.

v) An active civil society and a competent impartial and professional bureaucracy are twin pillars of a constructive relationship between the state and civil society. When comprehensive collapse of the state is a danger, these twin pillars may reduce the risk of further decay as well as placing it on the right path of recovery.

vi) The Central African sub-region is at the cross-roads of rapid deterioration in the state's effectiveness. Its manifestations can be seen in eroding civil service wages, heavy dependence on foreign aid, and patronage politics. These are some of the factors that have given birth to corruption and poor quality service delivery.

vii) Admittedly, achieving a turnaround in the effectiveness of the state is not easy; but remains a job that must be done in order to create a strong state system, without which there can be no reform and reconstruction. Therefore, the urgent priority for the sub-region is to build state capability through an overhaul of public institutions and credible checks on the abuse of power.

viii) To move forward requires improving the delivery of public and collective services; and this requires closer and stronger partnerships between the state, private sector and civil society. Such partnerships should be encouraged, nurtured and sustained through participation and responsibility, and equitable wealth sharing between the different actors, especially since these links currently are weak, underdeveloped and undemocratised (Forje 2003).

What is most important for the states within the sub-region is to prevent further state collapse by reinforcing and empowering civil society as an active and integral component part in the development process and as a way of increasing the resilience of social institutions. Unfortunately, the Central African sub-region is operating under a system of 'governance by religious sects' that help in perpetuating the state of 'Weak states' and holding the people hostage. The way forward is through decentralisation of power, coupled with democratisation and empowerment, as these have the inherent capability of transforming the local political landscape of the sub-region. A new model of governance should emerge. A new 'political will', action and total empowerment of civil society are needed.

References

Achebe, C., 1988, *Anthills of the Savannah*, New York: Anchor Books/Doubleday.

Bayart, J., 1993, *The State in Africa: The Politics of the Belly*, New York: Longman.

Boone, C., 1994, 'States and Ruling Classes in Postcolonial Africa: The Enduring Contradictions of Power', in J. Migdal, A. Kholi and V. Shue (eds.) *State Power and Social Forces: Domination and Transformation in the Third World*, Cambridge: Cambridge University Press.

Camilleri, J. A. and Jim Falk, 1992, *The End of Sovereignty*, London: Edward Elgar Publishers.

Cornwell, R., 1999, 'The Collapse of the African State', in J. Cilliers and P. Mason (eds.) *Peace, Profit or Plunder? The Privatisation of Security in War-Torn African Societies*, Johannesburg: The Institute for Security Studies.

Dauvergne, P., 1998, 'Weak States, Strong States: A State-in-Society Perspective', in P. Dauvergne (ed.) *Weak and Strong States in Asia-Pacific Societies*, Australia: Allen and Unwin.

Davidson, B., 1992, *The Black Man's Burden. Africa and the Curse of the Nation-State*, London: James Currey.

Davidson, B., 1989, *Black Star: A View of the Life and Times of Kwame Nkrumah*, New York, (Davidson 1964 reprint), Boulder: Westview Press.

Jackson, R., 2002, 'Violent Internal Conflict and the African State: Towards A Framework of Analysis', *Journal of Contemporary African Studies*, Vol. 20. No. 1, January.

Kohn, H., 1944, *The Idea of Nationalism*, New York: The Macmillan Company.

Migdal, J., 1998, 'Why Do So Many States Stay Intact?', in P. Dauvergen (ed.) *Weak and Strong States in Asia-Pacific Societies*, Australia: Allen Unwin.

Olowu, D., 1989, *Newsletter of the African Association of Political Science* (Lagos), April.

Skinner, Q., 1978, *Foundations of Modern Political Thought: Volume Two, The Age of Reformation*, London: Cambridge University Press.

14

Conflict and Violence in Central Africa: The Political Economy Behind Internal and External Networks in Fomenting War in the Sub-Region

Ian Taylor

Introduction

Central Africa is currently characterised by conflict and disorder, with concomitant social, political, not to mention ecological dislocation and displacement. The war(s) in the Democratic Republic of Congo and its borderlands are a catastrophe in the heart of Africa. The political economy of informal - as well as formal – regional and international networking has actively prolonged the conflict. At the formal level, the Southern African Development Community (SADC) is riven by tension and rivalries that profoundly call into question the 'official' region-building project. Yet at the same time, and in contrast to the fissures within SADC generated by the conflicts, another type of regional networking has been assiduously developed. This networking adds up to a form of regionalisation that seems as 'real' – if not more so – in the DRC than any *formal* regionalism. The type of regionalism emerging links up well-placed individuals and groups within Africa to outside interests, creating a milieu where a wide variety of networking involving states, mafias, private armies, 'businessmen' and assorted state elites from both within and outside Africa has developed.[1] These linkages may start locally, then regionally and finally encompass international connections, or they may develop in a variety of combinations. What is significant is that for all such networks to prosper, transboundary formations must be constructed. It is in this sense that international involvement in the emerging milieus are of crucial importance. Certainly, without quite extensive international activities and connections, the type of scenarios currently playing themselves out in the Congo would not be possible. International business has, through its contracts, deals and provision of all manner of means, served to finance and sustain those actors involved in the conflict. This fact should not be forgotten when we talk of 'Africa's First World War'.

Crucially, the forms of regional networkings, based essentially on a form of kleptocratic political economy, undermine coherent developmental projects and the prospects for peace and stability. They are what Shaw refers to as 'war economy' as one of his five typologies of regionalisation currently remaking Africa,[2] and are truly a reflection of the globalisation of African conflicts, with diverse actors encouraging and profiting from African misery. Indeed, the wars in Central Africa have thrown into sharp relief the involvement of international interests in helping perpetuate the continent's disorder, whilst influential voices – ignoring such roles – at the same time throw up their hands at the 'hopeless continent'.[3]

In this discussion, I would like to expand on how powerful international interests have helped stimulate a form of regional networking in Central Africa that we need to take on board if we are to attempt to comprehend (or at least start to) the conflicting processes currently reconfiguring the region. If we are to try and understand the multifaceted processes that mark out Central Africa's political economy, the political, private, social, ecological, and informal/illegal aspects of regionalising impulses, *alongside* the formal institutional (or what remains of it) and economic aspects need to be analysed and understood. In this sense, the type of transboundary connections discussed parallels Nordstrom's 'shadow networks'. Such networks are a combination of political, economic and socio-cultural forces linked to the international and are transactional in nature.[4] The actors involved share an inter-subjective understanding of their own roles and norms of exchange and alliance, as will be shown below.

In addition, we need to transcend the traditional boundaries taken for granted by African Studies, which invariably see state boundaries as frontiers of knowledge, converting geographic frontiers into epistemological ones.[5] The dynamics that have driven the regional and transnational networks, discussed below, are not confined to simply the entity known to us as the DRC. Neither is the regionalisation discussed restricted solely to the continent. Indeed, what is intriguing about the type of shadow networks present in Central Africa are the way that they are not restricted by notions of state or continental boundaries, but are regional, continental and global: the continent's boundaries are now truly transnational in scope, reflecting the intensification of the extraversion of the African state identified by Bayart.[6]

In this light, the article examines the forms of regional and transnational networks that are currently reconfiguring the Central African region and aspects of the African and global political economy. How and in what way can international interests be understood to have contributed to the current malaise in the region? How have international business networks worked to make things worse in the region? Obviously, this is not to suggest that Central Africa is simply acted upon by 'imperialism' or broad outside interests. Clearly, all the actors within the area under discussion possess varying degrees of agency and are not simply automatons carrying out the wishes of outside forces. How and in what way there are varying convergence of interests between outsiders and internal actors is an absolute key to understanding how global forces may be thought of as contributing to the scenarios that we may observe in the DRC today. Before delving further into this issue, a brief discussion of the literature on regionalism and how it pertains to our discussion on Central Africa will be attempted.

Regionalism and Central Africa

There are two regionalising processes that may be identified: 'regionalism' refers to the formal projects with particular plans and strategies and that often lead to institutional arrangements; 'regionalisation' on the other hand refers to the actual processes that result in forms of co-operation, integration, connectivity and convergence within a particular cross-national territorial area. Orthodox approaches to regionalising have invariably neglected this latter, often more informal, though no less tangible, set of processes.[7]

By focusing on the 'real' regions, recent work on regionalism has generated a useful set of analytical tools by which the diverse sets of regionalising processes may be better understood. In the context of this particular study, the recognition that regionalisms in Central Africa are multi-layered and can and do involve transnational networks that may or may not be legal, or that reflect Bayart's 'criminalisation of the state' in Africa is fundamental.[8] Such regionalisms involve the participation of a multitude of actors, both 'state' (whatever that may actually mean) and non-state players. This is essential, particularly in Africa, as much of the social and economic interconnectedness remain at the nexus of formal/informal, legal/illegal, national/global etc., constituting what has been called the 'three economies of Africa'.[9] In such a milieu, formal activities, quantifiable through orthodox analyses, only tell one part of the story: there is a conceptual gap that does not allow us to analyse the informality of trading networks that are typical of much of Africa's political economy, for instance.[10] As Shaw writes on recent analyses of regionalism:

> [Their] inclusion of non-state and non-formal interactions between the national and global levels enables it to treat the interconnections between more and less statist relations, as well as to transcend the official by recognising how the latter relates to the unofficial in a myriad of ways: the multiple conceptions of 'regions', as well as diversity of issue areas, from ecologies and ethnicities to civil societies and private armies.[11]

The complexities and heterogeneous nature of regionalisms in Africa clearly provide a study in how regionalising tendencies take on a variety of forms that play out at a diverse set of levels, not all of which are recognisably legitimate or constructive. Yet they are still forms of regionalisms and still reflect Central Africa's insertion into a globalising political economy. At the same time, and to varying degrees, such tendencies reflect the diverse manner in which outside interests have sought to exploit and exacerbate milieus within Central Africa as a means to extract profits and/or construct linkages and chains of influence and control in the region.

Neo-imperialism and Mobutu's Zaire

Any discussion of the Congo must start from the premise that it is potentially one of the wealthiest countries in Africa. It is one of the world's leading industrial diamond producers, provides about a quarter of the world's cobalt and holds 80 percent of world reserves of this mineral. It is also the world's sixth largest copper producer. In addition, zinc, tin, manganese, gold, silver, iron ore, and uranium are also found in abundance in the country. Lastly, the country has over 10 percent of the world's total hydroelectric potential. It is, in short, a very rich county, *in theory*.

However, since independence a combination of neo-imperialist machinations and possibly one of the worst examples of kleptocratic rule (put in place, nourished and supported to the very end by the West) has meant that the people in the Congo have never seen the benefits from such riches. It was the West's manoeuvring that put Mobutu in power in 1965 when, with the aid of the CIA, he betrayed and murdered Patrice Lumumba. Lumumba had made the mistake of calling for the Congo's economic as well as political liberation, a position that made him instant enemies, particularly when it became clear that Lumumba would not shy away from contact with socialist countries. Within weeks of formal independence from Belgium in 1960, the Congo was thrown into crisis by the secession of mineral-rich Katanga. Outside forces, through either direct interventions or via their subalterns, quickly rushed to defend their protégé time and again from uprisings of his own people. For instance, in 1977 and 1978, the country's main opposition movement, the Congolese National Liberation Front (*Front de la Libération Nationale Congolaise*; FLNC), operating from Angola, instigated two major invasions into Shaba (formerly Katanga) Province. Both affairs brought in outsiders to prop up Mobutu: from Morocco in 1977 and from France in 1978. 'Classic colonialism is a relic but its absence does not mean that there are no "colonial" interests to safeguard'.[12]

The careful cultivation of Mobutu as a 'friend of the free world', with its concomitant nod-and-wink to the construction of a highly personalised and kleptocratic regime is well known. The propping up of Mobutu's decrepit regime by the West was a major crime against the Congolese people—but something which has been largely forgotten back in the metropoles. Any reference to this is usually waved away with references to the Cold War milieu and that it is all in the past. But, what is more intriguing for any understanding of the political economy of contemporary Central Africa is the way that outside forces have maintained a steady grip on the regime post-Mobutu. Indeed, outside involvement has further stimulated a set of regional structures that now criss-cross Central Africa, some new but many with a decidedly older pedigree. Working hand-in-hand with global networks of extraction, local big men have 'blatantly advertised the economic motivations underlying their participation. Intervening states have sought a direct share in Congo's revenues from the extraction of mineral and other resources'.[13]

Such activity has built up a series of inter-linking connections in collaboration with outside i.e. extra-African forces, that have constructed what may be seen as a set of transnational networks centred in Kinshasa and extending outwardly to Geneva, Brussels, Lisbon, Paris, Washington and beyond. These shadow the type of networking and linkages that already exist 'from below' vis-à-vis the trading interactions between central Africa and Europe so excellently covered by MacGaffey and Bazenguissa-Ganga.[14] In regionalisation literature, the 'hubs and spokes' of connectivities are often discussed. Are such networks extending outwards from Central Africa anything less than a form of hubs and spokes, actively encouraged by international actors?

Such developments are not necessarily new per se: international forces have helped mould and influence domestic outcomes in Africa for a very long time. What is new in the contemporary post-Cold War era however is that the emerging regionalising networks are managing to develop their own links and ties to the international arena, often on their own terms. Whilst we should not overly exaggerate this agency, it has increased the space available to the type of shadowy manipulators and elites involved in the process and in tandem with diverse international actors. Whilst during the immediate post-independence period aid relationships granted donors a degree of latitude and influence over the receiving elites, in an era where Africa continues to be 'marginalised' and aid is rolled back in favour of (elusive?) 'trade', this patron-client linkage is dissipating. In addition, in a liberalising world, the ability of the dominant powers to manipulate the global market has somewhat declined, granting even greater agency to those actors involved in such networking.

The development of such forms of networking was particularly blatant in Laurent Kabila's case with the DRC big man assiduously constructing both domestic and international patronage networks to serve as resources through which clients might be rewarded for their support. These networks stretched beyond Kinshasa to link up with a variety of global players. For instance, in September 1998 Kabila decreed that all purchases of gold and diamonds must be in Congolese francs (brought in on 30 June) and go through a newly established state purchasing company. This allowed him to bring the country's revenue under his direct control and thereby offer the incentive of cash rewards to his supporters throughout the DRC.[15] Kabila also seized all the assets of the Canadian gold concession, Banro Resources Corporation, a company with which he had formed a contract before becoming Congo's president. The United Nations report by the panel of experts on the illegal exploitation of wealth in the DRC explicitly named, amongst others, the United States, Germany and Belgium as being leading consumers and purchasers of illegally exploited resources from the country, often via networks with the Kabila administration.[16]

Indeed, Kabila's interactions with outside business interests and the history of such interactions are a compelling part of the story regarding the rise and demise of Kabila senior and a precautionary tale for Kabila junior. Kabila renewed mining concessions to international companies even before the end of the civil war and his formal accession to the presidency of the 'Democratic Republic of the Congo'. One of the first major deals signed was with the US company American Mineral Fields– a $1 billion agreement for AMF to mine copper, cobalt and zinc. AMF is an intriguing example of an international interlocutor in the Congo war which has links with the very top of Washington's political elites. Whilst it was involved in the DRC its headquarters were in Hope, Arkansas, Clinton's hometown. Its senior stockholders comprised veteran political friends of Clinton.[17] The links between this influential company and American foreign policy in the region and Washington's role in the DRC conflict is important. According to Madsen, testifying on the war in the DRC before the Subcommittee on International Operations and Human Rights of the United States House of Representatives:

> America Mineral Fields directly benefited from America's initial covert military and intelligence support for Kabila. It is my observation that America's early support for Kabila, which was aided and abetted by U.S. allies Rwanda and Uganda, had less to do with getting rid of the Mobutu regime than it had to do with opening up Congo's vast mineral riches to North American-based and influenced mining companies. Presently, some of America Mineral Fields' principals now benefit from the destabilisation of Sierra Leone and the availability of its cut-rate 'blood diamonds' on the international market.[18]

Sensing which way the wind was blowing, Canadian-based Tengke Mining Corporation dumped its contract with the Mobutu regime for the copper and cobalt mines in Shaba and quickly signed an agreement with Kabila. Both times Kabila's 'generosity' in facilitating such contracts secured finances to pay for further military advances – at a price. As one commentary put it quite succinctly, 'it is hardly conceivable that mining companies would be financing Kabila if they thought he was going to take over the economy and run it in the interests of Zairian people'.[19]

Mobutu's downfall in May 1997 sprang from his failure to realise that whilst he had been useful during the Cold War as an alibi for all sorts of intrigues within the continent in the name of fighting communism, after the collapse of the regimes in Eastern Europe, his extravagance and arrogance could no longer be tacitly ignored. In particular, his venality and corruption came to be seen as embarrassing, particularly as it was combined with a continued refusal to go through the motions of democratisation—something which other African elites had long realised was a necessary rigmarole if continued support (and flows of finance) were to be secured. Whilst much of this was simply the recycling of elites, with no real change or progress, Mobutu baulked at even this cosmetic exercise, though at times he seemed to understand the game with on-off moves to multi-party politics obscuring his obdurance. But, ultimately, Mobutu proved to be an obstacle and needed to be removed.

Scratching around for a replacement, Laurent Kabila was elevated from nowhere and promoted as the new Congolese messiah, with considerable backing and support from the West. According to Madsen's testimony:

> [The] DIA [Defence Intelligence Agency] trained young men and teens from Rwanda, Uganda, and eastern Zaire for periods of up to two years and longer for the RPF/AFDL-CZ campaign against Mobutu. The recruits were offered pay of between $450 and $1000 upon their successful capture of Kinshasa... When the AFDL-CZ and their Rwandan allies reached Kinshasa in 1996, it was largely due to the help of the United States. One reason why Kabila's men advanced into the city so quickly was the technical assistance provided by the DIA and other intelligence agencies. According to informed sources in Paris, U.S. Special Forces actually accompanied ADFL-CZ forces into Kinshasa. The Americans also reportedly provided Kabila's rebels and Rwandan troops with high definition spy satellite photographs that permitted them to order their troops to plot courses into Kinshasa that avoided encounters with Mobutu's forces.[20]

Thus when Laurent Kabila took over the seat of government after Mobutu's inglorious evacuation, excited observers hastily proclaimed that Kabila was 'different' and that a formal regional project could use this difference constructively - hence the newly-named entity known as the Democratic Republic of the Congo being admitted post haste into SADC.[21] In many respects, Kabila's victorious entry into Kinshasa (supported by Rwanda and Uganda) marked out a victory for the 'Anglo-Saxons' over French interests, which had supported Mobutu until the very end. The international aspect of this supposed internal war in the Congo may be contextualised as part of the struggle between Washington and Paris for spheres of influence (and, particularly, markets) on the continent. Pro-American leaders in Asmara, Addis Ababa, Kampala and Kigali seemed to be constructing a new bloc of regimes friendly to Washington's interests, linking up with Thabo Mbeki's South Africa as a group of states that America could do business with.[22] Ironically, Paul Kagame of Rwanda, and Yoweri Museveni of Uganda, were touted as belonging to a new generation of African leaders who would help advance the 'African Renaissance'.[23] Sadly (inevitably?), they are now 'on the verge of becoming the godfathers of the illegal exploitation of natural resources and the continuation of the conflict in the Congo'.[24] Talking up such new elites was a major theme of Clinton's early presidency, yet:

> In reality, [those] leaders, who include the current presidents of Uganda, Rwanda, Ethiopia, Angola, Eritrea, Burundi, and the Democratic Republic of the Congo preside over countries where ethnic and civil turmoil permit unscrupulous international mining companies to take advantage of the strife to fill their own coffers with conflict diamonds, gold, copper, platinum, and other precious minerals - including one - columbite-tantalite or 'coltan' - which is a primary component of computer microchips and printed circuit boards.[25]

With tantalising commercial networks on offer to elites willing to partake, the turmoil in Central Africa demonstrated how quickly these so-called 'new leaders' succumbed to various opportunities on offer in partnership with international capital.

So, whilst Western corporations saw in Kabila a person who they thought would rein in the extravagant corruption that had developed under Mobutu, the shadow networks were to continue, particularly as it was thought that Kabila would be more 'reliable' as head of Kinshasa's government, especially if under the control of Uganda and Rwanda. However, premature optimism by international interests over the character of Kabila (talked up by Washington as a 'new leader' of Africa) was rudely disappointed, although international capital and the great democrat then ensconced in Kinshasa *did* enjoy a honeymoon period. Almost immediately, Kabila entered into deals with mining companies, such as American Mineral Fields and Anglo-American, and Belgian investors such as Texaf, George Forrest International, Petrofina and *Union Minière*. Indeed, the first major deal signed by Kabila was with the American company American Mineral Fields (AMF), a $1 billion agreement for AMF to mine copper, cobalt and zinc. International capital's involvement in the Congo debacle was clearly being run along 'business as usual' lines, reflecting a coincidence of interests between foreign interests and local elites. This was very much run along mercenary lines with little care for the policies and practices of the elites involved - unless they began to encroach too much on commercial operations. As Madsen writes,

> The United States has a long history of supporting all sides in the DRC's civil wars in order to gain access to the country's natural resources. [One report] presents a cogent example of how one U.S. firm was involved in the DRC's grand thievery before the 1998 break between Laurent Kabila and his Rwandan and Ugandan backers. It links the *Banque de commerce, du developpement et d'industrie* (BCDI) of Kigali, Citibank in New York, the diamond business and armed rebellion. The report states [that] in a letter signed by J.P. Moritz, general manager of *Societe miniere de Bakwanga* (MIBA), a Congolese diamond company, and Ngandu Kamenda, the general manager of MIBA ordered a payment of $3.5 million to *la Generale de commerce d'import/export du Congo* (COMIEX), a company owned by late President Kabila and some of his close allies, such as Minister Victor Mpoyo, from an account in BCDI through a Citibank account. This amount of money was paid as a contribution from MIBA to the AFDL war effort.[26]

The problem for Washington and its allies within Africa was that Kabila did not seem to be following the script and rather than rewarding those who put him into power, turned on them. Kabila rapidly turned out to be a forbidding dictator, causing profound alienation amongst former allies. Having alienated the Congolese and Rwandan Tutsis, Kabila was bereft of a proper military force of his own. Desperately in need of such a force, Kabila turned to Mobutu's former allies and enrolled in his armed forces 10,000 Interahamwe militias and Hutu soldiers of the former Rwandan army.[27] He then claimed that the DRC was being subverted by Rwanda and Uganda in the cause of a pan-Tutsi empire and on August 2, 1998 ordered all the Ugandans and the Rwandan Tutsis to leave the country post haste. This sparked a pogrom against Tutsis in all towns still controlled by Kabila's government. 'By 1998, the Kabila regime had become an irritant to the United States, North American mining interests, and Kabila's Ugandan and Rwandan patrons. As a result, Rwanda and Uganda launched a second invasion of the DRC to get rid of Kabila and replace him with someone more servile'.[28]

At the same time, Kabila also alienated potential foreign investors, particularly in the mining sector, by making deals and then reneging on them. Indeed, so frustrated had international capital become by Kabila's erratic behaviour and his repeated dishonouring of contracts he himself had signed with foreign businessmen, that (so the story goes) some companies offered Kabila $ 200 million to clear out of the Congo![29] Importantly, Kabila began constructing alliances on a private basis with both individual companies that shouldn't by rights, have benefited from Kabila's emergence and, with African regimes such as Zimbabwe and Angola that were, at best, ambivalent about the encroaching Western influence in the region and at worst (Mugabe in his more excited flourishes) rapidly 'anti-Western'. Those taking others' places had no intention of severing the highly profitable linkages that international capital had constructed in the Congo over many decades, even if it meant that new networks and regional spokes needed to be elaborated.

This was facilitated by the state of disorder region-wide and the opportunities this offered, as well as the already extant networks of power and patronage, affording a logical *modus operandi* for a variety of actors operating within areas where the formal state was in a process of eclipse.[30] These circumstances in turn increased the likelihood of what Reno referred to as 'warlord capitalism' and the 'shadow state',[31] which however retained enough substance to negotiate with and benefit from international capital's willingness to conduct business with such entities. Certainly, 'internal disorder need not impede commerce, especially if compact, valuable natural resources are present. A few entrepreneurs may even prefer minimal government control'.[32] The profits available can be remarkable and very tempting: 'if the risks are high in Angola or the Democratic Republic of Congo (DRC) where President Laurent Kabila's troops are battling rebel forces, the business rewards can be dazzling. These and other warring African countries, like Sierra Leone and the Republic of the Congo (Congo-Brazzaville) are rich in mineral deposits with scant, if any, regulatory restrictions – a glittering lure for foreign companies'.[33]

Transnational Networking and Central Africa

Such involvement in war-ridden spaces reflects the internationalisation of African conflicts, not only through 'normal' state-to-state (or rather 'state'-to-state) relations e.g. Paris with Kinshasa, but also through global business networks. These mesh outside interests with local elites' stakes. Indeed, we are seeing a 'quite distinctive form of... regionalism in Africa... the emergence of the minerals and mafias syndrome in which scarce resources are exchanged for protection, as well as regime enrichment and aggrandisement'.[34] Certainly, conflict-ridden spaces offer a form of competitiveness for both patron and client that can prove highly profitable.

In this sense we can say that the processes unfolding in conflict areas of Central Africa are constructed by local actors sharing particular interests and agendas but who do this in partnership with and enjoying encouragement and support from, global business networks. As Latham et al write, 'the Great Lakes conflicts, and especially the wars in the Congo, are... impossible to make sense of without accounting for the role of regional and transnational forces... [Such involvements] were neither peripheral nor determinative in the political trajectories of Uganda, the Congo and the Great Lakes region in general. They were, and are, constitutive'.[35] This is most apparent with regard to the big men involved in such processes who share an inter-subjective understanding of their own positions of power and prestige, concur on the logic that the state of which they have at least nominal control is 'theirs' to do with as they please, and court international capital in order to shore up such constructions. Their activities are permitted and sustained by the transboundary configurations such elites develop that enable huge profits to be evacuated, invariably outside of Africa, through networks leading back to the metropoles. Whether this is through the infamous tried-and-trusted 'confidential' Swiss bank accounts or through unscrupulous business partners managing such interests, the result is the same: more denuding of Africa's resources. But, in sharing such identities, the defence of one is the defence of all. Arguably, the socially constructed regionness advanced by Mugabe, Kabila senior, Dos Santos and Nujoma, in tandem with their various international business partners and political allies, is no less 'real' than other forms of regional identities and connections.

Paradoxically, just as regionalisation can be constructed upon joint interests and concerns, so too can it be *deconstructed*. This occurred in late 1999 when four days of fighting between Ugandan and Rwandan troops around Kisangani was blamed on money and egos, with both sides competing to support the RCD. The RCD split, with Wamba dia Wamba aligned to Uganda and based in Kisangani, whilst Emile Ilunga sided with the Rwandans and kept the majority of the RCD in Goma.[36] Reports have subsequently alleged that the fighting 'stemmed mainly from competition over access to Congo's valuable natural resources'.[37]

With the type of regionalisation in Central Africa based on corrupted abilities to lay claim to the mantle of state, it is doubtful whether many of the current elites in the formal region (or even the wider international community for that matter) can bring themselves to confront the reality on the ground, even if it stares them in the face. The use and abuse of the 'organised hypocrisy' of sovereignty has clearly allowed an assortment of actors to successfully construct a number of international commercial and military alliances involving state leaders and their courtiers as well as private corporations.[38] Indeed, 'global recognition of even very weak states' sovereignty and the role such recognition plays in the privatisation of diplomacy and internal security for these regimes, serves not only regime interests but also the interests of officials and investors in [outside] powerful states'.[39] This has, to a large degree, reflected the uneven manner in which Africa has been inserting itself (or been inserted) into an increasingly globalised world.

Globalisation and Central Africa

How does this type of regionalisation and transboundary networking tie in with global processes? Globalisation is obviously asymmetrical and variegated and its impact upon different spatial entities varies. As such it takes advantage of, indeed exacerbates differences as much as, if not more than, it produces a uniform new world. In doing so, counter-reactions and contradictions are generated. Certainly, what is going on in Africa is connected to processes associated both with globalisation and with the specific historical experiences of a particular space. Local and global processes are inter-linked, 'since any particular process of regionalisation in any part of the world has systemic repercussions on other regions, thus shaping the way in which the new world order is being organised'.[40] Within this context, globalising impulses push for a reconfiguration along the lines of (Western-derived) ideal types of socio-economic governance.

Ironically, the neo-liberal principles governing the global economy and that have been foisted onto the continent in the form of Structural Adjustment Programmes and other conditionalities, have provided the structural context that has helped cultivate the forms of regionalisation that mark out central Africa. Indeed, global liberalisation has stimulated a variety of regional linkages and cross-border networks, with transcontinental spokes linking such activities to the outside world. In this we can see a remarkable similarity between such regionalisations and the type of relations and forms of social, political and economic organisation that mark out the war economies, particularly in Central Africa. Thus instead of bringing about stability and (legitimate) growth, impulses generated by globalisation have contributed to the further deepening and development of criminal networks and decidedly quasi-feudal forms of political economy.[41]

As Reno has persuasively argued, two paradoxes are particularly evident in the neo-liberal approach to reform and development in Africa. First, rulers of weak states who face severe threats from strongmen and the most intense pressures from outsiders, are the most consistent and thorough in destroying any remaining formal institutions of state. Second, outside creditors, foreign firms, and even elites from 'stronger' states participate in or support hard-pressed rulers' attempts to deal with political events in this unexpected fashion.[42] This type of solidarity amongst the big men is an apt description of what has occurred in central Africa as the likes of Mugabe and Dos Santos rushed in to aid Kabila, thereby setting in motion the construction of a form of regionalisation not covered in any of the prospectuses of SADC. It seems that in many cases no longer is the state leader that necessarily interested or dedicated to a project that is devoted to establishing control over a specific recognised territory, with all the bureaucratic encumbrances and requirements to maintain some form of consensual balance.[43] Now, with their position threatened by the various tendencies associated with the penetration of globalising impulses, the informalisation of economic and political activity seeks to counterbalance the erosion of state capacity and power. By expanding internal *and external* clientistic networks in a form of networking, elites within conflict-ridden spaces pursue what Duffield refers to as 'adaptive patrimonialism'.[44] This regionalisation of course is not at all the type expected when the DRC was granted membership of SADC, although such phenomena are certainly a lot more relevant when discussing the DRC's role in SADC.

Returning to globalisation and liberalising impulses, 'liberalisation created new opportunities for private appropriation of public resources... More importantly, by reducing the role of the state, the donors both reduced its resources and the opportunities for access to those resources. At the same time the crisis [of development] did not reduce dependence on state resources for private accumulation. Corruption has tended... to go well beyond the appropriation of surpluses and extend to the looting of the very fabric of the state itself'.[45] In this sense, instead of representing the antithesis of what formal regional projects should look like, the type of alliances and transboundary networks currently reconfiguring Central Africa may well offer a prophetic vision of what may be in store for vulnerable and peripheral areas of the world. This is particularly so where there exist elites who are more than willing to craft shadow networks with international capital bent on the extraction of Africa's resources for private profit.

Ironically, such networks are held by the local protagonists as examples of their space's integration into the global capitalist economy and of their adherence to the hegemonic neo-liberal normative order. One can almost sense the indignation and frustration of a spokesman from a rebel group in the DRC when he protested that 'our system is a liberal system, we are not here to interfere, we just ask business people to have the proper documents to do business [in our sphere of control]'.[46] Is this activity any less damaging than the activities of 'official' foreign businessmen during Mobutu or, dare we say, the more pernicious effect of SAPs? It is certainly probably more in line with the mantra of neo-liberalism and an 'open economy'.

In a discussion of another area of Africa ravaged by such processes, it is asserted that under SAPs and post-Cold War scarcity in the continent, the African state 'shrinks – both physically... and sociologically (in terms of the groups it can afford to patronise). The regime's priority attention has to be given to maintaining loyalty among the security services'.[47] This elevates the role and power of those with weapons and prioritises their needs over the wider needs of society, cultivating an air of warlordism either in service to the incumbent who wears the (thin) mantle of sovereignty, or to challengers. Indeed, in an ironic twist, liberalisation may actually coincide with and/or facilitate a further slide away from formal regionalism. This is because those engaged in warlord capitalism will seek to reduce the provision of public goods as a means to abet a clientist culture of dependency in order to consummate business. This is typically centred around personalised networks and access to well-connected elites, rather than through 'normal' public service channels, which have been looted of any resources anyway.[48] Thus both the capacity to administer and advance regional integration projects at the formal and institutional level *and the rationale* are undermined, to be replaced in many cases by the informal and illegal.

From the perspective of the warlords and big men, pursuing some form of *formal* regionalism does not make sense as they are not interested in some regional public good or advancement. Furthermore, committing themselves to a formal regional pact may actually lead to inhibiting factors (norms, sanctions, even military interference from fellow member states upset by their behaviour) that could threaten the continuation of their activities.[49] The neo-liberal ingredients of globalisation may well then actually legitimise the peeling away of the state whilst at the same time helping to lay the foundations for decay and clandestinity, almost always aided and abetted by various international forces.

At the same time, such processes invite a re-evaluation of the very state in Africa. Just as Bayart talks of the criminalisation of the African state, so too does he assert that what might be emerging from the war-shattered spaces in Africa is an intriguing process of state *formation*, which although unrecognisable using our traditional Westphalian-inspired analysis, may well be an extraordinary 'alternative' model of the African state: 'dissidence, war and banditry... do not necessarily threaten the formation or existence of a state. They can, on the contrary [facilitate] its centralisation'.[50] Bayart links this to external intervention and interference quite explicitly, claiming that such processes are 'related to the manner in which Africa is inserted in the international system through economies of extraction or predation in which many of the leading operators are foreigners whose local African partners have to a considerable degree based their careers on the use of armed force'.[51] Indeed, the type of transnational linkages illustrated above may very well be the precursor to emerging forms of stateness in parts of Africa. This calls for a recognition of such 'real' processes, rather than bemoaning the demise of fixed normative conceptions of what an African state *should* look like. As one analyst remarked, 'what needs to be recognised is that the African state is not failing as much as our understanding of the state'.[52] In such cases, it is necessary to take on board Clapham's commentary on rethinking African states:

> The warlord phenomenon illustrates the integration of the different elements in modern African politics from which new systems of rule may be constructed, either in opposition to the inherited structures of colonial statehood, or indeed through the metamorphosis of post-colonial units into very different entities behind the cover of what Reno terms the 'shadow state'.[53]

Such 'shadow states' must, and this is where the international comes in, have military power both to ward off rivals and secure space in which to operate and pursue 'the development of a set of economic linkages to global trading networks'.[54] These links between such elites and international networks 'revive aspects of the 'imperialism by invitation' that Doyle describes in nineteenth-century Africa. That is, 'rulers during Africa's late pre-colonial period... commonly took advantage of access to and control over commerce with Europeans to increase their personal power'.[55] The difference, as Reno rightly points out, is that the international actors are anxious to gain 'legitimacy' through dealing with the 'sovereign' entity, internationally recognised as the head of state of the 'Democratic Republic of the Congo' or whatever imaginative name the elites think up for their crisis-ridden spaces. In essence, the Westphalian state system, foisted on Africa by imperialism, means that today there remains a new scramble for Central

Africa, only this time by leading political and economic actors anxious to secure the signature of the 'official' (as opposed to the unofficial) big man. In doing so, this new form of imperialism, interacting with local elites interests, has helped craft a distinctly unconventional form of regionalisation and may be constructing decidedly unorthodox versions of the state, one in which it is unlikely that the average African will be rescued from her distress. Responsibility for such a scenario is shared, for sure, but certainly the unscrupulous activities of international capital must be blamed for stoking the fires and perpetuating further misery for the ordinary person living in the heart of Africa. Without such transboundary networks, such unfolding processes centred around conflict would be severely compounded: 'war today, by definition, is constructed internationally. We may well speak of internal wars, but they are set in vast global arenas'.[56] Clearly, the type of regional networking and transnational linkages discussed above have helped sustain the war in the Congo. In this sense, international involvement in the continent continues to further Africa's tribulations. As the twenty-first century progresses, little - so it appears - has changed.

Notes

1. See ICG Africa Report No. 26, *Scramble for the Congo: Anatomy of an Ugly War*, Nairobi/Brussels: International Crisis Group, 2000; and United Nations Security Council S/2001/357 Report of the Panel of Experts on the Illegal Exploitation of Natural Resources and other Forms of Wealth of the Democratic Republic of Congo New York: United Nations, 2001. It should be noted that the UN report is seriously flawed by its concentration on the activities of the 'uninvited' combatants in the DRC (Rwanda and Uganda) whilst not interrogating sufficiently the role of the so-called 'invited' participants such as Angola, Namibia and Zimbabwe—see Ian Taylor 'The "Blind Spot" in the Recent Report of the Panel of Experts on the Illegal Exploitation of Natural Resources in the Democratic Republic of Congo', *Environment, Development and Conflict News*, June 12, 2001, http://www.padrigu.gu.se/EDCNews/Reviews/Taylor2001.html.
2. Timothy Shaw, 'New Regionalisms in Africa in the New Millennium: Comparative Perspectives on Renaissance, Realism and/or Regressions', *New Political Economy*, vol. 5, no. 3, 2000.
3. *The Economist* (London) May 13, 2000.
4. Carolyn Nordstrom, 'Out of the Shadows', in Robert Latham, Ronald Kassimir and Thomas Callaghy (eds.) *Intervention and Transnationalism in Africa: Global-Local Networks of Power*, Cambridge, Cambridge University Press, 2001, p. 218.
5. Mahmood Mamdani, *When Victims Become Killers: Colonialism, Nativism, and the Genocide in Rwanda*, Oxford, James Currey, 2001, p. xii.
6. Jean-François Bayart, 'Africa in the World: A History of Extraversion', *African Affairs*, 99, 2000.
7. Björn Hettne and Fredrik Söderbaum, 'Theorising the Rise of Regionness', *New Political Economy* Vol. 5, No. 3, 2000, p. 458.

8. See Jean-François Bayart, Stephen Ellis and Beatrice Hibou, *The Criminalisation of the State in Africa*, Oxford, James Currey, 1999.
9. Constance Freeman, 'The Three Economies of Africa', *African Security Review*, Vol. 9, No. 4, 2000.
10. For an excellent study of one such facet of this, see Janet MacGaffey, *The Real Economy of Zaire: The Contribution of Smuggling and Other Unofficial Activities to National Wealth*, London, James Currey, 1991.
11. Timothy Shaw, 2000, p. 401.
12. Abillah Omari, 'Ethnicity, Power, Governance and Conflict in the Great Lakes Region', in Sandra MacLean, Fahimul Quadir and Timothy Shaw, *Crises of Governance in Asia and Africa*, Aldershot, Ashgate, 2001, p. 253.
13. Jeremy Weinstein, 'Africa's "Scramble for Africa": Lessons of a Continental War', *World Policy Journal*, Vol. 17, No. 2, 2000, p. 17.
14. See Janet MacGaffey and Remy Bazenguissa-Ganga, *Congo-Paris: Transnational Traders on the Margins of the Law*, Oxford, James Currey, 2000.
15. 'War Turns Commercial', *The Economist* (London) Oct. 24, 1998, p. 88.
16. See United Nations Security Council Panel of Experts on the Illegal Exploitation of Wealth in the Democratic Republic of the Congo (DRC), November 13, 2001, http://www.un.org/Docs/sc/letters/2001/1072e.pdf
17. Richard Morais, 'Friends in High Places', *Forbes Magazine*, August 10, 1998, p. 50.
18. Wayne Madsen, 'Prepared Testimony and Statement for the Record of Wayne Madsen, Author, "Genocide and Covert Operations in Africa 1993-1999", Investigative Journalist, on 'Suffering and Despair: Humanitarian Crisis in the Congo Before the Subcommittee on International Operations and Human Rights Committee on International Relations, United States House of Representatives', Washington, DC, May 17, 2001, p. 7.
19. Jordi Martorell, 'Mobutu Overthrown: What Next for the New Congo?', http://www.marxist.com/Africa/Zaire.html
20. Wayne Madsen, 2001, p. 4.
21. See Ian Taylor and Paul Williams, 'South African Foreign Policy and the Great Lakes Crisis: African Renaissance Meets Vagabondage Politique?', *African Affairs* Vol. 100, issue 399, 2001.
22. On South Africa, see Ian Taylor, *Stuck in Middle GEAR: South Africa's Post-Apartheid Foreign Relations*, Westport, Connecticut, Praeger, 2001.
23. Marina Ottaway, 'Africa's "New Leaders": African Solution or African Problem?', *Current History*, May 1998.
24. *Business Day* (Johannesburg) April 18, 2001.
25. Wayne Madsen, 2001, p. 6.
26. Ibid.
27. Mwesiga Baregu (ed.), *Crisis in the Democratic Republic of the Congo*, Harare, SARIPS, 1999.
28. Wayne Madsen, 2001, p. 5.
29. Peter Strandberg, 'With the Rebels in Congo', *New African*, February 1999, p.18.

30. This scenario had been long developing within the Congo, where regionalisation tendencies based on tribalism and ethnic polarisation, stoked by ambitious local big men and tacitly tolerated by the centre in Kinshasa as a means of providing a skeletal form of 'governance' and control, had long been a feature of post-colonial Congo, accelerated under Mobutu – see Kalele-ka-Bila, 'Regionalist Ideologies' and Longandjo Okitakekumba, 'State Power under MPR Control: An Interpretative Essay', both in Kankwenda Mbaya (ed.) *Zaire: What Destiny?*, Dakar, CODESRIA, 1993.
31. William Reno, *Warlord Politics and African States*, Boulder, Lynne Rienner, 1998, p. 26.
32. William Reno, 'External Relations of Weak States and Stateless Regions in Africa', in Gilbert Khadiagala and Terrence Lyons (eds.) *African Foreign Polices: Power and Process*, Boulder, Lynne Reinner, 2001, p. 187.
33. *Financial Mail* (Johannesburg), Jan. 15, 1999.
34. Timothy Shaw, 2000, p. 406.
35. Robert Latham, Ronald Kassimir and Thomas Callaghy, 'Introduction: Transboundary Formations, Intervention, Order, and Authority', in Robert Latham et al, p. 2.
36. See 'Carve-up in the Congo', *Le Monde Diplomatique* (English edition), (Paris) October 1999.
37. 'Uganda Explains Clash with Rwanda', Associated Press (Kampala), Aug. 25, 1999.
38. Stephen Krasner, *Sovereignty: Organised Hypocrisy*, Princeton, Princeton University Press, 1999.
39. William Reno, 2001, p. 186.
40. Björn Hettne, 'Globalization, the New Regionalism and East Asia', paper delivered at the United Nations University Global Seminar 1996 Shonan Session, Hayama, Japan.
41. For a well-developed argument along this line, see Mark Duffield, 'Globalisation and War Economies: Promoting Order or the Return of History?', *Fletcher Forum of World Affairs*, Vol. 23, No. 2, 1999.
42. See William Reno, 1998, p. 7.
43. Mark Duffield, 'Post-Modern Conflict: Warlords, Post-adjustment States and Private Protection', *Civil Wars*, Vol. 1, No. 1, 1998.
44. Ibid.
45. Morris Szeftel, 'Between Governance and Under-development: Accumulation and Africa's "Catastrophic Corruption"', *Review of African Political Economy*, No. 84, 2000, p. 303.
46. Quoted in *Botswana Gazette* (Gaborone) April 20, 2001.
47. Paul Richards, *Fighting for the Rain Forest: War, Youth and Resources in Sierra Leone*, Oxford, James Currey, 1996, p. 36.
48. William Reno, 2000, pp. 442-443.
49. Ian Taylor and Paul Williams, 2001, p. 285.
50. Jean-François Bayart, 'Conclusion', in Jean-François Bayart et al, 1999, p. 115.

51. Ibid., p. 114.
52. Kevin Dunn, 'MadLib: The (Blank) African State: Rethinking the Sovereign States in International Relations Theory', in Kevin Dunn and Timothy Shaw (eds.), *Africa's Challenge to International Relations Theory*, London, Palgrave, 2001, p. 49.
53. Christopher Clapham, 'Rethinking African States', *African Security Review*, Vol. 10, No. 3, 2001, p. 14.
54. Ibid.
55. William Reno 2001, p. 200.
56. Carolyn Nordstrom, 'Out of the Shadows', in Robert Latham et al., 2001, p. 217.

Printed in the United States
73514LV00005B/97-99